Social Media Measurement and Management

This new textbook applies a critical and practical lens to the world of social media analytics. Author Jeremy Harris Lipschultz explores the foundations of digital data, strategic tools, and best practices in an accessible volume for students and practitioners of social media communication.

The book expands upon entrepreneurship, marketing, and technological principles, demonstrating how raising awareness, sparking engagement, and producing business outcomes all require emphasis on customers, employees, and other stakeholders within paid, earned, social, and owned media. It also looks to the future, examining how the movement toward artificial intelligence and machine learning raises new legal and ethical issues in effective management of social media data. Additionally, the book offers a solid grounding in the principles of social media measurement itself, teaching the strategies and techniques that enable effective analysis.

A perfect primer for this developing industry, *Social Media Measurement: Entrepreneurial Digital Analytics* is ideal for students, scholars, and practitioners of digital media seeking to hone their skills and expand their bank of tools and resources. It features theoretical and practical advice, a comprehensive glossary of key terms, and case studies from key industry thought leaders.

Jeremy Harris Lipschultz holds the Peter Kiewit Distinguished Professorship in the UNO Social Media Lab and School of Communication, University of Nebraska at Omaha. He is Book Review Editor for *Journalism & Mass Communication Educator*. His *Social Media Communication: Concepts, Practices, Data, Law and Ethics* (2018, 2015) textbook integrates theory and practice. Lipschultz's Rural Futures Institute project with Purdue University and the University of Nebraska-Lincoln is developing best practices for smaller communities to leverage broadband technologies and social media. Lipschultz received the AIM Institute College Tech Educator of the Year award in 2017, and was Omaha Press Club Journalism Educator of the Year in 2016. He has been a *Huffington Post* contributor, and currently blogs on LinkedIn.

Connect with @JeremyHL #SMMM2020 on Twitter, follow his Facebook pages, and send questions to: jeremy.lipschultz@gmail.com.

Social Media Measurement and Management

Entrepreneurial Digital Analytics

Jeremy Harris Lipschultz

Routledge
Taylor & Francis Group

NEW YORK AND LONDON

First published 2020
by Routledge
52 Vanderbilt Avenue, New York, NY 10017

and by Routledge
2 Park Square, Milton Park, Abingdon, Oxon, OX14 4RN

Routledge is an imprint of the Taylor & Francis Group, an informa business

© 2020 Taylor & Francis

Library of Congress Cataloging-in-Publication Data
Names: Lipschultz, Jeremy Harris, 1958- author.
Title: Social media measurement and management: entrepreneurial digital analytics / Jeremy Harris Lipschultz.
Description: New York, NY : Routledge, 2020. | Includes bibliographical references and index.
Identifiers: LCCN 2019007125 (print) | LCCN 2019008486 (ebook) | ISBN 9781351108072 (eBook) | ISBN 9780815363903 (hardback) | ISBN 9780815363927 (pbk.)
Subjects: LCSH: Online social networks—Research. | Social media. | Dyadic analysis (Social sciences) | Social sciences—Network analysis. | Marketing research.
Classification: LCC HM742 (ebook) | LCC HM742 .L57 2019 (print) | DDC 302.23—dc23
LC record available at https://lccn.loc.gov/2019007125

ISBN: 978-0-8153-6390-3 (hbk)
ISBN: 978-0-8153-6392-7 (pbk)
ISBN: 978-1-351-10807-2 (ebk)

Typeset in Warnock Pro
by Apex CoVantage, LLC

Visit the eResource: www.routledge.com/9780815363927

Contents

List of Figures   xi
List of Tables   xiii
Contributors   xv
Preface   xix

Unit One: Foundations of Social Media Measurement and Management

1

Social Crowds, Voice, and Personal Branding   3

Social Entrepreneurship and Personal Branding   17
Brand Evangelists and Ambassadors   20
Entrepreneurship and Digital Analytics   22
Awareness   23
Outcome Measurement   24
*Thought Leader Anna Vargas: Social Media Measurement and
    Management Help Land New Clients*   24
As Seen on YouTube   31
Useful Tools   31
Project Ideas   33
Discussion Questions   34

2 Concepts and Campaigns   35

The Barcelona Principles 2.0	38
Google Analytics and SEO	42
Social Media Target Marketing to Latinos and Latinas	46
Target Marketing Panel	47
Thought Leader David Kamerer: Get Started with Google Analytics	49
Strategies	54
The Digital Analytics Association (DAA) and the eMetrics Summit	55
Goals, Objectives, and Tactics	59
Social Media Events	60
Diffusion of Innovation	61
CMC and Social Media	62
Thought Leader Randa Zalman: Home Instead Senior Care Foundation: GIVE65 Fundraising Campaign Case Study	62
Social Media Marketing Data Science and Brand Engagement	72
As Seen on YouTube	75
Useful Tools	76
Project Ideas	79
Discussion Questions	80

3 Social Network Sites (SNS) Measurement and Management   81

Thought Leader Deepti Ganapathy: Focus on Goal-Oriented Measurement to Derive Desirable Outcomes	83
Hub and Spoke Marketing and SEM Audits	87
SNS Data Overview: Social Network Sites (SNS)	87
Hosting a Live Twitter Chat	91
Thought Leader Roberto Gallardo: Social Media, Intelligent Communities, and Management of Civic Engagement	92
As Seen on YouTube	98
Useful Tools	99
Social Media Marketing Entrepreneurs Should Listen to Customers	99
Project Ideas	102
Discussion Questions	102

Unit Two: Strategic Social Media Measurement Tools 103

Social Media Metrics and Management Tools 105

Simple and Advanced Measures 106
Social Media Dashboards and Advanced Tools 106
Thought Leader Jason Buzzell: Homepage Updating Focused
  on #TopTasks 106
Social Media Marketing, Employee Sharing, and New Business 110
Social Media Monitoring and Social Network Analysis (SNA) 112
PR Trust and the Social Media Marketing "Echo Chamber" 114
Thought Leader Stu Shulman: Text Analytics for Mining Twitter Data 117
Electronic Word-of-Mouth (eWOM) in Marketing Communication 118
Best Practices: Social Capital, Diffusion, Personal Influence, and
  Social Networks 119
Paid, Earned, Social, and Owned (PESO) Media 119
Social Media Audits and Thought Leaders 120
As Seen on YouTube 121
Useful Tools 121
Project Ideas 125
Discussion Questions 125

Academic Social Media Research 127

Quantitative and Qualitative Social Science Research 131
Testing and Replication of Data 132
Thought Leaders Roma Subramanian and Andrea Weare:
  #NotOkay 134
Thought Leader Sam Petto: A Social Media Use Research
  Project 141
As Seen on YouTube 144
Useful Tools 145
Project Ideas 145
Discussion Questions 145

Unit Three: Best Practices in Social Media Measurement 147

Integration of PR, Advertising, and Marketing Plans 149

Use of Email to Micro-Target Qualitative Relationships 151
Best Practices in Social Media Measurement 153
Integration of PR, Advertising, and Marketing Plans 154
Step-by-Step 156
Measurable Outcomes and Monitoring 160
SWOT Analysis 161
SMART Objectives 162
Reporting Results 165
Thought Leader Amanda Bright: Why You Should Stop Worrying
  about Disparate Audiences and Focus on the Universal Gap 166
As Seen on YouTube 169
Useful Tools 170
Project Ideas 170
Discussion Questions 170

Social Media Data Law and Ethics 171

Federal Trade Commission (FTC) Regulation 174
Uber and Lyft Passengers Were Secretly Live-Streamed 175
Digital Data Trails, Brand Insights, and Mobile Users 177
Case Law 181
The Future of General Data Protection Regulation (GDPR) 184
Media Ethics 185
PRSA Code of Ethics 185
A Return to Transparency, Independence, and Authenticity 187
Thought Leader Marc A. Smith: Cultivating Creative Connections in
  a Networked World – #ThinkLink 189
As Seen on YouTube 191
Useful Tools 192
Project Ideas 192
Discussion Questions 192

Customer Relationships and Content 193

Customer Relationships, Content, and Service	194
Small Business and Nonprofit Social Media Marketing Strategy	194
Customer Relations Management (CRM), C-Suites, and Corporate Social Responsibility (CSR)	196
Peter Shankman on Entrepreneurship	198
Media Storytelling, Content Sharing Blogs, and Microblogs	201
Thought Leader Dana Dyksterhuis: Influencer Marketing and the Future of Social Media Entrepreneurs	201
As Seen on YouTube	204
Useful Tools	205
Project Ideas	205
Discussion Questions	205

Unit Four: Social Media Planning and Campaigns 207

Employee Engagement 209

Engagement and Employee Advocacy	212
Effective Employee Mobile Communication	214
Employee Social Media Engagement May Help with Business Trust	216
Participation Marketing	218
Thought Leaders Donna Presnell, Betty Farmer, and Rylee Roquemore: Managing Social Media during the Death of a Leader—A Crisis Communications Case Study in Higher Education	218
Thought Leader Jennifer Grygiel: Why You Should Stop Trying to Justify the Cost of Social Media and Play More	231
As Seen on YouTube	237
Useful Tools	238
Project Ideas	239
Discussion Questions	239

10 The Future of Social Media Measurement and Management 241

Data Science	245
Tech Entrepreneurship on the Silicon Prairie	248
Thought Leader Todd Murphy: #SameRulesNewTools	254
Thought Leader Matt Tompkins: From TV to the Web—Omaha Live!	257
Messenger Bot Sequences	260
Thought Leader Jurge Cruz-Alvarez: Case Study—Extra Life	
Fundraising Campaign	262
Useful Tools	268
As Seen on YouTube	269
Project Ideas	270
Discussion Questions	270

Appendix A: Social Media Planning	271
Appendix B: Social Media Marketing Evaluation	273
Glossary	275
References	289
Index	305

Figures

0.1	BuzzFeed News Facebook post data	xxi
1.1	Fred Cook	16
1.2	Anna Vargas	25
1.3	Instagram Insights data	27
2.1	Gary Vaynerchuk	41
2.2	David Kamerer	49
2.3	Google Analytics top, time, acquisition, and pageviews	50
2.4	Gary Angel	55
2.5	Kuntal Goradia	56
2.6	Randa Zalman	62
2.7	#Give65 campaign	66
2.8	Jim Sterne	72
2.9	Howard Rheingold	75
3.1	Deepti Ganapathy	83
3.2	Facebook Insights	88
3.3	Instagram Insights	89
3.4	Twitter Analytics dashboard	90
3.5	Roberto Gallardo	92
3.6	Meltwater KPIs	94
3.7	LinkedIn audience data	97
3.8	Klipfolio Command Centre Dashboard	100
4.1	Jason Buzzell	107
4.2	Share Rocket network & Minneapolis data	110
4.3	Kevin Cook	114
4.4	Stu Shulman	117

5.1	Roma Subramanian	134
5.2	Andrea Weare	135
5.3	DiscoverText Data Collection	136
5.4	Sam Petto	141
5.5	Media use motivation data	143
6.1	Peter Barber	150
6.2	Amanda Bright	166
6.3	Twitter Analytics data	167
7.1	Jon Mills	174
7.2	Alan Knitowski	177
7.3	Marc A. Smith	189
8.1	Peter Shankman	198
8.2	Dana Dyksterhuis	201
9.1	Ray Long, *Connected to Chicago with Bill Cameron* podcast	211
9.2	Donna Presnell, Betty Farmer, and Rylee Roquemore	219
9.3	Jennifer Grygiel	231
9.4	Beth Trejo	238
10.1	Carol Fowler	251
10.2	MasterCard Conversation Suite data	253
10.3	Todd Murphy	254
10.4	Matt Tompkins	257
10.5	Jurge Cruz-Alvarez	262
10.6	Extra Life data	264
10.7	KETV newsroom social media desk data	266
10.8	Union Metrics data	267

Tables

1.1   Search engine results pages (SERPs)   5
1.2   NeilPatel.com marketing blog data example   13
1.3   Planning social media research   15
1.4   Social media governance of content   22
1.5   Content A/B testing   23
1.6   Google Analytics for website clicks   27
2.1   The seven principles   39
2.2   Continuous process measurement and evaluation   43
2.3   Alexa unomaha.edu data 2017–18   46
2.4   Overview Google Analytics data   50
2.5   Social media campaign template   67
3.1   Total unique visitors by platform (000s)   82
6.1   Mailchimp data   151
6.2   Email domain performance   152
6.3   Paid Facebook reach and engagement   157

Contributors

Amanda Bright is an academic professional specializing in digital journalism at the Grady College of Journalism and Mass Communication at the University of Georgia. Formerly, she was a professional journalist, a scholastic journalism adviser, the education editor for MediaShift, a journalism instructor and adviser at Eastern Illinois University, and the media content coordinator for Indiana State University Online. She also served as the social media director and web administrator for the Illinois Journalism Education Association.

Jason Buzzell is Digital Communications Director at the University of Nebraska at Omaha. He previously was a digital content strategist at the University of Alberta in Canada. He began his career as a sports content creator and web analyst.

Jurge Cruz-Alvarez graduated in Journalism and Media Communication (JMC) at the University of Nebraska at Omaha in 2019. He was named by JMC faculty as the outstanding undergraduate. He served as UNO Social Media Lab technician in 2018–19.

Dana Dyksterhuis is co-founder of Here For You For Them, Founder of Boasthouse and Fanzo (www.linkedin.com/in/danadyksterhuis). She was creator and executive producer at Foodie Empire and has worked in media and media relations. She welcomes email at: dana@boasthouse.com.

Betty Farmer is Professor of Communication and Public Relations at Western Carolina University. Located in Cullowhee, North Carolina, WCU is one of the 16 universities in the University of North Carolina System.

Roberto Gallardo (Ph.D.) is Purdue Center for Regional Development (PCRD) Assistant Director and Purdue Extension Community & Regional Economics Specialist. He holds a doctorate in public policy and administration, as well as a graduate degree in economic development and an undergraduate degree in engineering. His focus is on use of technologies to spark local and regional economic development. He previously served as Director of the Mississippi State University Intelligent Community Institute. Contact him at: robertog@purdue.edu.

Deepti Ganapathy (Ph.D.) pursues a multidisciplinary interest in social media, seeking to explore the use of social media for strategic political and corporate communication, climate change communication, news coverage of human trafficking and digital activism. Assistant Professor at NMIMS University's School of Business Management, Bangalore, she is a visiting faculty at the Indian Institute of Management Indore and the Indian Institute of Management Bangalore's Executive Education Program, where she conducts programs for senior bureaucrats and policy makers in the government of India. Her doctorate in social media and communication sparked work with scholars in Spain, New Zealand, Canada, the United Kingdom, Italy, and the United States.

Jennifer Grygiel (Ph.D.) is an Assistant Professor of Communications and Magazine, News, and Digital Journalism at the S.I. Newhouse School of Public Communications at Syracuse University.

David Kamerer (Ph.D.) is Associate Professor in the School of Communication, Loyola University Chicago. He teaches public relations, digital media, and online marketing. Kamerer consults small business and non-profit clients on successful social media strategies and tactics. www.linkedin.com/in/davidkamerer/.

Todd Murphy is CEO at Universal Information Services. He has developed innovative public relations and news monitoring client tools for more than 27 years.

Sam Petto is Associate Director of Editorial and Media Relations at the University of Nebraska at Omaha. A public relations professional and former television journalist, he is also a FEMA certified Public Information Officer (PIO) and crisis communications lead for UNO.

Donna Presnell is a social media and digital marketing manager at Western Carolina University.

Rylee Roquemore is a social media strategist at Western Carolina University.

Stuart W. Shulman (Ph.D.) is founder & CEO of Texifter. He was a Research Associate Professor of Political Science at the University of Massachusetts Amherst and the founding Director of the Qualitative Data Analysis Program (QDAP) at the University of Pittsburgh and at UMass Amherst. He is Editor Emeritus of the *Journal of Information Technology & Politics*, the official journal of the Information Technology & Politics section of the American Political Science Association.

Marc A. Smith (Ph.D. in sociology, UCLA) is an entrepreneur and data scientist. He directs the Social Media Research Foundation and Connected Action. He has spoken around the world about NodeXL and social network analysis.

Roma Subramanian (Ph.D., Missouri) is Assistant Professor of public relations and advertising, School of Communication, University of Nebraska at Omaha. Her science editing and PR relate to research focus on health communication, news about stigmatized disorders, impact of social and mobile media on health, and physician–patient communication dynamics.

Matt Tompkins is a cross-platform media producer and entertainer. He created *Omaha Live!* He graduated with a broadcasting degree from the University of Nebraska at Omaha.

Anna Vargas is the owner and Creative Director of Brand Her Style, LLC, a one-stop shop for women entrepreneurs that focuses on brand strategy, copywriting, social media, and web design. Brand Her Style helps businesses from the moment of launch, including creating pitch decks for potential investors, and during phases of rapid growth when it's time to upgrade their online presence because they've outgrown their starter sites. This is her third business in the last decade: she has experience as sole creative designer for a public relations firm in Chicago, where she worked with the new business, digital, consumer, and corporate teams.

Andrea Weare (Ph.D., Iowa) is Assistant Professor of Public Relations and Advertising, School of Communication, University of Nebraska at Omaha. She teaches strategic communication, media, and qualitative research methods. Her research focuses on digital and strategic.

Randa Zalman is the President and CEO of Canary & Coal, a marketing firm in Omaha, Nebraska. She is a recognized thought leader on the power and appropriate use of new media including social media and digital placement.

Preface

A Cambridge Analytica Facebook data scandal in the 2016 U.S. election seemed to shock people who were unaware of the ability to surgically target advertising on social media sites. In fact, the social media measurement and management industry has dramatically grown within advertising, public relations, and marketing because of its effectiveness as a business model. Instagram, for example, is a social media site that reaches young people with organic and paid messages that cost much less than less targeted, traditional media. Boston firm Crimson Hexagon, one of the earliest data collection and analysis tools, was suspended in mid-2018 by Facebook amid questions about its use of Facebook and Instagram data. Facebook explicitly claimed to prohibit development of "surveillance tools," but there are fuzzy areas within algorithms that are used to target audiences.

Zuboff (2019) has called this *The Age of Surveillance Capitalism*, defined as an economic order that "unilaterally claims human experience as free raw material for translation into behavioral data" (p. 8). Social media users typically ignore data collection, which now extends to one's facial recognition, the "smart home," vehicles, work, and other important physical spaces. With few meaningful regulatory controls, entrepreneurs have leveraged the freedom to measure and manage social media communication. Jay Baer, founder of Convince & Convert, for example, pitched a Cision measurement dashboard tool that optimizes influencer marketing effectiveness. AI and machine learning data science of social networks are applied to match paid influencers with their highly targeted audience of consumers. Clearly, there is a need to explore so-called "big data" from not only their utility, but also critical perspectives and ethical concerns.

By the beginning of 2019, journalists found that Facebook had sold Microsoft, Amazon, Google, and other technology companies access to user location and other private data, such as messages. Facebook, Twitter, and other social network site executives have admitted to journalists that the technology industry was overly optimistic and naïve about the power available to use the tools for good or bad. For example, it was disclosed that Facebook search and location data for millions of accounts also was accessed, but not immediately disclosed to site users. Facebook faced millions of dollars in Federal Trade Commission (FTC) fines for not protecting user privacy, as it had promised to do in 2011. Likewise, mobile phone software, such as The Weather Channel's app, according to a Los Angeles lawsuit, routinely tracked user location, and apparently sold data for advertising purposes. Google, meanwhile, was appealing a record European Union (EU) fine in France of $50 million. As this book was published, it was not clear if U.S. regulators would follow the EU and the state of California in demanding stricter data privacy laws. Clearly, it is both an exciting and challenging time to study measurement and management of social media data. As entrepreneur Gary Vaynerchuk suggested about Instagram popularity and relatively low-cost marketing during his IGTV *DailyVee* series (519, 2018, December 4), "It's so popular, it becomes the mirror of human shortcomings . . . it's exposed us."

Certainly, there are increasing levels of awareness, caution, and maturity about use and misuse of social media. A Buzzfeed News investigation of 2016 election data showed that left and right partisan political engagement on Facebook peaked around the presidential decision. Facebook, for example, appeared to realign filtering toward content created and shared by friends and family members rather than brands using content management tools for organic marketing. Facebook Community Boost traveled the country in 2018 to spread the message to small businesses that paid and boosted Facebook and Instagram Stories were the way to increase reach to greater numbers of highly targeted customers. The challenge is that few social media users understand the computer code and processes behind emerging machine learning communication technologies. In fact, one survey found that less than half of people in the United States could be certain when they were communicating with an automated chatbot. As automation continues to advance, the character of human–computer interaction (HCI) and computer-mediated communication (CMC) will continue to evolve and likely transform social media into a less human and more technological experience.

The data show an obvious and dramatic shift away from the traditional media landscape in the past two decades. *Social Media Today* reported that there were more than one billion Web pages, 3.5 billion daily Google searches, two billion Facebook users, and more than 71,000 videos viewed every second. Social media data are large, challenging to manage over time, and not always representative of an increasingly fragmented audience. The global numbers continue to rapidly grow—especially in India, China, and other large nations. Those who master search engine optimization (SEO) will find themselves at the heart of an $80 billion U.S. industry in 2020. These facts support the need to develop this academic field of study, as well as for this book—more universities

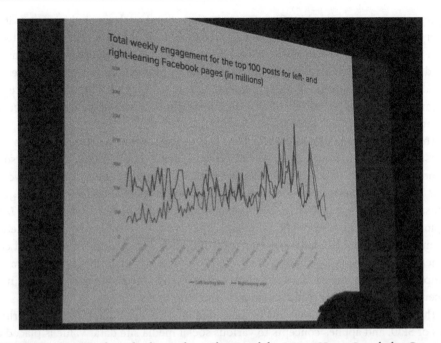

FIGURE 0.1 *BuzzFeed Facebook post data. Photograph by Jeremy Harris Lipschultz: Courtesy Buzzfeed News Media Editor Craig Silverman (@CraigSilverman), keynote speaker at the Association for Education in Journalism and Mass Communication (AEJMC) in Chicago 2017.*

and colleges are developing new measurement and management courses. At the same time, small and large businesses or nonprofits have invested in social media listening and engagement "command centers"—hiring individual managers or teams of analytics specialists. SEO is a way of thinking for students and industry professionals that aligns with state-of-the-art social media measurement and management techniques, such as social network analysis (SNA). It groups conversation into clusters with top influencers at the center of graphs.

This book expands on and applies a social media communication (SMC) perspective to the study of measurement and analytics. The textbook is designed for courses in social media measurement, digital marketing analytics, applied media research, social media management, and media entrepreneurship. Innovation continues to be at the heart of ongoing transformation of how social media are measured and managed. We must understand that the "hacker culture" that built and continues to grow Facebook and other social media sites views the Internet and new communication technologies from a libertarian approach to business. *Social Media Measurement and Management: Entrepreneurial Digital Analytics* is grounded in a view that: 1) SMC practices represent a fundamental shift; 2) data measurement and analyses are key skills within emerging media models; 3) SMC management is critical for business or nonprofit success; and 4) media entrepreneurship represents a behavioral model for responding to rapid and ongoing change. As such, students and professionals face daily challenges and opportunities. The book reflects the increasing value of traditional social science research concepts, such as reliability (data consistency) and validity, in the proper use and interpretation of available social media data.

The book is divided into four parts. *Unit One* introduces foundations of social media measurement and management—social crowds, share of voice (SoV), and personal branding; campaigns and concepts, such as SEO; and application to social networks. *Unit Two* focuses on strategic social media basic and advanced tools for monitoring and measuring outcomes, as well as recent developments in academic research. *Unit Three* explores best practices in public relations, advertising, and marketing. These include organic and paid social media within a legal and ethical framework of social and customer relationship management (CRM). *Unit Four* develops planning for a social media campaign through electronic word-of-mouth (eWOM), media storytelling, and influencer engagement that includes customers and employees.

The book provides an overview of measurement, teaches Google Analytics principles of SEO, and applies concepts to various social media site data. Value is placed on an introduction to social marketing from a communication perspective, a roadmap for the project planning process, and a readable text that takes students and professionals from introductory ideas to advanced analytics. This book incorporates communication theory and application through a focused set of key industry thought leaders and online YouTube video. It translates the complexities of digital analytics for use by students in public relations, advertising, marketing, and related fields. Other traditional media majors, such as in journalism and broadcasting, also increasingly need data analytics skills and practices to be successful.

The increased interest in social media curricula includes courses covering social media measurement, metrics, and management strategies and tactics. New courses, certificates, and programs are being driven by industry trends to use rigorous social science and behavioral data in applied research. Students need to learn the state-of-the-art in techniques and tools. As Richard Gershon (2017) observes in his entrepreneurship textbook *Digital Media Innovation, Management and Design Strategies in Communication*, disruptive technologies alter processes: "It redefines the playing field by introducing to the marketplace a unique value proposition" (p. 3). His focus is on product, process, and business model innovation, with limited attention to social media and digital analytics. The purpose of this book, however, is to serve upper-level undergraduate and introductory graduate students in media communication fields with a media entrepreneurship framework that bridges social media measurement and engagement.

The book owes much to my teachers and colleagues over decades at the University of Illinois, University of Evansville, Southern Illinois University, and the University of Nebraska at Omaha (UNO). It draws heavily from UNO's original "Social Media Metrics" course launched in 2009, as well as the "Social Media Measurement and Management" course taught to undergraduate and graduate students since 2015, and the "Media Entrepreneurship" course launched in 2018. Omaha, located on the "Silicon Prairie" with Kansas City, Des Moines, St. Louis, Chicago, and other Midwestern tech hubs, has been a hotbed for entrepreneurs and social media activities. We have learned from industry leaders at Edelman Digital, Golin, and other large agencies, as well as smaller local firms B2 Interactive, Canary and Coal, and Universal Information Services. Our students have cultivated skill sets on how to build professional and successful social media campaigns based upon data and entrepreneurship. I am thankful for our UNO Barbara Weitz Community Engagement Center, local nonprofit and business partnerships, service-learning experiences, and collaboration with Nebraska's Rural Futures Institute (RFI) that helped the UNO Social Media Lab (@unosml) and our students in Maverick Social Media (MSM) organize a body of knowledge found within these pages. Book Thought Leaders Amanda Bright and Jurge Cruz-Alvarez helped format some of the book data images. My colleagues Roberto Gallardo at Purdue University and Charlotte Narjes at University of Nebraska-Lincoln, as well as community and nonprofit clients, continue to ask important questions.

For more than 35 years, my spouse Sandy has collaborated to balance family and work. In many ways, this book is a reflection of my professional transformation from a teaching, research, and service focus of traditional media toward our emerging discipline of digital and social media innovation.

Jeremy Harris Lipschultz (@JeremyHL), Omaha, Nebraska

January 2019

UNIT ONE

Foundations of Social Media Measurement and Management

Social Crowds, Voice, and Personal Branding

> *Branding is the perception of your position in the market, including all of your content and imagery.*

—Andy Crestodina (@crestodina, 2018, p. 15)

> *There is a barrier keeping most companies from really getting value out of their analytics investment . . . It's getting the wider org (not just the analytics team) to adopt a data-driven mindset in a way that actually changes the way folks go about their day-to-day business.*

—Jennifer Kunz (@33Sticks, 2018, via ObservePoint, 2018, p. 9)

Data-driven branding decisions reflect an organizational understanding that valuable insights offer a competitive advantage. The simple act of clicking a "Like" button on a post sends valuable targeting data to Facebook and its paying businesses. Unfortunately, the historic legal freedom to use targeted online data is very effective at the same time as it may unethically promote dangerous political polarization around the world

(PBS, 2018). Some businesses reaped huge profits by understanding and then "gaming" Google, Facebook, and other social media **algorithms** to drive traffic to their owned media websites. For example, it appears that **clickbait** sites that share sensationalized content remain popular and profitable (Roose, 2018b). It should be obvious that students as well as social media users should learn about the high stakes behind social media measurement and management. Social media literacy skills and practices are the first line of defense against the tyranny of data access and use. The European Union (EU) **General Data Protection Regulation** (**GDPR**) online privacy framework seeks to offer consumer protection, and U.S. businesses with a global reach are moving toward compliance with data protection rules. Still, rapid technological innovation offers huge corporations, such as Amazon, massive data that track human behavior. Smaller businesses and organizations tend to lack knowledge, skills, and practices to keep up.

Measurement is central to social media management of successful businesses outcomes. Drawing from the field of public relations, "practitioners use measurement to demonstrate their value to organizations," which explains why data have "occupied a central place" for decades and are considered as evidence of "impact" (Hopp & Gallicano, 2016, p. 127). Likewise, the fields of advertising and "data-driven marketing" and decision practices measure "social influence" to strategically increase revenue and meet other goals (Quesenberry, 2019, pp. 11–12). Social media campaigns and ongoing work may leverage the power of social crowds through **branding** and **crowdsourcing**. Employee **brand storytellers**, for example, may be activated in "participation marketing" through online "advocacy" (Brito, 2018, p. 14). The so-called positive or negative "megaphoning" by consumers, employees, and others appears to be associated with deeper relationships and situational context (Kim & Ni, 2013, p. 139).

The field of marketing has developed decades of research exploring the social power of brands and branding to increase **reach** and a **share of voice** (**SoV**) for a product or service. Twitter, for example, was used by television newsrooms for promotion and branding (Greer & Ferguson, 2011). Content marketer Andy Crestodina (2018) observes that outbound "traditional marketing" began to shift online in 1994, and "web-centric" marketing offered new data from "**pay-per-click**" (**PPC**) advertising, email, and **search engine optimization** (**SEO**)—social media was added to the mix in about 2010 (pp. 4–5): "That's why content marketing is emerging as a winner over advertising. It's a friendlier, more credible and more sensitive way for us to connect with information . . . including the information that drives purchasing decisions" (p. 6). Crestodina's work is driven by an emphasis on branding and marketing. His quote at the beginning of this chapter is followed by his @crestodina Twitter handle. Throughout this book, readers can use these account references as suggestions on who to follow for the most current ideas about social media measurement and management.

SEO resides within the broader search marketing area (Jansen, 2011). Specifically, **search engine marketing** (**SEM**) is defined as using "paid strategies," whereas SEO is based upon organic promotion (Yesbeck, 2018, para. 8). SEM and SEO are utilized to improve page rankings by increasing views and clicks. PPC marketing through Google Ads clicks is considered a SEM "tactic" that builds, and test ads based upon keywords (para. 10). Since 1998, Google searches, as well as those from competing search engines, have produced organic **search engine results pages** (SERPs), and this still happens within modern SEO. For example, a SERP analysis of a brand **keyword** phrase for a university reveals ranking of top pages, estimated visit data, as well as social shares and a domain authority score:

TABLE 1.1 *Search engine results pages (SERPs)*

Rank	SEO Title URL	Root Domain	Est. Visits	Soc. Shares	DA
1	UNOmaha.edu	http://www	4499	3851	51
2	Wikipedia.org	http://www	2397	6	92
3	Niche.com	http://www	1440	0	58
4	Facebook.com	http://www	975	0	99
5	USNews.com	http://www	694	0	64

Source: https://app.neilpatel.com/en/ubersuggest/serp_analysis

In this example, a keyword search of "University of Nebraska at Omaha" found only a handful of Wikipedia social shares beyond the owned media website. The "Best Colleges" listing ranked in terms of page visits, but not social shares or domain authority. Students can check their campus with this valuable free tool.

Top-of-page results that are most likely to be seen in a search increasingly happen because of paid SEM. On the organic side of SEO, keywords and content drive on-page SEO, coders improve technical SEO, and links and backlinks create **authority** needed to optimize off-page SEO. In fact, many social marketing businesses organize around three departments: content, coding, and SEO.

When you shop at a local grocery store, how do you decide which brands to buy? Are you most influenced by family, friends, advertising, or social media conversation and posts? Personal influence is an important communication research area that spans decades (Katz 1957, 2006). Sometimes a sale or special offer leads consumers to try a new product or switch brands. This **adoption** and spread of new products, processes, services, and ideas through **diffusion of innovation** happens through our personal and social networks (Rogers, 1995). There are at least 337 resources and tools available to the social media manager (Quesenberry, 2018), but the key is to focus on those that add value to this important work.

America's Test Kitchen, which publishes cook books and produces public television shows, found it could connect through social media with loyal fans. Its marketing efforts depend upon growing the number of online memberships. "From a digital marketing perspective, turning online engagement into measurable action starts with increasing website traffic from social" (Sprout Social, 2018a, para. 4). In order to know what is happening over time, a brand must **benchmark** data, track data over time, and develop strategies and tactics for "moving the needle" through an increase of numbers defined as important for a business or organization. This requires a great deal of planning and execution skills.

Sometimes a social crowd represents a wave of persuasion through a spread of personal influence or public opinion. Other times, a long family history of brand experience drives a purchasing decision. Increasingly, **organic** (naturally developing) and **paid** (promoted or boosted) social media campaigns seek to influence our decisions about products and services. In the end, a brand **sentiment** (positive, neutral, or negative) may influence behavior, but such affective or emotional responses are extremely difficult to measure with **reliability** or consistency. Social scientists conduct research to answer these questions through data collection and analysis. The simplest definition for research is finding answers to questions, and the best social media managers apply answers to future management decisions. Large brands, such as Southwest Airlines, Target, and McDonald's, were early adopters and leaders in development of **real-time social media listening** and **engagement**. In simple terms, they recognized that reputation management now requires brands to listen and quickly respond to customer concerns and complaints, as well as engage with appreciative fans (Fertik & Thompson, 2015). One estimate found, however, that content engagement dropped by half over three years, as many brands prefer to broadcast messages rather than engage with consumers (Tran, 2018b). This may be because of the time and resources required to either use human resources or develop machine learning **artificial intelligence** (**AI**) **chatbots** for these tasks. We will return to these issues at the end of the book, as most thought leaders predict that AI will dominate **computer-mediated communication** (**CMC**) and social media in the future. As it is, online interaction has been found to cloud perception of psychological traits, such as introversion, extroversion, and neuroticism (Amichai-Hamburger, et al., 2002). We are re-creating social life on the Internet (Bargh & McKenna, 2004), and global participation continues to grow.

There were more than 7.59 billion people in our world toward the end of the first decade in the twenty-first century, and more than two-thirds of the global population use mobile phones. *WeAreSocial* estimated that among the more than four billion Internet users, more than 3.2 billion were active social media users, with most of them accessing sites through mobile devices. Mobile news adoption, consumption and usage varies across age groups (Chan-Olmsted, et al., 2013). Bloomberg reported that by 2020,

Instagram and its more than one billion users will account for 20 percent of Facebook sales and revenue (Frier, 2018). Billions of accounts operated by humans and automated chatbots generate so-called **big data**—massive amounts of observations every minute. The size of data, however, does not guarantee quality, and many social media managers prefer to focus on development of relationships.

Active social media and mobile social users are estimated to be the fastest growing population, as the planet continues to shift from rural to now a majority urban population. Surviving rural communities have adopted an "intelligent community" model of leveraging broadband online access to global markets: "Digital technologies are insensitive to location and distance and potentially offer workers a much greater range of opportunities than ever before" (Gallardo, et al., 2018, para. 3). The adoption of a "hacker culture" mindset by the younger tech sector is driving social media success through creativity and experimentation: "Hacker, in the Facebook sense, means building something quickly or testing the boundaries of what is possible" (Gershon, 2017, p. 229).

For people living and working in cities and smaller urban centers, mobile smartphone apps and social media communication are essential tools. The current fascination with entrepreneurs and entrepreneurship is important because the words are commonly defined around the work of organizing, managing, and innovative risk-taking. One need look no further than the last Toys R Us, Sears, or Blockbuster Video store in America to see why technological disruption must be met with openness to rapid change (Abrams, 2018). Blockbuster Alaska announced in a Facebook Post closing its remaining stores:

> To all of our valued customers,
> We regret to inform our customers that Blockbuster Video will be closing both the College and Debarr stores starting July 16th. We will reopen for our inventory sale on Tuesday, July 17th at 12 noon and will run through the months of July and August. These are the last two Blockbuster stores in Alaska that survived, and it is sad to say goodbye to our dedicated customers. We have thought of you as family for the past 28 years. Both Kelli Vey and I (Kevin Daymude) have been with the company since 1991 and have had great memories throughout our career. Thank you for sticking by us throughout all these years. I can't tell you how much it means to us. We hope to see you at our stores during the closing, even if it's just to say "Hello". What a great time to build your media library and share some Blockbuster memories with us.
> We will miss all of you!
> Thank you again,
> Kelli Vey
> District Manager
> Kevin Daymude
> General Manager

Within a week, the post had 510 comments, 955 shares and thousands of Facebook reactions. As retail shoppers adopted Amazon, Target, and other online purchasing sites, there were winners and losers in diffusion of technological innovation. By 2019, Sears and Kmart had joined a long list of brick and mortar retailers failing to adapt to Internet change. At the most fundamental level, social media measurement and management is essential for organizational survival in this digital age that is dominated by information sharing and online commerce.

From retailers to media companies, digital and social media alter the playing field for business or nonprofit success and failure. Initial impression, anticipation about future interaction, and perceived loyalty, for example, are important variables in building long-term relationships (Foster and Cadogan, 2000; Ramirez, 2007). Social media managers need to assess risk by collecting and analyzing data and contextually interpreting online interaction and opportunity. If they embrace the entrepreneurial challenges behind continuous innovation, then it can be enjoyable and very rewarding work. Social media interaction of people, messages and AI technologies involve human values. For example, Facebook engineers drove a small startup to become a global corporate giant with billions of users by embracing behavioral data of newsfeed users, learning from experiments, and refining company products, processes and business models. Social media have *play* between physical and virtual boundaries, and the notion of "embodying technology" offers one explanation of a complex, yet flexible space (p. 144). This may offer new competitive "economic reality" of "big data and big analytics" driven by "**cloud computing** and the **Internet of things**" (**IoT**) (Ezrachi & Stucke, 2016, pp. 11–18), which do not always allow for predictable behavior:

> to perfectly price discriminate with incomplete data, any prediction would likely be based on assumptions, such as consumers having stable premises and a preexisting reservation price. The problem is that multiple dispositional and situational factors can affect purchasing decisions, and consumers may not even know their reservation price.
>
> (p. 97)

Social media communication (SMC) was revolutionary, and IoT are transformational. The point is that people frequently act in reflexive and irrational ways, and this may be true when it comes to our examination of social media behavioral data. For example, as we will see, when people copy and paste links from social posts without tracking code, these may be incorrectly measured as direct website traffic (**dark social**), diminishing the perceived value of content shared through social media sites (Quesenberry, 2017). It is frequently difficult for social media managers to know as much as a social scientist should about hidden data proprietary practices that communication scholar David Kamerer, a thought leader in this book, says are "behind the curtain."

In other words, a lack of transparent research methods should lead us to be skeptical about data and findings.

The potential for error becomes even more pronounced when we explore the global, transnational, and cultural nature of social media (Darling-Wolf, 2015). Research suggests that rural media users, for example, may consciously differentiate themselves from the urban: "They distanced themselves from the YouTube obsessed, Facebook fixated Twittering crowd of the city" (p. 156). While broadband mobile access increasingly is available, some "negotiated their local/rural identities in relationship to the urban and national, as well as the global" (p. 156). Still, we find local business people needing to understand that survival depends upon technical skills and knowledge to leverage a variety of digital tools, including social media measurement and management. So, from the largest brands to the smallest family business, social media knowledge, skills, and practices are essential.

An important challenge within social media measurement and management is to recognize the basic limitation of social research data analysis. While "applied research" is seen as a benefit for public relations and advertising work, for example, "a commercial or client-driven need" may be less "pure" than basic academic research interests in discovering and creating knowledge for its own sake:

> Most advertising and public relations research is applied research, intended for a specific purpose or application, often in a particular, proprietary situation. You may still avail yourself of all the research methods and approaches that are available, just applied to a specific situation or problem.
>
> (Jugenheimer, et al., 2014, p. 5)

For example, the *2019 Edelman Trust Barometer* suggests a growing gap between the "informed public" and the "mass population" (Edelman, 2019, p. 8). So-called news "amplifiers" are defined as those sharing or posting "several times a month or more" (p. 18). The survey found that 76 percent of respondents agreed that "CEOs should take the lead on change rather than waiting for government to impose it" (p. 21). The connection between this finding and the business model of the world's largest PR firm, which includes advising CEOs on business practices, cannot be overlooked in review of the study's methods, instrument, and specific questions.

For social media managers, it is important to strive for rigor in measurement of quantitative data and interpretation of qualitative data. This requires an emphasis on critical thinking, explicit frameworks, and planning processes. Simple data points, such as the number of Twitter followers, have large amounts of error. In 2018, for example, Twitter announced by email that the "daily follower change" data "may have shown a very big drop in your followers" of 1 to 6 percent. Twitter Counter Chief Omer Ginor, however, added that drops were much larger for those who had purchased followers, but also celebrities who had not: "There's no need to be alarmed: Twitter just deleted and suspended millions of alleged fake accounts," Twitter explained. "This drop may happen again as Twitter is not done with the cleanup" that was "in response to public pressure to crack down on fake news and public opinion manipulation on social media." Twitter's **Chief Executive Officer (CEO)** Jack Dorsey (@jack) lost a whopping 14 percent of followers, as public figures and celebrities tended to be hit hardest by the effort. Entertainer Ashton Kutcher (@aplush), for example, lost about 6.2 percent of followers. In social science, we call this cleaning the data, and these methods are starting to be seen more than a decade into the social media revolution. At the same time, CEO Dorsey expressed remorse about Twitter's decision to emphasize the follower count metric to users: "They want to make it go up" (Slashdot, 2018, para. 2).

> It is actually incentivizing you to increase that number. That may have been right 12 years ago, but I don't think it is right today. I don't think that's the number you should be focused on. I think what is more important is the number of meaningful conversations you're having on the platform. How many times do you receive a reply?
>
> (para. 3)

Dorsey's emphasis on engagement coincided with his concern about likes, which may motivate unhealthy user behavior. Co-founder Ev Williams claimed some of the blame through stoking numbers by displaying follower accounts in user profiles, offering following suggestions, and gaining media publicity (*Recode*, 2018b). "It really put in your face that the game was popularity" (para. 3). Social media popularity, as well as verification check marks, clearly have had an impact upon the personal brand and organizational data measured and managed. So, it is an empirically verifiable overstatement to suggest that vanity metrics, such as followers and likes, had little or no branding value. Business reflection and self-evaluation, though, are important entrepreneur attributes in the need for continuous improvement of social network site use.

There are a variety of sources and tools used to measure online activities, including social media content. The media measurement field increasingly expresses concern for rigor in research methods. This includes greater disclosure of research methods that is common within the academic setting. The goal is to explain how data were collected and analyzed, so that outsiders can judge the value of results. Academics enforce rigor through what is called "blind" peer review before acceptance of results for publication. For applied research, though, we should demand transparency of methods and disclosure of client and other interests. This is challenging for companies in confidential relationships that use proprietary data sets and computer algorithms—especially public companies with a fiduciary interest to maximize profits for shareholders. They have a competitive motivation to keep company secrets about innovation and business practices.

Smartphones have moved to the center of data because mobile devices are the most common way to access social media sites, websites, blogs, and video. Typically, analysts use data to examine site visitor **demographics**. Other, deeper filters include location (**geographic** or geo), psychographic, and use data. For example, health perception and lifestyle behavior are important within **psychographics**. Meredith (2017) summarized Hubspot's marketing suggestion that psychographic data may be obtained by interviewing existing clients and exploring website analytics. Testing can be used to identify motivation for clicking onsite objects, and these data can be important in building stronger marketing strategies and tactics. For products and services, important goals include attracting new users and then retaining them, hopefully, as loyal fans. Data may provide important evidence of movement toward **conversion** to an idea, process, product, or service.

In social science data, we talk about **variables** as measures that reflect this type of **empirical** or observable evidence of human behavior. Researchers are interested in measuring change over time. **Independent** variables typically measure potential causes or predictors of future outcomes of effects, as seen through the measurement of **dependent** variables. Most social media data do not reflect cause and effect, but they may offer patterns of change. Within these complex measures, a set of independent variables, as well as potential **intervening** variables, may begin to allow us to explain what is happening. It is helpful to define our observation through a set of explicit **research questions**, if not outright predictions you may know as **hypotheses**. It is common for social media managers to have taken a social science methodology course during their undergraduate or graduate school training, and this is recommended for professional advancement.

In the area of social media measurement, academics are beginning to study concepts, build models, and structure theories that may help us to predict future outcomes. Traditional communication research textbooks have started to add the topic of social media research methods, but these tend to be at the broadest level, viewing social media as "a research site," a "research tool," and an ethical concern (McIntosh, 2019, pp. 151–156. While traditional survey research addresses sampling and other **measurement error**, social media numbers may be considered **population data**—if a complete set of data can be collected. Frequently, however, social media data also involve sampling that may not satisfy **random** conditions required for generalizing from a sample to a population. For example, the Twitter **application programming interface** (**API**) has allowed free collection to some tools of about 18,000 tweets on any search over the most recent ten-day period. This may allow us to collect complete population data for a local query of a word, phrase or **hashtag**, but may be less than one minute of tweets from an internationally trending topic. A researcher might decide on a method of randomly sampling the population data over time. Alternatively, researchers may pay for more complete data that approximate the population. That said, *all* social data have error, and all measurement tools are at the mercy of platform API computer code.

The same can be said for website analytics data collected with the two most popular tools—Google Analytics and Adobe Analytics. The Evolytics firm recommends frequent analytics audits to determine if data are correctly collected. Their *AUDIT* framework is:

Align—goals, key metrics and user flow

Understand—implementation

Document—data gaps and improvement opportunities

Identify—priorities to fix and enhance

Tell—the story and share findings

Porter (2018) concluded that, "It doesn't matter how much analytics code is on your site if it's not sending the right data in the right format at the right time to the right analytics platform" (para. 3). **Tracking calls** are used by site developers to observe accuracy and debug website journeys. If you received an email today with a link to a website page, the tracking begins when a user clicks that automatically attach tracking code. To see this, click on a link. Everything after the "?" in the web address **uniform resource locator (URL)** at the top of your browser is your tracking code. This is important because we want to know if social media content effectively sent visitors to websites, and what happened once there. This also is a consideration when examining any social media platform insights data. Facebook, for example, essentially is a highly interactive website and mobile data app. While Facebook Insights offer user reactions, the company retains user journey data as proprietary for advertising purposes. We constantly must keep limitation of social data in mind. Facebook behavior may be linked to personality traits, self-presentation and impression management (Rosenberg & Egbert, 2011).

Khatibloo, et al. (2018) link measurement of dirty data to trust because personal data can be viewed as "a ticking time bomb" (para. 5). While digital marketers latched onto the value of personal data, governance, and accountability fell behind these technologies. While data-driven efforts frequently demonstrate results, consumers may want to guard personal information: "43% say they're likely to cancel an online transaction if they see something they don't like in a privacy policy" (para. 9). Forrester uses a matrix of "identifiability," "sensitivity," and "scarcity" of data to determine if use of data are "risky" or "toxic" (paras. 16–19). Among the potential risks in data collection are inappropriate use of personal data, use of out-of-date data, and ignoring customer interest in an expectation of privacy. Additionally, the use of inaccurate data remains a common problem.

The concern with social media data is that most proprietary data collection and analysis tools offer no way to measure an estimate of error. Without this form of scientific rigor, quantitative data may be meaningless. Often analysts are left to quickly move from quantitative measures to qualitative interpretation. This is less scientifically objective, and more aligned with potentially rigorous, yet subjective analysis.

From small organizations and businesses to large corporations, budgeting requires that managers identify a **return on investment (ROI)** of money, time, and other resources. It is common to talk about **monetization** of social media content or realizing a flow of money in exchange for the time and effort. For example, social media buzz and conversation likely contributed to the sale of more than 100 million products during the July 2018 Amazon Prime Day event. Online engagement helped remind consumers to visit the site during a 36-hour promotion window. The creation of a mid-summer event helped Amazon surpass Black Friday and Cyber Monday revenue later in the year. In this use case, the company relies heavily on devoted customers subscribed to its Prime paid program and in the habit of regularly visiting the site, but social media may attract new potential customers and sales.

Likewise, the NeilPatel.com marketing blog (Patel, 2018a) for one month reported the following data:

TABLE 1.2 *NeilPatel.com marketing blog data example*

2,510,893 **visits** → 1,609,314 **unique visits** → 5,890,103 **pageviews** → 1,942 **leads**
→ 262 **companies budgeting** + $5,000 per month marketing
→ $972,860 **contract value** (12-month *revenue*) – *expenses* = **profit**

Patel's data are not completely granular—there is no discussion of the specific impact on profit of Facebook, Twitter, LinkedIn, and other traffic driven to the agency blog. However, the most shared posts data indicate a high value for Facebook, as well as smaller shares for Twitter, Reddit, and LinkedIn. Patel (2018a) employs a blog model that includes 2,000–3,000-word posts packed with **keywords** that are important to Google, and the Google Analytics data report new users of the blog site. In one highlighted Facebook post, organic reach was 22,499, with an additional 5,431 from paid and targeted $400 promoted posts. Email posts also continue to extend reach. Patel says he leveraged his personal brand and influence, earning consulting jobs paying more than one million dollars because of his millions in monthly blog views, YouTube subscribers and video views, and other social media (Facebook, Twitter, and LinkedIn) followers and fans (Patel, 2018c). Still, he regrets that his strong personal brand overshadows the businesses he built. "None of my companies have as much traffic, and they don't have anywhere near the social following as my personal blog" (para. 8).

> And here's the kicker: It's also harder to sell a company when it is named after a person. And if you are one of the lucky people who are able to sell a business based off of a personal brand, the multiple won't be as great because the buyer knows that when the personal brand leaves, so will some of the revenue.
>
> (para. 78)

Patel's personal branding success continues because his daily podcast, blog, weekly YouTube videos, public speaking engagements, guest posts, and global reach keep content flow current and relevant. Brands were driven by consultants to push company faces into the social crowd that connects as individuals: "It's about relationships over reach" (Rubel, 2017, para. 4). "The businesses that stress a storytelling approach that prioritizes delivery through credible, authentic and proximate peer faces [versus] faceless brands will be more successful" (para. 8). The emphasis on relational communication over algorithm gaming is important.

Adobe commissioned a study by Forrester (2018) to demonstrate ROI from the use of Adobe Analytics and Adobe Audience Manager software. The data suggested increases in site traffic, conversion rate, average order value, upselling, reduction in **cost per click (CPC)**, and overall ROI. It makes sense that use of tools helping social media managers organize and be strategic would have positive economic impact. Still, the data are a snapshot within a rapidly changing field. Constant algorithm changes at Google are complicated by its desire to sell Google Ads—more than $ 95 billion in 2017 revenue (Patel, 2018b, para. 7). SEO data may fluctuate due to changes in weighting of search criteria but paying attention to the mobile shift and your audience for content demonstrate empirical success in the marketing space. Patel (2018b) recommends a "prune and crop" strategy for older content by observing social media shares within a spreadsheet of specific URL page data. Optimization sometimes involves the decision to delete content and redirect online traffic. By paying attention to a growing global market and brand strategies, individuals and organizations may gain competitive advantage through effective social media measurement and management. An entrepreneurial approach of quickly responding to data shifts should help managers develop innovative solutions to business challenges.

The decision to spend on social media is weighed against other needs. The same is true for nonprofit organizations or government agencies. Leaders must be able to read a profit and loss (P&L) statement and make a sound judgment about the value of social

TABLE 1.3 *Planning social media research*

Problem ID →	*Research Methods* →	*Data Collection* →	*Data Analysis* →	*Outcome*
History	Approaches	Timeframe	Interpretation	Action
Theories	Multimethod	Budget	Skills	Feedback
Concepts	Quantitative/Qualitative	Observation	Analysis	Business

media within a specific context. Nonprofit PR organizational adoption should happen within a larger strategic planning framework (Curtis, et al., 2010). When developing a social media campaign, the planning process is impacted by identification of **key performance indicators (KPIs)**—those data points that are most central in achieving specific organizational goals. For example, a Facebook post may feature a link to a website with a goal of driving traffic from a social media post to a business page. One KPI might be the number of clicks on a webpage that encourages a potential customer to complete a form with contact information. In doing so, she has become a sales lead at the top of what is known as the **marketing funnel**. As we build a research plan, it is important to consider the cost of research against its potential value to an organization. At the highest corporate level, social media management teams may wish to influence a chief executive officer, **chief marketing officer** (**CMO**), and others in the **C-suite** to invest in building social media measurement and management assets within the larger public relations (PR), advertising, and marketing budgets. Especially for lean nonprofits or start-up businesses with a sole social media manager who frequently has other duties, time needed to accomplish rigorous measurement must be considered. A linear research process model is a useful starting point in understanding knowledge and skills.

Rigorous research is a continuous process that takes outcomes as feedback to refine problem identification, methods, data collection, and analysis. Social scientists typically begin with an explicit purpose statement for the research. From there, they conceptualize the problem through a comprehensive **literature review** of all published results. By exploring previous findings, it is possible to develop theory-based research questions (RQs). Only then can we collect meaningful data, answer questions, and interpret the data over time within a research program. In business, on the other hand, research may not be driven by clear concepts and **operational definitions** of procedures. Instead, it is more common to connect research data to short-term business goals. In this book, we argue for a synthesis of academic and industry research driven by scientific rigor, a search for new knowledge, and application of research findings. As a student, it is too easy to forget about rigorous methods after the final examination in a research course, but it is worth resisting the tendency. Whether you take research skills onto graduate school coursework or a job in public relations, advertising, or marketing, the use of good data should lead to better decision-making. A social science mindset demands vigilant attention to research method principles of reliability and validity of data. A healthy skepticism is needed when viewing and interpreting all data with an emphasis on what we do not know.

Sometimes, social businesses offer a free e-book or white paper online download ("**freemium**") in hopes of ultimately leading to **conversion** of a new or returning customer. The idea is to move a person through a sales process that converts her or him into a buyer of products or services. White papers are an important resource for social media managers to keep up with the latest trends, and it is worth noting those sources cited within this book.

Increasingly, social media are new tools that align with traditional media advertising, email lists and other modes of communication with brand representatives. KPIs should be continuously monitoring within social media and sales or other data. Social media data must be connected to larger business goals and strategies for growth. Social business places social media within the more traditional context of **word-of-mouth** (**WOM**) branding. Social media conversation offers paths toward cultivating brand loyalty by consistently delivery convenience. Social media **influence** appears to have reach via amplification across social networks. Engaging content within **social network sites** (**SNSs**) may be measured and connected to brand influencers. A scientific **social network analysis** (**SNA**), such as the academic and business NodeXL tool, visualizes top influencers as at or near the center of a social media conversation. One brand strategy might be to monitor these networks and engage with influencers. Specific tactics may be employed by a social media manager or team to offer incentives to an influencer. At this point,

FIGURE 1.1 *Fred Cook (@fredcook). Photograph by Jeremy Harris Lipschultz, courtesy Fred Cook.*

ethical issues arise over paid influencers willingness to be transparent in disclosing to followers and fans any exchange of financial value. For example, one report suggested that some influencers promote fake brand deals as a way to seek credibility with advertisers (Lorenz, 2018b). Paid amplification of branded messages should happen within a set of rules that do not violate the trust of followers, fans, customers and others using selectivity and filtering (Yun & Park, 2011). Edelman, Weber Shandwick, Golin and others among the largest global firms have devoted resources to being sensitive about the value of brand reputation and trust (Lipschultz, 2018). Chairman of Golin Fred Cook was an industry innovator when the firm in 2011 developed "The Bridge" as an integrated real-time social media listening space for clients served by its Chicago office.

Golin uses art and science in its restructured vision of how a PR firm should meet client needs. Cook later authored the book *Improvise, Unconventional Career Advice from and Unlikely CEO*. His message to students was to not be afraid to take chances. An entrepreneurial mindset and some courage to innovate are valuable assets within social media measurement and management.

Organic and original consumer content, for example, must be distinguishable from co-created messages. In other words, behind measurement of social media data spikes, managers must be aware of the qualitative conditions responsible for successful efforts. From promoted posts to other paid techniques for boosting social media content reach, it is important to clearly label the role money plays in reaching more eyes and ears, as well as the context of engagement.

Not all goals are profit-oriented. For example, non-profit journalism thrives on limited resources and collaboration of "sharing through distribution" (Konieczna, 2018, p. 134). ProPublica, for example, created rules for page view tracking code attached to free content—essential in establishing "**impact measurement**" for stories: "One element of this has been encouraging news organizations to use the kind of impact-based measures increasingly common in the foundation [fundraising] world in general, bringing a kind of market logic to the nonprofits studied here" (pp. 212–213). Successful philanthropy has embraced the need for entrepreneurial personal branding through social media, as well as the data behind the efforts. Some fundraising campaigns have embraced social media as a tool to achieve goals.

SOCIAL ENTREPRENEURSHIP AND PERSONAL BRANDING

This book also recognizes the value of social entrepreneurship as "a process by which citizens build or transform institutions to advance solutions to social problems" (Bornstein & Davis, 2010, p. 1). Historically, urban forces of social change "compelled traditional structures to relinquish some control over social and commercial activity" (p. 3), in a way that "intensifies economic change" (p. 11). Social media are no less an agent of transformational leadership and change. The so-called "creative class" behind social media entrepreneurship drives adoption of new technologies and practices. "Social entrepreneurs depend on a responsive media to spread new ideas and challenge existing attitudes and behaviors" (p. 119). The argument is that leadership in any new area requires open-mindedness, listening skills and a willingness to act on great ideas—even if repeated failure is a path to learning. Entrepreneur Gary Vaynerchuk (@garyvee) gained millions of Instagram and IGTV views by targeting young men and women with simple messages about health, happiness, and doing what you love. Social media entrepreneurship is successful when passion meets hard work and persistence. Social media data guide content decisions within a fragmented and highly competitive marketplace.

Crestodina (2018) takes a content marketing approach to branding market perception: "It should be consistent from the first impression throughout the entire experience of each of your visitors and customers" (p. 15). Message and visual consistency are central in cultivating your personal brand, as well as those of associated organizations. The analytics behind consistent brand data may include social conversation and sharing of content, tracking site visitors and sources of online traffic, and movement of customer or fan behavior. Personal brand cultivation, then, can be empirically observed within the context of a set of values expressed through consistent brand voice within a variety of social media spaces. For example, podcasts and webinars have become popular ways to reinforce brand messages and may be integrated with blog posts, company, or organizational white papers and other branded content.

Martin and Osberg (2015) suggest that "government-led" efforts are a different form of "social transformation" from those projects that are "business-led" (p. 56). Specifically, government social entrepreneurship is focused on citizens and social benefits. Businesses, on the other hand, tend to focus on customers and profit. In either case, though, entrepreneurship has an openness to continuous change and adaptation: "A vision is not something to be changed lightly. But social entrepreneurs show remarkable versatility in adapting the way they deliver on their visions. They alter their methods, even as the core vision remains unchanged" (p. 121). In other words, "beating a dead horse" by use of traditional methods should be less attractive to entrepreneurs than continuously innovating new approaches that respond to rapid technological and social change. Market competition requires that we constantly observe and respond to social innovation by others (Bornstein & Davis, 2010). The metaphor of sports battlefield frequently is used to understand real-time responsiveness and market survival of those best positioned for what happens next. Responsive or "incremental" innovation may be seen through low-cost products and services (Nicholls & Murdoch, 2012, p. 4). Such efforts may be crowdfunded through relatively small campaigns. Larger campaigns may be designed to upend "institutional" market structures, or even be "disruptive" in changing fundamental thinking "to alter social systems and structures" (p. 4). So-called "social innovation" begins with an individual, but may diffuse throughout an organization, a "network/movement" or system (p. 7). Social media measurement and management offer tools for strategic "value creation," and "stakeholder accountability" that may be achieved through private or public resources, as well as "public–private partnerships" (pp. 10–11). Social media offer individuals an avenue to activate change:

> Just as markets draw on the energies and creativity of entrepreneurs willing to risk money and prestige, so does social change draw on the often-invisible fecundity of tens of thousands of individuals and small groups who spot needs and innovate solutions.
>
> (p. 47)

Successful individual entrepreneurs understand that entrepreneurship is a process that may lead to creation of a "socially oriented business" (p. 261) that helps people and the larger society from its earliest "introduction," through "growth," launch or "take-off" and "maturity" (p. 282). **Corporate social responsibility (CSR)** is an important foundation for innovative businesses that earn profits at the same time as moving society forward through a progressive vision.

The use of data, key metrics and analytics help transform campaign tactics into serving a focused set of goals and objectives. In social media measurement and management, efforts begin with individuals cultivating personal branding that can produce power through thought leadership. Readers of this book will meet thought leaders representing important values. Media students and professionals need to develop a **personal brand**—an individual online identity (Turkle, 1995)—that aligns with keywords commonly used within their work and by their employers or clients. **LinkedIn** has become a primary tool for cultivating personal brand. The SNS offers tips and measurement of progress on the personal branding process. Additionally, the use of LinkedIn to blog through articles (as well as **Slideshare** presentations) as an industry thought leader may amplify message reach, assist in growing a personal social network through new connections, and offer opportunities for professional engagement with other thought leaders. In this sense, social media are key to building new relationships. Likewise, businesses utilize **customer relationship management (CRM)** software tools within customer service and support functions. A social network perspective means that individuals engage in *bridging* connection to others through online interaction. Personal branding suggests that individual and brand identities are important in cultivating a broader sense of community.

Other blog sites, such as WordPress, Medium, Blogger, and Tumblr, also may be useful in personal branding. Regardless of the site, though, content marketers have discovered some commonalities that help explain the stickiness of social media content.

One analysis of 6,000 blogs used the SEO Writing Assistant Tool, which is a Google Docs and WordPress extension. The study found that:

- The average blog length is 810 words in which bloggers spent an average of two hours, 32 minutes optimizing content.

- Bloggers used an average of two keywords, or 95 percent of target keywords.

- Bloggers used an average of 15 "semantically related keywords," or 97 percent of recommendations.

- At least one targeted keyword was found in 76 percent of headlines.

(Vasileva, 2018, paras. 13–18)

The use of content marketing techniques to spark action, including social media sharing, also apply to a YouTube or Vimeo video channel, a SoundCloud audio file, iTunes, or other audio podcasting platforms, or other **rich media** sites. These allow individuals to become recognized through **multimedia storytelling** within professional fields, or even as general public media figures. At the author's campus, faculty spent years redeveloping curriculum around a focus on media storytelling skills and practices. These undergird the work of social media managers, as they develop into content creators and data scientists.

Google suggests that best practices, include seeing YouTube video, increasingly are the start of a customer journey during the information-seeking process. For example, Google Advertising claims that a car dealership can use video to drive visits to local dealerships at a significantly lower cost of reaching more people than local television advertising. As we will see later in this book, the use of machine learning further targets content audiences and IoT devices through previous interest. Instagram's IGTV followed a similar model of refining viewer interest over time—an approach that keeps viewers on site longer and delivers them to potential advertisers. This is basic stimulus–response (S–R) psychology model in which user outcomes offer feedback into future content focus. Targeted media content also benefits a thought leader who can use Facebook, Twitter, Instagram, Reddit, Pinterest, and other social media sites to broaden content reach, raise awareness, spark engagement, and trigger a desired outcome based upon explicit goals and tactics.

BRAND EVANGELISTS AND AMBASSADORS

A social media manager seeking to improve data would identify influencers who may function as a **brand ambassador** by regularly posting favorable content through positive megaphoning. In some cases, brands turn to celebrities, which is nothing new. It can be argued that the 1962 revealing photo of Elizabeth Taylor and Richard Burton and its resulting global conversation ("The photograph signified an adulterous relationship") launched our current "celebrity culture," which in this century plays out on Instagram and other social media sites (Cashmore, 2014, pp. 53–54). The digital shift creates a "more fluid" relationship between iconic celebrities and their fans, "involving a collaboration and exchange of ideas between celeb and audience" (pp. 98–99):

> Ideas like restraint, prudence, and modesty have either been discredited or just forgotten. Celebrity culture has replaced them with impetuosity, frivolity, prodigality. Human impulses like these were once seen as vices; now they are almost virtuous . . . Celebrities have energized our material expectations, helping shape a culture in which demand is now a basic human experience.
>
> (p. 341)

Celebrity culture can be seen either as a framework for successful social media management or a concern that should be resisted. It depends upon personal and organizational brand values. It would seem that celebrity video on IGTV and YouTube have been the epicenter of this cultural transformation. From MySpace to Facebook, iconic personalities applied traditional media use theories about para-social interaction, or the tendency of fans to see stars within a social network as intimate friends (Kassing & Sanderson, 2015; Raacke & Bonds-Raacke, 2008). Athletes and their fans, for example, may be seen as sport community members. For brands, celebrities frequently are seen and paid as influencers. Micro-influencers with fewer followers also create celebrity personas that become their own personal brand. At the same time, U.S. cultural values must be understood against the "cultural nuances" reflected in other countries and regions (Lim & Soriano, 2016, p. 7). For example, Asia is not monolithic. China, Japan, India, South Korea, and other countries offer distinct histories and perspectives when they evaluate and act within the Internet and social media.

In the U.S. model, increasingly, employees and other **brand evangelists** may collaborate on content sharing and social media engagement. Current examples of how data are used to plan, measure, and utilize strategies include activation of employee social networks to broaden content reach. Dynamic Signal, for example, is a **mobile app** that aligns approved social media content with employee interests and make it easier to share to their social networks. Employees may be activated to raise brand awareness, help educate customers, participate in word-of-mouth (WOM) marketing, raise search engine "visibility," and ultimately improve business or non-profit metrics (Brito, 2018, p. 42). Managers develop a **social media policy** or set of **governance** documents that

TABLE 1.4 *Social media governance of content*

SMC Policies →	*Campaign* →	*Brand Media Storytelling* →	*Social Media Sharing*
Rules & boundaries	Strategies, goals, & tactics	Content & platforms	Reach & outcomes

outline what an employee may do, and this framework becomes the basis for developing campaigns and content.

Typically, companies consider using paid, earned, shared, and owned (PESO) media, as "social employees" help the marketing effort across their social networks (Brito, 2018, pp. 46–54). Happiness of employees may be improved through engagement with other thought leaders. Entrepreneurs may value more employee freedom within social media, and this engagement offers opportunities to learn from customers and stakeholders and further innovate. In this sense, entrepreneurship requires a great deal of trust between individuals.

Social media policies and procedures should reflect law and ethics within a specific industry context. A social media campaign begins with a marketing analysis. Social media data should drive strategic campaign goals and objectives, and these are reflected within a set of tactics. A blog post that includes a link to a video, for example, may be a form of brand media storytelling that serves campaign objectives. The social media sharing of this content offers new opportunities to measure effectiveness.

ENTREPRENEURSHIP AND DIGITAL ANALYTICS

From Silicon Valley on the birth and development of the personal computer during the last century, to a global market driven by digital and mobile media, we have seen the emergence of entrepreneurship—defined as a business desire to respond to the market with new ideas, innovation, and continuous improvement. Entrepreneurial thinking in business start-ups, as well as within all forms of business, nonprofit, and government organizations, challenges existing practices and assumptions. Digital data leave trails of evidence that should be useful for leaders and managers. The rapid growth of social media analytics since about 2010 was based upon earlier Internet Web analytics and the search for digital breadcrumbs that reveal insights into consumer behavior. Social media began as an attempt to leverage free advertising through **electronic word-of-mouth (eWOM)**. Brand enthusiasts and fans tend to use social media to talk about their love for products and services, and digital analytics are a systematic way to observe and respond to brand engagement.

Kim Kosaka (2018), director of marketing at Alexa, argues for "lifecycle marketing tactics" that transform "one-time customers into loyal advocates" for a brand through: awareness, engagement, evaluation, purchase, post-purchase, and advocacy (paras. 1–6). We could group these into three distinct stages:

Stage 1: Raising social *awareness* and *engagement* in breaking through message clutter.

Stage 2: *Evaluation* and *purchasing* as a social process of discernment and individual action.

Stage 3: *Post-purchase* and *advocacy* as social psychological reinforcement, as well as influence upon others.

In practice, these stages are not entirely linear, and may overlap. For example, sometimes a consumer may decide to return a product, as evaluation continues. Social media messages could be important in all steps. It also is likely that feedback loops play a role in overlapping processes across individuals and groups—all with potential **social capital** to spend.

AWARENESS

The simplest social media campaign goal is to raise awareness. A nonprofit, for example, might develop a campaign around raising public awareness about an annual event through use of an email list, website content, and its Facebook page. Social media posting may be a useful tactic in taking existing data and measuring effectiveness. The more advocates posting consonant media messages (Noelle-Neumann, 1984), the greater the potential reach across individual social networks. The long-term impact may be greatest when authentic content and trusted relationships develop and lead to collaboration within and across organizations.

Howard Rheingold (1993) valued development and cultivation of online communities, and it is fair to suggest that relationships translate into valuable quantitative and qualitative data. In the example above, existing benchmarked data are those points measuring awareness prior to a strategic marketing campaign. It is common for social media managers to maintain data sets over long periods of time. **Facebook** and

TABLE 1.5 *Content A/B testing*

Benchmark Awareness (Time 1a) → **Post** Strategic Content → **Measure** Awareness (Time 1b)
Version 2 (Time 2a) → **Post** Content Iteration → **Measure** (Time 2b)

Instagram Insights from a fan page, for example, show continuous branded site data. By exporting these data to a Microsoft Excel spreadsheet, a social media manager may track weekly, monthly, quarterly, or annual data across large amounts of content. It may be that audience engagement is seasonal. If so, data peaks (spikes) and valleys may be partially explained by seasonal fluctuation, changes in the organic Facebook algorithm, content **optimization**, or use of paid promotion. Or use of Facebook and Instagram Stories, photographs and video may boost reach and impact, as these sites force traffic away from the newsfeed.

OUTCOME MEASUREMENT

Thought leader Brian Solis observed in 2013 that communication between consumers and branded websites or Facebook pages was poor. If we think of online experiences as journeys, then integration of advertising, public relations, and marketing principles makes sense. The Public Relations Society of America (PRSA) offers APR accreditation to members based upon a process called **research, planning, implementation, and evaluation (RPIE)**. When it comes to social media measurement and management, we must begin with research that informs the planning process. This involves setting goals and objectives that lead to specific tactics for strategic action. Once implemented, there should be evaluation based upon empirical data that feedback into future research. In other words, there is an ongoing research process that guides social media effectiveness (Broom & Sha, 2013). Social media audits are utilized in the refinement of outcomes. Entrepreneurs must bring macro-level principles into play when working with clients and building new businesses and business models through product and process innovation.

 Thought Leader Anna Vargas

Social Media Measurement and Management Help Land New Clients
Social media are such a powerful marketing tool, especially because use can be absolutely free at first. I rapidly grew my second business on Snapchat, but with the introduction of IG story, we have now fully focused on Instagram. Because of the constantly changing nature of social media, we are always open to trying new approaches. We are not afraid to go all-in when a new feature has launched, work with it a bit, and decide how it makes the most sense to focus our efforts. That's exactly what we did with

the mid-2018 launch of IGTV; it's a platform with potential, but I personally am not drawn to watching these videos, so right now our time is best spent focusing on what works for us in IG story. We also have tutorials hosted on YouTube and featured on our website in order to better connect and build trust. We think it's great to have a presence on all social sites, but the focus should be on impact. It's really about finding out where your perfect future client is spending their time, then focusing a majority of your time strategizing and staying consistent on that medium.

Our agency is 100 percent remote, and our clients come from Facebook Groups (one that we run, and others where women entrepreneurs hang out), our Instagram Business page, my personal Instagram/Facebook pages, and referrals from our friends on the internet! We know that putting time into social media helps us land new clients. Our agency has only responded to two request for proposals (RFPs) since we were created in 2017. Both of those RFPs were sent to us by my personal Facebook friends. We have a full client roster now, and it's because we know our target audience, we're transparent and authentic, and we've created a voice for our brand. Even though we are an agency of creatives and developers, Brand Her Style has its own unique voice, as if it were another member of our team. Here are some best practices that we have learned to follow:

FIGURE 1.2 *Anna Vargas (@mrsannavargas, Twitter; @annavargas, Instagram). Photograph by Amy Lynn Straub, courtesy Anna Vargas.*

- Provide value over asking for a sale. I ask myself if what I'm posting will serve a purpose for my target audience. If not, it won't be posted. It's okay to self-edit!

- We speak to our clients' pain points and show them how we can fix their problems. Were they burned by a bargain logo creator? No worries; they will get logo options from three designers who follow a process. Our design process includes a brand questionnaire, mood-boarding, audience profile research, sketching, and, finally, logo creation.
- Followers don't equal clients. Sure, it equals more visibility, but we'd rather do stories and posts that will lead to website clicks and direct messages (DMs) asking for our rates.
- People follow people, not brands. We have our own BHS voice. We focus on the people we work with and frequently highlight the creatives who will be working with on their projects.
- Post consistently. Don't ghost your followers. It's hard to build credibility and trust if you're invisible. Building relationships through trust and communication is how you succeed on social media.
- Quality over quantity. I'd rather see a beautiful photo or a heartfelt caption than three blurry photos in a row from someone I'm following. I ask myself, what would I give a "heart" to? What images would catch the eye of our audience, or what kinds of stories would resonate with their needs? What's going on with current events and if BHS would have an opinion about it. If a post does well, we aren't afraid to re-use the same photo or same caption. Our top two performing posts in terms of reach are actually the same image! We noticed our illustrated pieces perform well for reach, so now we make sure that every sixth post is an illustration.
- Switching up hashtags. You are able to use 30 Instagram hashtags per post. If your goal is growth, use those hashtags! The algorithm is forever changing, so if you want to be seen by new people, do research on hashtags and constantly switch them up so you don't get shadow banned. If you use the same hashtags for every post, IG will think you are a bot and ban you from that hashtag.
- Don't be a spammer, ever. It's not cool, and people see through it. Authenticity wins people over; being constantly in their faces begging to work with them does not. Instead solve their problems and create relationships.

FIGURE 1.3 *Instagram Insights data. Image courtesy Anna Vargas.*

How we measure ROI:

- Likes and follows.
- Website clicks: We use Google Analytics to track website clicks.
- We track our design request form via Bit.ly and can see where the clicks come from and when (possibly a certain post, IG story or when a previous client posts about us).

TABLE 1.6 *Google analytics for website clicks*

Traffic Source	No. of Clicks (%)
1. Social	514 (54.7%)
2. Direct	306 (32.6%)
3. Organic Search	97 (10.3%)
4. Referral	19 (2.0 %)
5. Other	3 (0.3%)

Source: Anna Vargas, Google Analytics

We create monthly creative strategies based on trends and real-time feedback from our followers. If we notice that our views have been down, a great way to bring them up again is to make sure we are posting IG stories consistently. We also use the poll feature and ask our audience directly what they want to hear from us. We keep it on topic and follow our business pillars, but we want to make sure our content is really what our audience actually wants. The key factor here is to make sure to follow through with that content.

We create measurable goals based on giving value and signing new clients. We use our Business Insights on Instagram to see which photos get the most likes. Across all social media, everyone's goal is visibility. Increased following and measuring page likes is an easy way to set goals each month, but we also know that followers don't equal clients. In terms of the data we collect from our insights, we use that to target our content. If we had a topic or photo that did well, we aren't afraid to use it again. We've noticed that if we share more tips and stories or focus on quick snippets, we'll get more likes but that won't help us get more sales. Our goal is to absolutely get more visibility and that comes through more follows and likes, *but* we care more about having a full client roster and being booked months in advance. We make sure to have **calls to action (CTA)** quite often. We like to keep it in our top nine posts so when someone comes to our page it's always in our feed without them having to scroll. We keep our CTA short and sweet by letting them know we have openings for the month, how many slots we have left, and that if they miss out they'll have to get in line for next month. This bit of urgency helps nudge those who may be interested to actually begin the process with us. We also do stories reminding our audience of our services in language that they use as if they were chatting with their best friend who happens to know a ton about branding. We keep it millennial-style copy and to the point.

Word of mouth amplified is what has us booked months in advance
Previous clients have talked about the whole process of designing and creating their websites, because that's what we do on our social. We show behind-the-scenes (BTS) moments to hype up our clients and help direct our

followers their way. When we launch, they talk about it on their Instagram stories with their audience. And once we complete projects, we notice an influx of forms being filled out for our services. Our clients will get DMs asking, "Who did you work with?!" and our clients will talk us up in a private message. These kinds of leads are super-valuable, because the trust and relationship with us has already been established, even before we ever chat with the possible client. Social media is about relationships, so when our clients share their experience throughout their launch, potential clients can see themselves in their stories. Connecting with our followers and creating relationships with them is key when landing a new client, and our previous clients are doing a lot of the leg work to help us build trust.

Our previous clients speak about us because they love us, and they do it without wanting anything in return. It's the power of an old-fashioned referral, amped up by the visibility that social media provides. Most people who are running businesses on social media already understand this, so there's an unspoken code of supporting other entrepreneurs because you think they are dope and need a shout out. We talk about our clients because we truly like them, they do the same for us, and everybody benefits. And since our process is the same for each client, our future clients can easily picture themselves when we post these types of posts.

What we've learned to do was to make sure to spread out our launches, so we have a steady flow of clients and don't have everyone messaging us all at once. Although we meet clients directly on social media, we do make sure to get their information and begin an email communication and then a 20-minute call. Social media can help form connections quickly, but most of the actual client work is still handled through personal conversations, whether online or by phone.

Almost all of our clients consent to us highlighting the process of their branding, because it hypes up their launch or rebrand and can help build an audience before the time of launch. However, we have clients that have us sign non-disclosure agreements (NDAs), and then we have to wait to post until their launch. We can use this to our advantage by building up the intrigue a bit. When the brand launches, it's more of a big reveal and our audience is excited to finally see what we've been spending our time on. All launches have shown to be great for our website traffic as well, so it's worth the wait.

We have yet to buy promos on IG story, but we have done FB ads. We are open to anything in the future, including running ads if we feel it would be best for our growth. For now, word-of-mouth referrals and building relationships with our clients has been extremely successful, and we see the highest ROI using these methods. We schedule one to two hours a day to search through hashtags we use and hashtags our target audience is using, and we find possible new clients through them. We will go to their page, and we'll know intuitively if they seem like a fit, based on style, interests, and goals. If they seem like a fit, we'll like a few photos, tap through their story, and follow them if we really like them. If we really, really like them and want to work with them, we will comment on a few photos, add them to our spreadsheet, and share one of their photos and tag them in a story, *or* we will feature them in our "follow Friday" IG stories for the week. This is how we continue to find our ideal clients, creating relationships first and giving them value. When seeking out connections, it's always about them before it's ever about us. If they like our vibe, we are confident they will choose us for all their creative and website needs.

Anna Vargas is the owner and Creative Director of Brand Her Style, LLC, a one-stop shop for women entrepreneurs and small- to mid-size businesses that focuses on brand strategy, branding, copywriting, social media, and web design. Brand Her Style helps businesses from the moment of launch, including creating pitch decks for potential investors, and during phases of rapid growth when it's time to upgrade their online presence because they've outgrown their starter sites. This is her third business in the last decade, and all of them have been able to exist because of social media. She has experience as a sole creative designer for a public relations firm in Chicago, where she worked with the new business, digital, consumer, and corporate teams. Vargas left her design job at the firm to pursue a passion of empowering small business owners in building their brand strategies, brand identity, and digital presence. She currently lives in Silicon Valley with her husband. Social media followers in 2018 mourned the passing of her popular 17-year-old gray tabby cat, Siri.
https://www.linkedin.com/in/annavargas/

Instagram Stories ushered in a new social media wave of interest in developing engagement over time. Barnhart (2018) reflected this in Sprout Social's *Ultimate Guide*. Instagram had more than 400 million daily Stories users, and Facebook appeared to capitalize on the Snapchat idea of stories that disappear after a day. "Stories' sequential format makes them perfect for step-by-step, how-to style content" (para. 21). This includes sharing user-generated content of follower-influencers, offering behind scenes views, and highlighting special events. Barnhart (2018) suggested a set of best practices:

- Remind followers to check Stories.

- Use compelling visuals.

- Experiment with text sizes, fonts, and colors.

- Increase interactivity with polls and stickers.

- Adobe Spark, Boomerang, and other apps brighten photos.

- Paid Instagram advertising is hyper-targeted.

AS SEEN ON YOUTUBE

Assignment

Watch the UNO Social Media Lab (@unosml) content marketing interview with Andy Crestodina to learn more about content marketing collaboration: https://youtube/ISRKpqUdRjo

Questions

1. How could you link your website traffic to a larger social media campaign?

2. What would be strengths and weaknesses of Facebook, Instagram, or other social media sites that you could use for content sharing and engagement?

USEFUL TOOLS

LinkedIn is perhaps the best available social media tool in terms of usefulness for cultivating personal branding. AGM CEO Julbert Abraham has a personal brand as "The LinkedIn Guy," and he says the beginning of a calendar, fiscal, or academic year is the perfect time to refresh a LinkedIn profile. He identifies four "starter tips" that may need attention:

- Start with uploading a professional headshot photograph.

- Add a background image to the default blue at the top of your profile page that helps amplify your story.

- Take a "deep dive" into the summary and focus on value of "skills and capabilities" you offer others.

- Seek recommendations from your social network.

LinkedIn is more than an online résumé. It has become a publishing site for blogs, photographs, and video. Why should college students and professionals take the time? "Oh, it's very simple," Abraham says. "If they're planning on getting a job, or getting internships or getting mentorships, LinkedIn is the place to go." Employers combine a Google search with a LinkedIn check "before they do anything," Abraham says. That is why establishing a personal brand online is so important for employees and entrepreneurs. As with other social media, it is important to have a LinkedIn plan developed with clear goals backed by measurable outcomes. Small businesses, for example, use LinkedIn to look for new talent, Abraham says. It also is useful in social networking and development of business opportunities, or even partnerships. It begins with a LinkedIn "refresher" check-up:

> *If you haven't been using LinkedIn a lot, maybe go online, look up some YouTube videos, learn exactly . . . what changes are happening on LinkedIn and update your profile. And, also even look through your network, and maybe follow-up with some people that you haven't spoken to in awhile.*

—*Julbert Abraham*

Abraham recommends developing three-month plans with specific goals for each quarter of the year. While Facebook and Instagram users focus on friends, family, and entertainment (Hutchinson, 2016), it should be all business on LinkedIn. Some users are looking for work. Or, you may want to know what's new with others. The Microsoft acquisition of LinkedIn in 2016 for $26 billion signals further development of the platform in the months ahead, Abraham says. Native video, for example, is a response to the current "age of video" across online sites. As with other sites, LinkedIn offers data to "measure your success," Abraham says. "You know what's working because you're getting feedback." Abraham anticipates that video advertising will be coming in the next wave of development. LinkedIn is likely to make it easier in 2018 to target paid message strategy. Even though LinkedIn was one of the earliest social media sites, its slow evolution might turn out to be core strength. Established businesses tend to be cautious in adopting new tools, and LinkedIn is still gaining traction in the marketplace for cultivating business opportunities.

Finally, LinkedIn may also be useful in cultivating social business leads. A LinkedIn advertising campaign, for example, may have a goal of collecting "downloadable leads" (Abraham, 2018, para. 3). The process begins with a free download that collects user LinkedIn profile data into a form. LinkedIn sponsored content campaigns may be created with a native advertising blog post, an advertisement, or messages targeted at individuals. A lead generation form can be connected to promoted content, images or video. The call to action outcome takes a variety of options—sign-up, apply, download, get quote, learn more, subscribe, or register (para. 13). In terms of ROI, the marketing funnel process not only collects basics information, but it also allows for additional questions designed to qualify new sales leads.

LinkedIn is not the only business networking or blogging site. Indeed, GlassDoor, CareerBuilder, Monster, and others connect employers with prospective employees. Bloggers grow their personal brands on Medium, WordPress, Tumblr, Blogger, and other popular sites. The combination of thought leadership through engaging content and a strong social media brand adds value.

PROJECT IDEAS

View a recent Facebook Live event. How did the creators promote the event before, during, and after it happened? Which elements were engaging or not? Was the video designed to be organically shared across other social networks? Did the sponsor pay Facebook to promote the video on the newsfeed? What can be learned from "likes" and other Facebook reaction data? How does the video compare with similar video found on other social network sites Instagram, IGTV, YouTube, and Snapchat? Use research to propose a future Facebook Live event that would achieve a larger social media share of voice (SoV): How could the focus by placed upon raising audience awareness and engagement? How could the organization build stronger online relationships?

DISCUSSION QUESTIONS

1. Review the LinkedIn profile of a prominent local media personality in journalism, advertising, public relations or marketing: What are the key strengths and weaknesses of this personal branding? Why?

2. Read social media comments on a local news or blog site: How could you improve the quality of the engagement?

Concepts and Campaigns

> *We live in the most data-intensive period in this history of mankind . . . Just as this wave of Big Data is changing how we live our lives, it is changing how firms develop, grow, and innovate.*

—Russell Walker (@RussWalker1492, 2015, p. xiii)

> *Growing a digital business and proving the ROI of your digital efforts can be tough. Learning and putting growth methodologies and tactics into practice can help your business get ahead of the curve.*

—Krista Seiden (@Kristaseiden, 2018, via ObservePoint, 2018, p. 11)

Big data return on investment (ROI) happens only when social media measurement and management are strategically focused through entrepreneurial efforts to innovate through data-driven decisions. Social media managers need to develop a framework for organizing strategies, goals, objectives, and tactics within each social media campaign.

For example, the management tool Hootsuite recommends that managers for large **enterprise** businesses consider the nature of the social customer experience, including response to private or direct messaging:

1. Map the entire social customer journey—82 percent of companies surveyed responded that social channels are vital to their business, but about half lacked a defined strategy.

2. Secure early wins with social—data offer customer intelligence about their experiences.

3. Expand strategies beyond brand awareness—less than half of companies used social media for customer service.

4. Look beyond surface metrics—align social media metrics with business goals.

5. Focus on training, culture, and collaboration.

(Hootsuite, 2018, paras. 5–15)

Even small businesses should use strategies to explore data complexity. For example, a local cupcakes shop posted a Facebook photo of "S'mores Cupcakes. YUM!," as part of a fall "full of flavor" campaign. The business obtains organic and paid boosted reach and engagement data. However, there often are no direct data points on cash purchases, so inferences would need to be made about marketing effort direct effects on sales data. As location, facial recognition, and other data evolve, though, these data are likely to become more available.

The need to identify a set of events through a social media calendar includes benchmarking data and building measurable outcomes. To fully explore social media data, qualitative analyses examine celebrity culture (Cashmore, 2014), "technological innovation" and science driving the spread of social and cultural change:

Along with the cool scientific detachment (which is ethically questionable), there is the assumption regarding innovations that are potentially catastrophic, that humans with their reason will solve any problem, because these are technical processes that humans invented and so humans will have ultimate control over them.

(Hassan & Sutherland, 2017, pp. 190–191)

The "postmodernity" description of "nasty and brutish," however, also must be considered "in a fast-moving network society where the time for reflection and caution and due consideration of a problem or issue is, to say the least, dwindling" (pp. 200–201). From the headlines, for example, Andersson (2018) reported that developers of social media apps design them to be addictive, as confessed by a former employee: "It's as if they're taking behavioral cocaine and just sprinkling it all over your interface and that's the thing that keeps you like coming back and back and back" (paras. 1–2). With this in mind, enthusiasm over data growth should be tempered by the risks.

When it works, social media addiction may be similar to a slot machine or smoking cigarettes. The data allow social media managers to surgically track user behavior and leverage insights in future content and campaigns. So, as a manager develops skills and practices, this ethical dilemma of "sticky" content and audience response must be kept in mind. The paradox is that we know how, for example, to track users from a social media post to a website and through a purchase marketing funnel or monetize content in other ways; but it is not always ethically defendable to use specific social marketing tactics.

Traditional media research is divided into qualitative or quantitative methodologies. The various approaches, however, generate unique questions and answers: "First of all, all human actions can be considered communication in their own right. They may be intentional statements, or incidental behaviors in which others associate meaning, or they may belong to the considerable grey area between the two" (Jensen, 2012, p. 13). Generally, we acknowledge that research "techniques" may be influenced by the moment: "The pressures of fad and fashion are as great in science, for all its logic, as in other areas of culture" (Kaplan, 1964, p. 28). In the relatively short history of social media research, we need to address concept "sharpening" for core terms— engagement and influence—while refining the "fuzzy" nature of our words, a need for "successive definition," and progressive movement toward a higher level of "precision" (pp. 76–77). Careful social scientists avoid causal thinking, measure estimated error, test and re-test ideas through *repeated observation*. As social media communication data evolve through machine learned chatter, our measurement and management tool usage should be constrained by "the tendency to forget that statistical techniques are tools of thought, and not substitutes for thought" (p. 257). In other words, our abilities to critically think about social media data should be stronger than the desire to adopt the newest "cool" tools.

Increasingly the introduction of AI chatbots and other mechanisms blur lines between human and non-human communication. It is common for email marketing campaigns with MailChimp or other tools to track **open rates** and clicks on website or social media channel pages. While an email campaign may not reach a 30 percent open rate, marketers also have turned to SMS text messages with open rates as high as "a simply staggering" 99 percent (Baer, 2019, para. 4). At the same time, AI with all platforms may use machine learning to further target consumers based upon responses and non-responses to a variety of probe questions. Bots are frequently used to filter customer questions, offer quick responses, and channel concerns to customer service personnel. Among the most important marketing functions appear to be: 1) appointments and reminders; 2) customer questions; 3) upsell opportunities; 4) customer feedback; and 5) customer problem-solving (Baer, 2019). This highlights mobile phone numbers and email as valuable touch point data. Technologies also generate large scale communication data that is open for ongoing narrative and sentiment analysis, which are expected to have improved reliability as the science develops.

Big data dimensions include "a completeness" of "scale"; a "holistic measurement of market and consumer behaviors" through "frequency and velocity"; a "passive" data collection used in "active" creation; with "direct and indirect measurement"; "precision in dimensions"—"customer tags, geophysical location, and temporal occurrence"; and "data fusion," that is "integration on customers, operations, and channels, be it internal and external to the firm" (Walker, 2015, pp. xxii–xxiii). These dimensions help explain why data have enormous business value and are central to strategies that help a company make money or a nonprofit achieve its goals:

> Managing and participating in the process of viral data distribution is important for firms in handling not just disgruntled customers, but complex operations, and large markets. The most powerful feature of the viral distribution of data is the scale in which social users can reach each other and firms. The ability of firms to deal with the viral distribution if data is alarmingly poor.
>
> (p. 24).

Intimacy of most social networked conversation is surprisingly tilted away from mass media in its character—"The median ratio of Facebook views to shares is only 9 to 1" (p. 24). Research suggests that content consuming is much more likely than creation, and unfollowing boring content producers is common. Big data exist in this evolving space because of concerns about privacy, ownership, and automation through AI.

THE BARCELONA PRINCIPLES 2.0

The International Association of Measurement of Communication (AMEC) developed and updated the Barcelona Declaration of Measurement Principles 2.0 as an "overarching framework" for "measurement and evaluation programs" (2015, Slide 4; 2010). The industry faced serious challenges to the early practices of value "equivalencies" and "multipliers" within data, and the principles became widely used best practices (Slide 5). After five years in use, AMEC concluded that goals and objectives focused on outcomes remained most important.

The emphasis should be on "quality" and "transparent" measurement (Slide 6). AMEC became more proactive in addressing practices designed for public relations integration with advertising and marketing. "Evaluation and insight" now include qualitative methods (Slide 7).

TABLE 2.1 *The seven principles*

Original Principles (1.0)

1. Importance of Goal Setting and Measurement

2. Measuring the Effect on Outcomes is Preferred to Measuring Outputs

3. The Effect on Business Results Can and Should Be Measured Where Possible

4. Media Measurement Requires Quantity and Quality

5. AVEs are not the Value of Public Relations

6. Social Media Can and Should be Measured

7. Transparency and Replicability are Paramount to Sound Measurement

2.0

1. Goal Setting and Measurement are Fundamental to Communication and Public Relations

2. Measuring Communication Outcomes is Recommended Versus Only Measuring Outputs

3. The Effect on Organizational Performance Can and Should Be Measured Where Possible

4. Measurement and Evaluation Require Both Qualitative and Quantitative Methods

5. AVEs are not the Value of Communication

6. Social Media Can and Should be Measured Consistently with Other Media Channels

7. Measurement and Evaluation Should be Transparent, Consistent and Valid

Source: AMEC (2015). Barcelona Principles 2.0, Slide 8. https://amecorg.com/wp-content/uploads/2015/09/Barcelona-Principles-2.pdf

AMEC's update reflects a growing recognition that social media measurement of data are important within the field of PR, and should be included within the "fundamental" effort to set goals (AMEC, Principle 1). Campaign "outcomes" are considered important in understanding the measurement of "outputs" (Principle 2). Organizational effectiveness may be measured (Principle 3), and this includes quantitative and qualitative "evaluation" (Principle 4). Here, industry leaders align with the growing academic norm that multi-method approaches in research analyze quantitative measures, and also utilize rich qualitative data interpretation.

AMEC continues to reject **advertising value equivalency (AVE)**, which PR measurement historically used to estimate client earned value from news media coverage:

> AVEs would commonly measure the size of the coverage gained, its placement and calculate what the equivalent amount of space, if paid for as advertising, would cost. Often a multiplier would also be used—commonly in the range of 3 to 10—to allow for the credibility factor of news coverage over advertising.
>
> (SourceWatch, 2008, para. 1)

AVEs were controversial because they did not always reflect negative **sentiment** (positive, neutral, or negative) of news media coverage, and the multipliers used to manipulate the data were "rejected as arbitrary and unscientific" (para. 2). "AVEs are not the value of communication" (AMEC, Slide 5). The final two principles are central to our interest in social media measurement and management. First, "consistent social media measurement should be happening along with other media channels" (Slide 6). This is challenging because so many measurement tools use proprietary algorithms and inconsistent methodologies. Measurement standards, as we have in social science academic research, have yet to develop for social media measurement, and this principle remains an ideal more than reality. This point goes to the final and most important AMEC principle: "Measurement and evaluation should be transparent, consistent and valid" (Principle 7). This aligns with what a student might read in a traditional media research textbook. While open peer-review is common academic practice at conference presentations and in journal articles, PR firms tend to guard their data and methods.

Part of the competitive advantage of a firm tends to be seen as offering value that is perceived to be exclusive. In practice, nearly all PR professionals follow a set of best practices that include collection of observable data:

- **SMART Goals (Specific, Measurable, Attainable, Relevant, and Timely)** are a basis for evaluation.

- Quantitative and qualitative measurement identifies "who, what, how much, by when."

- "Holistic" measurement focuses on "changes in awareness among key stakeholders, comprehension, attitude, and behavior; and impact on organizational results."

- Integration and alignment of campaigns and ongoing PR work are measured "across paid, earned, shared and owned channels where possible" (AMEC, Slide 9).

Modern PR campaigns use targeted advertising and marketing strategies and tactics. For social media measurement, this means attempting to link outcomes to business data. AMEC treats qualitative data analysis as a method for determining "impressions among the stakeholder or target audience," as we assess the communication value of tone, credibility, relevance, and prominence (Slide 12). A social media manager, then, must track data effectiveness over time. This includes content analysis, SEO, customer relations management (CRM) data, and surveys (Slide 14). Within social media data, "Focus measurement on engagement, 'conversation' and 'communities,' not just 'coverage' or vanity metrics such as 'likes'" (Slide 14). It is not that a Facebook "like," for example, has no value, but these must be placed within the context of goals and objectives.

Entrepreneur Gary Vaynerchuk has suggested that people need to dig beneath the motivation for popularity to find a sense of self-awareness:

> People are living towards the numbers. How many likes? How many followers? How much capital have I raised? It becomes a numbers race, and it usually leads to bad behavior. When you do something for money, you quit. When you do it because you love it, you do it forever.
>
> (Vaynerchuk, 2018)

When correctly managed, social media build long-term professional relationships. Social media motivation, then, should be seriously considered ahead of any specific campaign or event. Raising awareness often is an important first step along a relationship-building journey with followers, fans, donors, customers, or other stakeholders. For

FIGURE 2.1 *Gary Vaynerchuk. Photograph by Shot Alive (Justin @Shotalive), courtesy Vayner Media and Gary Vaynerchuk (@garyvee).*

these reasons, measurement ethics remain important and will be addressed throughout this book. AMEC has not strayed from the view that there should be social media measurement "discipline," and that there is "no 'single metric' " for conversation and communities. Data transparency and reproducible results continue to be important, even as the measurement industry moves deeper into AI automated tools. More than eight in ten Americans surveyed said transparency is important and relate it to openness (59%), clarity (53%), honesty (49%), authenticity (26%), integrity (23%), and communication (19%) (Sprout Social, 2018b, p. 2). Not surprisingly, research attempts to examine trust built within ongoing relationships. Given what we already know about the complexity of face-to-face interpersonal relationships, it makes sense that online interaction can be problematic. For brands, transparent social media communication appears to drive consumer expectation. While these data paint with broad strokes, ongoing research is needed to move analyses beyond self-reports and perception.

Behavioral social media measurement addresses strengths and weaknesses and recognizes the existence of **measurement error.** Since the 1950s, social scientists have explored the limitations associated with data and statistics—sampling bias, averages, graphing of data, and simplistic explanations for complex phenomena (Huff, 1954). Visualization of data, for example, may "exaggerate the impression" (p. 72). As the tools for measuring and managing social media continue to become more sophisticated, these basic dangers do not diminish. It is possible, for example, to become distanced from observation by using data manipulation tools that suggest easy interpretation. Exact and causal social measurement is not possible, so we seek to measure and estimate sources of error. Nevertheless, a lack of precise social media measurement standards continues to be a problem. The marketing of engaging online content begins with a clear set of business goals and a "measurement framework" (Brito, 2018, p. 117). **Subject matter experts (SMEs)** may help raise awareness by increasing social media reach (p. 143).

GOOGLE ANALYTICS AND SEO

Google is in the search business. The company cornered the web browser space by developing intricate systems for matching search interest with available content. Google offers courses and certification—including an important beginners' course for students. Google suggests building a structure for data collection and analysis. The use of digital analytics is important for businesses seeking continuous improvement within social media customer conversation. Awareness, interest and engagement may trigger new business or assist with retention of existing customers.

Consistent with current social science, quantitative and qualitative data help analysts observe behavior and offer explanation for it. In the second lesson of its Digital Analytics Fundamentals course, Google offers common businesses objectives—online sales, lead generation, site visits for publishers, customer support information, and branding though awareness, engagement, and loyalty. Data value are found within a continuous process:

TABLE 2.2 *Continuous process measurement and evaluation*

Measurement	→	Reporting	→	Analysis	→	Testing	→	Repeating

Setting aside the previous discussion about measurement and reporting error, social media managers should treat data as rough estimates of behavior. Google suggests the use of data **segmentation**. For example, an analyst may want to separate mobile and desktop site visitors. Further, it is common to **benchmark** data through site history or industry expectations. This allows for tracking future growth or decline and provide contextual explanation for change.

At the heart of search are **keywords**—the words we use to find what we are looking for on the Internet. Alexa is a company that offers social media managers free and paid tools for **optimizing** content. The Alexa Keyword Difficulty Tool helps find the best words to use on a website in order achieve a higher **ranking** in search. This is because people searching online tend to avoid industry jargon and use common words. By knowing and using the best keywords, content managers increase the likelihood of being found.

Google Analytics uses the construct of a customer journey that now includes use of mobile devices. Avinash Kaushik (2010), author of *Web Analytics 2.0*, offered the seminal definition:

1. the analysis of qualitative and quantitative data from your website and the competition,

2. to drive a continual improvement of the online experience of your customers and prospects,

3. which translates into your desired outcomes (online and offline) (para. 11).

In this model, insights are viewed as a core goal in measuring **clickstream** for multiple outcomes, testing content variation, listening for customer voices, and gaining a competitive edge. Whether a social media manager is working for a business, nonprofit, or other organization, the noisy spaces of social media require strategic use in order for messages to be heard. Data can be helpful in developing organic or paid content campaigns. The typical goals are to raise awareness, build interest, spark engagement, move toward goal conversion, and retention of customers and others. Social media is seen as placing customers at the center of focus in the shift away from the traditional marketing funnel. The Google Analytics Academy, which offers free training and certificates, suggests that historical data provide internal context for realistic goals and benchmarking.

An important SEO concept is data **attribution,** or the source of an online click or other "micro conversion" action. So-called **last-click attribution** refers to, for example, the credit given for a product or service sale that is a "macro conversion." In this environment, we can see the value of developing a planning process that may include a targeted demographic or psychographic audience. A current view of analytics is that the entire contextual path from first to last click must be understood through rigorous data analysis techniques. Only then can a social media manager make judgments about the budget, and whether to focus on organic social media efforts, paid advertising, or both. Google Analytics recommends that measurement step needed include:

1. Define your measurement plan.

2. Document your technical infrastructure (i.e. service space and mobile apps).

3. Create an implementation plan.

4. Implement your plan.

5. Maintain and refine.

Google is consistent with other thought leaders in suggesting the need to articulate explicit business objectives, strategies and tactics, KPI metrics, data segmentation, and targeting. A long-term strategy allows social media managers to make quick adjustments in response to rapid change, at the same time that the organization remains on course to meet its goals.

Google's JavaScript code on websites enables user tracking. The code activates Google Analytics collection of browser and device type, user location, and other useful data. Some sites now solve the cut and paste URL address tracking issue by automatically attaching original attribution code. That said, a lot of dark social lack of attribution exist—perhaps more than half of all traffic: "Eight out of ten consumers' outbound sharing from publishers' and marketers' websites happens without referral data" (Quesenberry, 2017, para. 4). In response, shortened address link, sharing buttons, and dark social tools helped fight the persistent issue. Marketers want the data, but some users seek their data privacy.

While webpage data are built around page views, mobile data track activity. Data collection and processing called "configuration" or data "transformation" lead to reporting results. Google uses two types of data:

1. **Dimensions** include user characteristics (demographics), sessions and other action.

2. **Metrics** are quantitative user, session, and action numbers.

One important dimension is the traffic source that led a person to visit a site. For example, a visitor may have clicked on a Facebook post that linked to site content, she may have searched Google to find it, or typed or spoken the site name or URL web address.

When someone visits a site, the Google Analytics default is to define a session as lasting 30 minutes. Google Analytics then tracks interaction **pageviews** and events, such as video watching, which keep the visit active. A "time on page" can be estimated by measuring time between pages or other events. When a site visitor lands on a home page but leaves without doing anything, then Google Analytics measures a **bounce rate** as the "percentage of sessions with only one user interaction." If you expect people to visit more than one page, then a high bounce rate is not good. However, if the goal is to drive users to a single page, then it may not be a problem. For example, PR event planners sometimes need to send potential participants to an information page or a blog post published during the earliest stages of interest. Later, of course, it would be best practice to engage visitors with a registration form and other information pages.

State-of-the-art Google Analytics includes the use of content experiments. The Google Optimize tool is useful for:

1. **A/B tests**—a randomized experiment on two web page versions, these must control for time of day, targeting and other intervening variables.

2. **Redirect tests**—a comparative A/B test of two different URLs to see which performs best.

3. **Multivariate tests (MVTs)**—attempt to test and control for multiple combinations of variation.

(Google Optimize, 2018)

Account managers can create My Container, which is a virtual bin in the cloud to store various Google Optimize experimental data.

A company website is one example of what the industry calls **owned media**—online content that an organization controls and manages. A Google search will reflect the branding keyword success of organic activity on the page. The frequently changing Google algorithm examines location and other user data to match interests in a keyword search. To see how a particular webpage performs against competitors, use the Alexa.com site information tool to measure page rank. For example, the University of Nebraska at Omaha unomaha.edu webpage had its United States rank drop significantly from 2017 to 2018:

TABLE 2.3 *Alexa unomaha.edu data 2017–18*

Measure	2018	2017
U.S. Rank	15,147	5,789
Global Rank	50,864	29,216
Percent Visitors U.S.	75.9	86.4
Percent Visitors India	3.6	3.5

These data require further analysis over time because unomaha.edu had moved 13,548 positions during 2017. So, it may be that older data were an anomaly. Given the global growth of the Internet and increase in the number of sites in many large countries, U.S. rank data may be more useful in the short term. While India had the second largest percentage of site visitors for both years, the Philippines (2.2 percent), Nigeria (1.1 percent), and Malaysia (0.7 percent) all passed percentage of site visitors from Australia, the United Kingdom, and Canada. These data offer the opportunity for rich, qualitative data analysis to better understand trends.

The university site had a high **bounce rate** of 51 percent (+ 17%), average daily pageviews of 2.66 (– 26%), and daily time on site of 2:30 (– 21%) suggesting that visitors do not find as much engaging content to remain and leave fairly quickly. Much of the site traffic comes from search—38.2 percent (+ 16%), and the top two keywords included Canvas. The university had recently switched from Blackboard to Canvas for courses, and the data appear to show that a lot of site search is from students trying to find the new information portal. Overwhelmingly, students had come to the site from Google (40.1%) with no social media sites among the top five. A year earlier, Facebook had been the fifth most important site driving unomaha.edu traffic. It can be argued that engaging content and navigation may be problems, because the technical side of the site, as indicated through speed of load time, suggests it is among the top one-third. More granular data show that more than half of visitor traffic appears to be from current students, faculty and staff logging into password protected pages, while less than 7 percent appear to be potential campus visitors. Once online visitors leave the page, they are most likely to go to the Chinese site Sina.com.cn, academic jobs at Wikia.com, sports at ESPN.com or news at CNN.com. As we will see later, the campus faced a need to rebuild the site with a focus on its growing Latino and Latina metropolitan student population.

SOCIAL MEDIA TARGET MARKETING TO LATINOS AND LATINAS

Social media managers must consider the community context when beginning to understand site data. The growing Latino and Latina market is increasingly important in the measurement and management of social media assets. The U.S. immigration debate did not reflect the larger trend. In Omaha, Nebraska, for example, Latino and Latina population growth is expected to *triple* by 2050. And in some towns across Nebraska, Latino and Latina students already are the majority in their public schools. An AAF Omaha panel, Advertising to the Latino Market, urged businesses to embrace change and learn how to market through traditional and social media. Immigrants come from many different towns and cultures in Mexico, Guatemala, El Salvador, Cuba, and other countries, and each target group is unique.

Target Marketing Panel

A 2016 advertising panel focused on the changing nature of community, as Latino and Latina populations grow throughout the United States. "Know the community," Abril Avilés Garcia, Mundo Latino Publications in Omaha, says. "Start knowing all the groups, their organizations, the churches, and then based on that (you can) create your message." Target marketing to Latinos starts with, "just learning the culture, how can you send your message in a way that . . . you have to embrace it, instead of trying to fight it," University of Nebraska at Omaha Marketing Specialist Yanira Garcia says. Still, businesses need to start with market research. "Generalizing your message is the biggest mistake you can make," Radio Lobo 97.7 Account Executive Sole Salas says. Beyond traditional media, social media may have a positive impact. Businesses targeting Latinos are increasingly interested in website traffic, and they are starting to use Google Analytics to track site visits coming from email newsletters and social media sites.

Four Spanish-language publications and radio stations in Omaha are all growing. "The numbers are there, the businesses are there," Armando Salgado, Lingodocs Marketing, says. "Communication is the biggest issue, (and) the biggest barrier." For most businesses, the first need is to hire Spanish-speaking employees, and Lingodocs launched a "virtual assistant" service for businesses wanting to reach out to Latinos. The company offers a Spanish-language telephone and online staff. Young Latinos are growing up with both languages at school and in the popular culture. "I grew up with the pop culture," Salgado says, but it is everything from Spanish music to Drake. "The outside, sometimes, is a little bit more dominant. It's a nice mixture of both."

Obviously, it has to be a catchy ad in order to work. If you have something free to try it at first, or a great discount, but coupons, they don't work at all . . . with our paper—Abril Avilés Garcia

"When it comes to Latinos and marketing to Latinos . . . it's a comfort level," Salas says. "We want to be included, we want to belong, we want to be invited to your business, we want to feel good about it." Instead of starting with an advertising buy, Latino experts urge companies to build marketing plans around educating staff. It is not enough to advertise on Spanish-language radio stations. "You have to really educate your staff about why you're doing it and how you're going to go about it," Salas says. "All it takes is for somebody to look down to us, and we're not going to come back."

Omaha Spanish-language radio is growing online through website views and Facebook likes, and available social media data offer new business opportunities. **Click-through rates (CTR)** within Facebook appear to be higher—perhaps because it seems safer than the open Web for Latino users, one Omaha businessman suggested. From a purely social media marketing perspective, Latino businesses and consumers offer a growing target market. Quantitative data explaining qualitative results provides an important and valuable cultural context. It is clear that social marketers must take into account the complexities of this unique and growing demographic group, and the focus begins with website analysis.

Reference

Lipschultz, J. H. (2016, November 11, 14). Social Media Marketing to Latinos. *Huffington Post*, www.huffingtonpost.com/entry/social-media-marketing-to-latinos_us_5828c806e4b02b1f5257a4d8

Google Analytics offers a dashboard for tracking effectiveness:

- **Site visitors**—unique new or returning users

- **Site visits**—sessions with interaction

- **Pageviews**—each page viewed and interaction "events"

- **Time**—time on page, visit duration, and "bounce rate" (percentagr of sessions with only one action)

t(( )) Thought Leader David Kamerer

Get Started with Google Analytics

As our communication activities have moved to the digital realm, we now have an unprecedented opportunity to measure success. If you want to improve performance, you must know what needs fixing. And nowhere is this more important than on owned media, particularly our websites. Fortunately, we have access to web analytics, which can provide us with powerful data on how people use our website.

Google Analytics is the market leader, in part because it is a powerful, sophisticated tool, and in part because it is free. To get started, sign up for your account at Google.com/analytics, obtain your tracking code, and install

FIGURE 2.2 *David Kamerer (@DavidKamerer). Photograph courtesy Loyola University Chicago.*

it on every page of your site. This may sound daunting, but it may be easy, because content managers such as WordPress only require the code to be installed in one place, such as a header or footer, which is served with every pageview.

Your code will start reporting visits in about a day. While there are unlimited ways to use analytics, here are three essential reports to help you get started. Before you look at any report, adjust the time frame to a meaningful period, and always note the time frame when discussing results.

1. Top-Level—Overall Performance
To view this report, log in to your analytics dashboard and go to Audience > Overview.

This report shows the broadest overview of how people are interacting with your site—it's the "runs-hits-and-errors" report. How many people visited your site, how many clicks did they make, and how long did they stay?

TABLE 2.4 *Overview Google Analytics data*

Users	1,361,199
New Users	1,320,024
Sessions	4,935,463
Number of Sessions Per User	3.63
Pageviews	19,531,812
Pages/Sessions	3.96
Average Session Duration	00:02:38
Bounce Rate	17.82%

FIGURE 2.3 *Google Analytics top, time, acquisition, and pageviews. Google Analytics data images courtesy David Kamerer.*

Do they come back? The bounce rate refers to the percentage of sessions that only had a single page view. Bounce sessions are often, but not always, associated with a poor online experience. Analytics expert Avinash Kaushik (2018a) concludes that, "anything over 35% is a cause for concern and anything above 50% is worrying" (para. 24).

Be wary of comparing your top-level analytics with data obtained from different sources. It's best to look at month over month, quarterly or annual comparisons. This can be done by setting the appropriate time frame and clicking on the "compare to" button just under your time window.

2. Acquisition—Where Do Your Visitors Come From?
To view this report, go to Acquisition > All Traffic > Channels.

Now that you've got a handle on overall use of your site, you may want to look at where your visitors are coming from. The acquisition report is especially useful as a check on your digital marketing programs, which should be referring people to your website. A healthy website gets traffic from a variety of sources, including search, referrals, direct visits, and campaigns, which can include social, email, or online advertising.

Think of your web traffic as a financial portfolio, and each of the four buckets as a position. You want a balanced portfolio that minimizes risk and maximizes return. If one channel is weak, you'll know that you might need to work on it. Let's take a look at each channel.

Direct Traffic

These visitors know you and are familiar with your site. They typed your URL into their browser or bothered to bookmark you. To further enhance your direct traffic, choose a short, easy-to-remember and easy-to-type URL and promote it abundantly in your offline materials—letterhead, business cards, newspaper ads, wherever you have a presence offline. Analytics expert Kaushik (2018b) also recommends that direct traffic should be in the neighborhood of 20 percent (para. 26). However, relative to other channels, there's not a lot you can do to improve direct traffic. You should note that visits are also logged as "direct" when there is no referrer—these are the occasional visits from an app or from a link in a PowerPoint presentation. If Analytics can't tell where the visit came from, it gets recorded as direct.

Referral Traffic

These visitors come on a link from a website. A savvy marketer builds links because they pay two dividends—they send quality traffic to your site, and they are a signal to search engines that your site should rank over other sites with fewer or weaker links. How do you build these links? Reach out to webmasters, either offline or online. Comment on a blog post or guest author an article. Link back to strong, relevant websites that have appropriate content. You can also ask friends to link to you, or research others who should be on that list, and build relationships with them. Kaushik says your referral traffic should be around 20 to 30 percent; however, many smaller sites perform well below this standard.

Search Traffic

When people first look at their analytics, they're often surprised at how strong their search traffic is. Kaushik says 40–50 percent is normal. For many sites, it's even higher. This is why most digital marketers begin with SEO before other marketing activities. Increasing traffic in this bucket is the major goal of search engine optimization. In addition to link building, we work to make our content as relevant as possible to searchers, and as visible as possible to Google and other search engines. We do this by using relevant keywords in our copy, and by using them in places, such as the page title or first paragraph, that search engines view as important.

Too much dependence on search engines can be bad, however, because just as Google giveth, Google can also taketh away. Search is a fast-moving area and change is constant. You could be one algorithm change from losing a chunk of your traffic. So, by all means, get as many visits from search as possible, but also try to diversify your visitor portfolio.

Campaign Traffic

By default, you will have no campaign traffic. So this area is the purest test of the marketer's success. Every business or organization uses a different combination tactics to create campaign traffic. If you send targeted emails, the referrals will show up here. Other kinds of campaign traffic may come from paid search, display advertising or social media referrals. Kaushik suggests that campaign traffic should total about 10 percent of all visits.

3. Top Content—What Pages Are People Visiting?

To view this report, go to Behavior > Site Content > All Pages.

When you see this report, you'll think "finally—I can tell what content people are seeing." To get the most from it, be sure to go to the bottom of the report and extend the number of rows to 50, 100 or more, depending on how much content your site features.

You're likely to see your home page (represented as "/") and other pages linked from the home page, at the top of your report. But you might not. This is because of the role of search, which provides the most relevant results to searchers. You may find you have "hit" content that you didn't know about. Knowing this may help you create a better user experience.

Beyond how popular your top pages are, it's helpful to know how well they are performing. You want your top pages to have low bounce rates and low exit rates. You can assess this manually, or by clicking on the "comparison" tool on the upper right of the content report next to the "advanced" label. The resulting table shows the performance of each page relative to the site average. The goal: to not be leaking visitors from the site's most popular pages.

A few caveats.

Analytics reports are most useful when you use the information to drive change to your site. You should adopt a culture of continuous improvement. Over time, you will learn what changes to the site can improve its performance.

Don't stress too much if your overall acquisition pattern doesn't match the ideal. Overall, your goal is to grow your traffic, and to improve the channels that severely underperform.

This article does not discuss the most important aspect of your site's performance—conversions. Every site has some activity they want visitors to do, whether it's to buy something or provide personal information (lead generation). You should identify what is important to your site and build your measurement plan around this.

Analytics, for all its power, only measures page views. Analytics are good at the "what" but not so good at the "why." For this, you need to also use some qualitative tools to verify that visitors are having a good experience. As with all research methods, it pays to use multiple methods to learn the other kinds of truths about your website. So don't neglect other tools, such as surveys, user testing or competitive analysis, as you work to make your website as good as it can be.

References

Kaushik, A. (2018a). Excellent Analytics Tip #11: Measure Effectiveness of Your Web Pages. Occam's Razor.
www.kaushik.net/avinash/excellent-analytics-tip-11-measure-effectiveness-of-your-web-pages/

_____ (2018b). Beginner's Guide to Web Data Analytics. Occam's Razor.
www.kaushik.net/avinash/beginners-guide-web-data-analysis-ten-steps-tips-best-practices/

*David Kamerer, Ph.D., is Associate Professor in the School of Communication, Loyola University Chicago. He teaches public relations, digital media, and online marketing. Kamerer consults small business and non-profit clients on successful social media strategies and tactics.
www.linkedin.com/in/davidkamerer/*

STRATEGIES

Strategy is crucial in the social media measurement and management functions. Facebook, Instagram, Twitter, and other social media platform data all have different meanings, and some metrics are grossly inflated. "Those reach metrics aren't meaningful, and until we start making those distinctions," consultant Gary Angel says, "we're going to be misleading the people who need this information the most." Company and nonprofit executives either accept flawed data, or they simply dismiss it. Angel, Digital Mortar CEO, told the eMetrics Summit in Chicago that giving the same name to fundamentally different metrics is not standardization: "You've got to do some work to make reach metrics comparable, and if you're not doing that work you really haven't standardized the metrics you are giving people."

The Digital Analytics Association (DAA) and the eMetrics Summit

Too often, social media managers decide to adopt unique best practices designed years ago.

FIGURE 2.4 *Gary Angel (@garyangel). Photograph by Jeremy Harris Lipschultz, courtesy Gary Angel.*

> *Best practices are no way to make important decisions. Best practices are what other people learned in their business. Your business is unique and distinct. That's what analytics is about. I have started countless best practices . . . I know how crappy most of them are, how specific to unique situations they often are. Best practices are guidelines that happen to work for somebody else.*

—Gary Angel

Instead, Angel tells clients to use current analytics in decision-making. "Best practices should be used to sort of set the broad table for the research questions you want to look at, not to be adopted wholesale." Strategic priorities instead must be "translated" into KPIs. A focus on business customers, for example, means understanding why people care about your product or service, as well as competitors. "What's the story you need to tell them?" Angel asks. "If you're

FIGURE 2.5 *Kuntal Goradia (@PayPal). Photograph by Jeremy Harris Lipschultz, courtesy Kuntal Goradia.*

not answering those questions when you talk to creative people," Angel tells analysts, "you're not setting the table for them to do a good job."

"Stop making up KPIs," Angel rants. "If you pick engagement as a metric, you darn well better be able to prove that you're really measuring engagement, and that engagement has some kind of positive relationship to business outcomes." He's talking about the hard work it takes to be taken seriously in the C-suite. If analytics move up an organizational chart to executives, too often the data are never sent down to site developers to learn what worked, Angel suggests. This is one piece of the communication problem large organizations have because of silos and poor management practices. Angel also says it is natural to look for easy measures—time on a page, scrolling to the bottom, or completing a form—but "those metrics almost always suck, they don't mean anything."

The eMetrics Summit founder and author Jim Sterne described how a small group of web analytics professionals first met in Santa Barbara, California in 2002. The field later became known as digital analytics. Digital Analytics Association (DAA) Executive Director Marilee Yorchak says there are now 14 local chapters with quarterly events around the nation, and a new chapter may open in Vancouver. PayPal Director of CX Analytics and Experimentation Kuntal Maya Goradia offered examples of how digital analytics involves a continuous process.

It may be that too often social media managers lack time and other resources to bring scientific rigor to their measurement and management activities. It takes strong organization support for the value of improving data quality. Without it, we cannot expect valuable business insights.

References

Lipschultz, J. H. (2017, April 9). Social Marketing: It's Personal. *Huffington Post*. www.huffingtonpost.com/entry/social-media-marketing-its-personal_us_58ead152e4b0acd784ca59d4

Lipschultz, J. H. (2017, July 9). Misleading Social Media Engagement Metrics and 'Crappy' Best Practices. *Huffington Post*. www.huffingtonpost.com/entry/misleading-social-media-engagement-metrics-and-crappy_us_5962dc19e4b085e766b513f1

Frequently, the process begins with listening. Partner and Evolytics President Carey Wilkins says successful organizations have strong connections between stakeholders. That involves cultivating solid relationships. The DAA is not the only group of skeptical marketers. Jeff Bullas says number of social shares, for example, serve as social proof of credibility. Yet Facebook inflated the numbers to include a view as seeing just one pixel for three seconds. Bullas called the metrics "hope and optimism." Better to just recognize flawed data as crap. Only then may we begin with a strategic focus on goals and objectives. From there, organizations may be able to measure what really matters in their unique situation. Watching the president's daily tweets, we must see that social media continue to evolve. "There's this guy named Donald Trump who, if you didn't know what Twitter was, you do now," social marketer Jim Sterne says.

Sterne (2010) wrote *Social Media Metrics: How to Measure and Optimize Your Marketing Investment*—opening the book with "100 Ways to Measure Social Media" (p. xx). The list can be considered one of the earliest attempts to formalize social media measurement. As measurement matured, social media managers began to recall media research fundamentals, move beyond measuring "buzz," with a focus on goals, strategies and tactics. Brand marketing communication may be more sophisticated, but Sterne told students that there remains no good way to separate human from chatbot followers, although we can analyze growth and find meaning in context, emphasis, and sentiment. "So, the analysis part is always necessary, and measurement is a piece that you use to get some raw material." Statistical analysis may help social media analysis develop a predictive social marketing mix model that focuses on outcomes and business value. An effective social media engagement strategy moves beyond reach and instead focuses on conversation and relationships. Social media real-time listening helps brands to move in the direction of *audience*-centered communication—"talking about what they are talking about," Sterne says. Planning, then, is about meeting customers where *they* are, and reflecting their words. Sterne says trusted brand representation, for example, distinguishes between "exploitive" and "meaningful" hashtags, and it requires planning and organization before events happen.

Even for small nonprofit organizations with a Facebook page and a website, specific tactics depend upon, "what are you trying to do with it," Sterne says. Knowing the answer should drive a plan that helps guide measurement goals. For every brand, there is a "baseline conversation," and the easiest place to begin is with social media customer service and support, Sterne says. "Let them know that you are available and make it somebody's responsibility to respond." From there, a brand may work on "outbound promotion." Nonprofits have a need to cultivate donor relationships through social media channels. The key is to "learn just enough to engage with them in a personal way, maybe post a fun picture that those people will share with their friends . . . that's the power of social." Thus, eWOM can be used to raise awareness and spark social media engagement that move people toward desired actions. This may begin with earned and owned media channels that eventually inform an organization how to leverage limited resources for paid and promoted social media posts. Too often, organizations pay for advertising without knowing the most effective ways to reach and engage brand fans.

> *I'm going to go out and engage with people and get them to spread the word. That's earned attention . . . Who is your target audience? Where do they hang out? And, that's how you reach them. So, the goal is first, the audience, second . . . the channel, and finally the message.*

—*Jim Sterne*

Sterne, as with a lot of social marketers, suggests photographs, gif animation, and video as effective tactics once an organization locates its target audience and social media channels. While marketing ultimately requires great content, it may fall flat with the wrong audience on the wrong channel. Short, digestible social media content tends to be viewed and shared more often than long-form media. In the competition for marketplace attention, content tone matters, Sterne says. Public relations may try to push their tone on the audience by crafting messages: "it's disingenuous, it is hard work, it is not necessarily valuable," Sterne argues. "The real challenge is not can I get you to take on my tone, but can I take on a tone that's appealing across the board, and it's not corporate speak." We're just beginning to understand the impact of big data on social media marketing. Sterne places "an orange flag" on some claims because social media marketers need more research on the effectiveness of artificial intelligence (AI) in the process. In the long run, Sterne believes we all will have our own AI "assistant" negotiating with brands about what information to send, and even paying consumers to receive desired content. Consumer empowerment through personal filtering may take the edge off of data privacy concerns. It is clear that micro targeting based upon consumer needs and wants is the future of personal social media management communication.

GOALS, OBJECTIVES, AND TACTICS

Too often, social media managers post content without a clear set of goals and objectives. A nonprofit, for example, should begin with an organizational strategic plan that is built from an extensive planning process that involves all stakeholders. Quesenberry (2018) outlines a simple process: 1) situation analysis (target market, social media audit, business objectives); 2) develop key insights and a big idea (create engaging content of value); 3) select social media channels (add and subtract for target and big idea); 4) integrate with other business functions and traditional marketing; and 5) link business objectives to social media metrics (then budget, schedule, and run). If we begin with business goals, it is much easier to select relevant data and tools needed. A social media manager then aligns these with available resources and existing organization events.

Often, organizations have an existing calendar of events throughout the year. These can be the basis for building a **social media calendar** that aligns with those important opportunities to engage with the community and build lasting relationships. A calendar can be constructed as an Excel spreadsheet, or as part of a Hootsuite or other management tool guide. A calendar should include relevant and branded hashtags linked to broader marketing strategies that are focused on audience interests, hashtag analytics, and optimized posts (Samuels, 2019).

Typically, a social media calendar is linked to a larger organizational public and private events schedule. Influencers, for example, may spark interest in annual or special events. Stitt (2018) suggested that the future of influencer marketing includes transparent disclosure, use of podcasting, and cultivating relationships with e-sports gamers on platforms, such as Twitch:

> The days of vanity metrics are long past. So as the industry evolves so must we, from the tedious task of compliance, fraud protection to which is the next big group of influencers to look out for. We're on a mission to make influencer marketing data-driven and transparent so that companies can transform the way they do business to harness the power of digital influencers.
>
> (para. 3)

Clearly there are new opportunities to engage with younger social media users by creating authentic and compliant events that align a brand through social media metrics with new audience interests. Development of goals, objectives, and specific event-based tactics reflect an eye toward strategic management.

SOCIAL MEDIA EVENTS

Social media efforts have the best opportunity to be effective when engagement happens that is aligned with existing events. The CMC idea of human–computer interaction (HCI) frequently focuses on the act of information sharing (Barnes, 2003). In particular, group communication increases the likelihood that interest will be higher (Lieberman, 2013) throughout a set of social network site (SNS) connections (boyd & Ellison, 2008). While it may be possible to use online tools to form new networked connections, such as through LinkedIn, SNSs often are used to activate or enhance existing social relationships. The research speaks of online communities that may be cultivated through ongoing networked interaction and leadership (Huffaker, 2010). SMC may be a participatory and symbolic meaning-making process that utilizes metaphor and memes to building common shared communication (Lipschultz, 2018).

Relationship-building appears to be a function of interpersonal disclosure, transparency and trust.

The spread of new ideas and practices, though, happens within a context of place. In the case of social media communication, mobile apps drive users to a select set of popular online communities. Apple iPhone data help social media managers target online platforms, and a raw measure would be the list of top free app downloads: 1) YouTube; 2) Instagram; 3) Snapchat; 4) Messenger; 5) Facebook; 6) Bitmoji; 6) Netflix; 8) Google Maps; 9) Gmail; 10) Spotify Music (Bell, 2018, para. 4). Other top-twenty social media apps included WhatsApp (13), TikTok (16), and Twitter (20). While some social media platforms, such as Twitter, have reached a plateau, other new apps like TikTok seem to be on the rise. Social media managers must constantly watch trends for change brought about by adoption of new products and processes.

DIFFUSION OF INNOVATION

Diffusion and adoption through the spread of ideas and practices may be enhanced through the use of broadband technologies. S-shaped data patterns of adoption help us to see the rise in awareness and interest that may lead to evaluation by an individual. Rogers (1995) showed that diffusion curves normal curve shape are driven by the speed of product, process, or new idea acceptance. Social media adoption through interpersonal communication and media usage involve trends (Hunsinger & Senft, 2014). Snapchat, for example, became very popular among early adopters before the app had difficulty acquiring new users and retaining existing ones. The result was that the rate of adoption slowed, and the diffusion curve flattened. Still, YouTube, Instagram, and Snapchat success reflect a deeper pattern of the interest in recorded and produced video. As streaming video compression technologies improved, online video offered opportunities for audience engagement. Social media communication data include video views, but also likes, shares, and other useful measures.

The rising popularity of TikTok (formerly Musical.ly), a Chinese app, is one example of the rise of social media video. Roose (2018a) noted that its rise may be related to the initial lack of advertising and would-be social media influencers: "Users create short videos set to music, often lip-syncing along, dancing or acting out short skits" (para. 5). Music video has the power to transcend language and local culture by replacing it with a global and youth-oriented message. Yet, despite the adoption of the relatively new app, it contains older social media measurement data points—followers, likes, comments, and hashtags. This reflects a deeper aspect of socially mediated communication that mimics face-to-face oral tradition.

CMC AND SOCIAL MEDIA

Computer-mediated communication (CMC) tends to lack the information richness of face-to-face communication (f2f) and human relationships (Huynh, et al., 2013). Social media **memes**, for example, may be shared because they can to be easily interpreted within cultural norms (Shifman, 2013), yet sense of humor is a matter of racial and other subcultural agreement about what is funny or not (Anderson & Hitlin, 2016). Therefore, the examination of social media data must be placed within these important social and cultural contexts for emerging media communication (Chaffee and Metzger, 2001). Individuals within social networks have the power to create and share content that has standardized cultural meaning-making. Humans thousands of years ago awakened an oral tradition and social consciousness. Social media are simply a new way to communicate with massive and global audiences—sometimes with the perceived intimacy of tribal face-to-face conversation. A social media manager should reflect this understanding within broad goals and objectives, as well as specific campaign tactics.

ᵗ📡 Thought Leader Randa Zalman

Home Instead Senior Care Foundation: GIVE65 Fundraising Campaign Case Study
Every day, approximately 10,000 Americans turn 65 years old. The tremendous growth in this population means a tremendous growth in need from the population's most vulnerable members. While government programs like Social Security exist to serve this population, one in seven seniors still live in poverty according to the supplemental poverty measure from the U.S. Census bureau. Private programs can help. From meal programs to senior centers, and exercise classes to housing assistance, privately funded senior-related nonprofits are stepping up to provide important support for U.S. seniors. Recognizing the growing

FIGURE 2.6 *Randa Zalman (@randazalman). Photograph courtesy Canary & Coal.*

need, in 2016, Home Instead Senior Care Foundation (HISCF) created GIVE65. Every July, over a 65-hour timeframe, this crowd-sourced fundraising plat-form raises awareness and funds in support of services for the over-65 population.

Through GIVE65, HISCF partners with more than 90 nonprofits dedicated to helping preserve seniors' quality of life. GIVE65 partners are united by the goal of allowing seniors to age independently and with dignity. Each focuses on one or more of six key areas: 1) exercise and health; 2) housing and home improvement; 3) in-home care and visits; 4) nutrition and meals programs; 5) seniors care; and 6) adult day center and services.

After managing the inaugural year's campaign internally, in 2017 HISCF partnered with a professional social media practice to assemble a strategic paid social media blueprint for the fundraising event. The aim of the part-nership was "to engage the target market nationwide via implementation of a tactical social media plan that achieves identified goals and incorpo-rates Google and Facebook analytics to measure success."

Three major project goals were established:

Project Goal No. 1: Increase Awareness for the Needs of Our Senior Population
Rationale: Every day, 10,000 Americans are turning 65. In designing the GIVE65 event, HISCF asked its nonprofit partners to identify the top needs of the seniors they serve. Six were named and became the elements around which the awareness portion of the campaign is organized: 1) exercise & health; 2) housing & home improvement; 3) in-home care & visits; 4) nutri-tion & meals programs; 5) seniors centers; and 6) adult day center and services.

Project Goal No. 2: Encourage Philanthropic Support of Nonprofit Programs And Services Meeting the Needs Of Our Senior Population.
Rationale: Both government and philanthropic funding are being strained by the increasing demand for senior-focused programs and services. In con-versations with nonprofit professionals, GIVE65 representatives heard how difficult it is to raise money to help seniors—especially for smaller grassroots organizations. According to the U.S. Foundation Center, less than 2 percent

of funding from the nation's largest grant makers is focused on seniors. Many nonprofits noted that the under-representation of senior programs in grant awards is a longstanding trend in the U.S.

Project Goal No. 3: Create a Fun, Exciting, and Compelling Campaign that Builds Momentum and Revolves Around Helping Our Senior Population

Rationale: Home Instead Senior Care is a global organization with the stated mission to "change the face of aging." As the corporation's associated foundation, HISCF is helping to fulfill that strategic intent by financially supporting efforts to make aging hopeful, successful, and dignified for all seniors. This approach is inherently optimistic as it assumes that seniors' quality of life can be improved if the right resources are made available. The GIVE65 program makes this optimism tangible by creating a rewarding experience for sponsors, site visitors, donors, and the GIVE65 nonprofit partners. Organizer hope that the positive environment created by GIVE65 can be a catalyst for powerful and lasting social change.

With these goals established, the GIVE65 team turned to developing the campaign strategy required to meet each.

A paid placement campaign blueprint was drafted to strategically outline social media outreach. The blueprint provided a purposeful framework for goal-based budget allocation between social media platforms, content topics, target audiences, and key performance indicators for pre-event, during-event, and post-event communication.

Strategy for Project Goal 1

One-third of the social media content was devoted to building awareness for the top six areas of need: 1) exercise & health; 2) housing & home improvement; 3) in-home care & visits; 4) nutrition & meals programs; 5) seniors care; and 6) adult day center & services. With assistance from several of the participating nonprofits, the GIVE65 team shared powerful personal narratives from individuals positively impacted by programs in each area. Social media advertisements were placed nationally extending awareness to audiences across the country.

Strategy for Goal 2

To help maximize potential donations to the campaign, a segment of social media outreach was dedicated to delivering senior-driven messages to specific target audiences identified as likely-donors. Ad managers within each social media platform allowed us to select demographic, psychographic, and geographic variables to narrow the placement focus to those with a propensity to donate. In addition, through application of available research and an examination of prior fundraising results, select posts were delivered to a specific audience of women, age 35+ and living within a specified proximity of our participating nonprofits to leverage established program name recognition.

Prior to the GIVE65 Event, we reached out to the participating nonprofits to solicit examples and associated stories to humanize the need and to amplify the personal nature of the request. Twelve of the participating nonprofits provided images, videos, and a summary of their need and how the money raised would impact their organization and help the senior population overall.

In all messages created for this segment, the content and visuals of the posts carried a clear and emotionally compelling call to action encouraging users to click through donate and make a positive difference.

Strategy for Goal 3

Several campaign elements were strategically constructed to help build anticipation and enthusiasm around the event for both the participating nonprofits and the contributing donors. Numerous countdowns were posted to generate excitement for the start of the event. Playful challenges were issued to encourage donors to beat previous year's donation totals.

To help "change the face of aging" a number uplifting human-interest stories were shared to help highlight the services, the senior need and to explain the positive impacts of donations both large and small. Accompanying images illustrated the diversity and worth of those whose lives are being improved.

Home Instead Senior Care Foundation in 📍 Newark, Delaware.
Published by Randa Zalman [?] · July 13 at 6:05am · 🌐

A donation of $11 or more to Lori's Hands will help connect college students with seniors in their community living with chronic illnesses. Not only does this create a helping relationship between the pair, but it shows the value in being a compassionate and caring person. This organization is near and dear to Liz Bonomo – which is why she's Board Treasurer – and she's asking for your support right now during the #GIVE65 Event!

LH $11 TO $7,000!

Hello, friends and family!
 As most of you already know, Lori's Hands has been a big part of my life since my sophomore year of college when my good friend Sarah approached a group of us with a simple, brilliant idea. I served as a...

GIVE65.ORG

FIGURE 2.7   *Give65 campaign. #Give65 campaign image, Courtesy Canary & Coal.*

Results

Through targeted and compelling social media content, more people not only visited GIVE65.org to learn about the nonprofits and the life-changing services and programs they provide, but more donations were given in support of their senior-focused missions.

TABLE 2.5 *Social media campaign template*

Activity to Support Project Goal	Reporting Requirements	Campaign Results
1. Create and optimize a Facebook ad campaign and sponsor well-performing posts that utilize one-third of the grand budget.	**Social Media Traffic** will help us understand how many GIVE65.org visitors are coming from Facebook or other social media platforms. **Utilize Facebook Ads Manager** to continually monitor Results, Reach, Engagement, and People taking action due to the ad.	A total of 77 posts were shared over three major social media platforms for the GIVE65 Event. For the 2017 GIVE65 Event, we learned that our average donor *looks like:* Woman, 35+ Urban area One-third of the budget was utilized to place Facebook ads to emphasize the top five areas of senior need, identified above. Results are as follows: Impressions: *The number of people who had an opportunity to see a campaign Facebook ad (reach) multiplied by the number of times they had an opportunity to see it (frequency).* Facebook: 3,516,577 Instagram: 60,786 Twitter: 66,799 Reach *The number of unique Facebook users who had an opportunity to see a campaign Facebook ad.* Facebook: 1,180,961 Instagram: 57,462 Engagement: *The number of actions taken by Facebook users with a campaign ad. Actions can include, but are not limited to: likes, Facebook reactions, comments, retweets, shares, etc.* Facebook: 9,929 Instagram: 4,619 Twitter: 257 Link Clicks: *The number of user clicks from a social media platform to the GIVE65.com donation page.* Facebook: 1,445 Twitter: 21

(Continued)

TABLE 2.5   (Continued)

Activity to Support Project Goal	Reporting Requirements	Campaign Results
2. We have the capability to create a series of ads/sponsored posts that focus around "needs categories" and a "needs category specific URL link" to GIVE65 nonprofit partners raising funds within these needs categories. The categories can include needs such as those mentioned in the rationale above.	**Audience Engagement** allows us to measure a visitor's time spent on a page, the total number of pages visited, and return visits. **Link Clicks** will help us understand how many Facebook users are engaging with sponsored posts and taking action by clicking the accompanying link to learn more, donate, apply to participate in GIVE65 Event, etc.	Needs-specific social media advertisements were created for each of the identified categories. Total Engagement Actions: *The number of actions taken by Facebook users with a campaign ad. Actions can include, but are not limited to: likes, Facebook reactions, comments, retweets, shares, etc.* Facebook: 29,788 Instagram: 13,858 Twitter: 771 Total Campaign Link Clicks: *The number of user clicks from a social media platform to the GIVE65.com donation page.* Facebook: 4,335 Twitter: 63
3. Create and optimize a Facebook ad campaign that utilizes one third of the grant budget.	**Social Media Traffic** will help us understand how many GIVE65.org visitors are coming from Facebook or other social media platforms. **Utilize Facebook Ads Manager** to continually monitor Results, Reach and People Taking Action (visiting GIVE65.org) due to the ad.	One-third of the budget was utilized to place Facebook ads to emphasize the top six areas of senior need, identified above. Results are as follows: Impressions: *The number of people who had an opportunity to see a campaign Facebook ad (reach) multiplied by the number of times they had an opportunity to see it (frequency).* Facebook: 3,516,577 Instagram: 60,786 Twitter: 66,799 Reach *The number of unique Facebook users who had an opportunity to see a campaign Facebook ad.* Facebook: 1,180,961 Instagram: 57,462 Engagement: *The number of actions taken by Facebook users with a campaign ad. Actions can include, but are not limited to: likes, Facebook reactions, comments, retweets, shares, etc.* Facebook: 9,929 Instagram: 4,619 Twitter: 257

Activity to Support Project Goal	Reporting Requirements	Campaign Results

		Link Clicks:
		The number of user clicks from a social media platform to the GIVE65.com donation page.
		  Facebook: 1,445
		  Twitter: 21

4. Convert Facebook consumers to donors.	**Audience Engagement** allows us to measure a visitor's time spent on a page, the total number of pages visited, and return visits.
	
	Link Clicks will help us understand how many Facebook users are engaging with sponsored posts and taking action by clicking the accompanying link to learn more, donate, apply to participate in GIVE65, etc.
		Total Engagement Actions:
		The number of actions taken by Facebook users with a campaign ad. Actions can include, but are not limited to: likes, Facebook reactions, comments, retweets, shares, etc.
		  Facebook: 29,788
		  Instagram: 13,858
		  Twitter: 771
		
		Total Campaign Link Clicks:
		The number of user clicks from a social media platform to the GIVE65.com donation page.
		  Facebook: 4,335
		  Twitter: 63

5. Attract and engage the right audience. Attract and engage repeat donors, donors that will increase their donation and new GIVE65 donors.	**Cart Abandonment** helps us understand how many visitors begin the process to donate, but do not complete it. In 2016, only 5 percent of potential GIVE65 donors did not complete the giving process. This assures us that we are communicating with the right audience. We can measure **repeat donors**, **increased donations**, and **new donors** that have joined the GIVE65 movement.	**Percentage of Cart Abandonment:** **Number of Repeat Donors:** **Percentage of Increased Donations:** **Number of New Donors:**

(Continued)

TABLE 2.5   *(Continued)*

Activity to Support Project Goal	Reporting Requirements	Campaign Results
6. Create and optimize a Facebook ad campaign that utilizes one-third of the budget.	**Social Media Traffic** will help us understand how many GIVE65.org visitors are coming from Facebook or other social media platforms. **Utilize Facebook Ads Manager** to continually monitor Results, Reach, Engagement, and People Taking Action due to the ad.	One-third of the budget was utilized to place Facebook ads to emphasize the top five areas of senior need, identified above. Results are as follows: Impressions: *The number of people who had an opportunity to see a campaign Facebook ad (reach) times the number of times they had an opportunity to see it (frequency).* Facebook: 3,516,577 Instagram: 60,786 Twitter: 66,799 Reach *The number of unique Facebook users who had an opportunity to see a campaign Facebook ad.* Facebook: 1,180,961 Instagram: 57,462 Engagement: *The number of actions taken by Facebook users with a campaign ad. Actions can include, but are not limited to: likes, Facebook reactions, comments, retweets, shares, etc.* Facebook: 9,929 Instagram: 4,619 Twitter: 257 Link Clicks: *The number of user clicks from a social media platform to the GIVE65.com donation page.* Facebook: 1,445 Twitter: 21
7. GIVE65 digital properties include a built-in countdown clock, dollars raised counter and financial prize leaderboard that	**Audience Engagement** allows us to measure a visitor's time spent on a page, the total number of pages visited, and return visits.	Total Engagement Actions: *The number of actions taken by Facebook users with a campaign ad. Actions can include, but are not limited to: likes, Facebook reactions, comments, retweets, shares, etc.* Facebook: 29,788 Instagram: 13,858 Twitter: 771

Activity to Support Project Goal	Reporting Requirements	Campaign Results
provides real-time data to engage and motivate audiences to support the GIVE65 movement. Promotion drives audiences to these popular gamification features with the hope of them clicking to donate once they land on the main GIVE65. org page.	**Link Clicks** will help us understand how many Facebook users are engaging with sponsored posts and taking action by clicking the accompanying link to learn more, donate, apply to participate in GIVE65, etc.	Total Campaign Link Clicks: *The number of user clicks from a social media platform to the GIVE65.com donation page.* Facebook: 4,335 Twitter: 63

Among the general public, social media was the most significant driver of success for the 2017 GIVE65 fundraising campaign. Overall awareness activities were amplified and reached a diverse group of people who now understand that the senior population is often overlooked and underserved, and we as a society need to work together to ensure every senior is able to age safely, independently, and with dignity.

The following chart outlines the tactics and results of the seven primary campaign segments of the 2017 GIVE65 social media campaign. The impact this campaign generated continues to benefit seniors as the GIVE65 team works to build on its success with ongoing efforts to inspire greater awareness and charitable giving in support of seniors. In coming years, GIVE65 promises to be a catalyst that spurs society to take ever better care of our aging parents and grandparents.

Randa Zalman is the President and CEO of Canary & Coal, a marketing firm in Omaha, Nebraska. She is a recognized thought leader on the power and appropriate use of new media including social media and digital placement.

Successful campaigns require social media managers to cultivate positive and constructive online communities. Given the noise of social channels, this can be challenging. The focus should be on filtering worthless content and leveraging value. An entrepreneurial mindset allows a social media manager the freedom to explore, test, and create valuable content and relationships within meaningful communities. It is about being explicit in creation of goals and objectives for use of social media.

Social Media Marketing Data Science and Brand Engagement

Too many organizations maintain a Facebook page, at times without much thought about strategy. Small business and non-profit social media managers typically squeeze in posts around many other job duties. Still, much can be learned from those developing the art and science of social business goals, objectives and tactics. Brian Massey, founder and managing partner at Conversion Sciences, focuses on business website performance data analysis. "The Conversion Scientist" (complete with his lab coat) explores the marketing funnel—from lead generation through the optimization of the conversion process.

FIGURE 2.8   *Jim Sterne (@jimsterne). Photograph by courtesy Jim Sterne.*

"Quality leads," he says, allow marketers to "use a combination of user testing and A/B testing to prioritize and refine those ideas." Improvement is defined as those tweaks that increase business revenue. It involves a constant process of innovation to respond to market changes driven by social media and other forces. Mobile smartphones are a location-based sensor constantly measuring contextual consumer behavior. From inexpensive content testing panels to big data pools, entrepreneurs are developing new tools to help marketers.

We're talking about someone who understands how to evaluate data, how to collect data, how to make decisions based on the data they're collecting and integrate that into their design process.

Facebook target advertising offers social marketers' access to millions of potential customers based upon demographic and psychographic filters. For businesses, that translates into qualified prospects. For nonprofit and local government organizations, targeting is an efficient way to reach interested citizens, raise issue awareness, and spark new community engagement. Success on Facebook, though, requires advertising experiments and effective "landing experiences" on websites, Massey says. Instead of "spray and pray" blasts, "marketers have to embrace this experimentation culture."

You may not be ready to wear a lab coat, but Massey makes a good point about Facebook targeting as, "interrupt advertising, as opposed to search, which is intent-driven based on the keywords that are entered." A strategic campaign integrates words, site design and images, brand management and data. In short, we need to embrace granular, contextual data. The beauty of testing is that it allows a creative team to respond to data by developing bolder campaigns, Massey says. "We can take those risks because we're doing it with user testing and small experiments."

An ObservePoint analytics summit made this clear. Forrester Research Principal Analyst James McCormick emphasized that strategic metrics should be coordinated through standards and best practices. Optimization of KPIs are grounded in digital intelligence platforms. Understanding "digital touch-points," he has written, should lead to "optimizing and perfecting experiences delivered, and decisions made by brands during moments of engagement."

Meanwhile, Massey focuses on site personalized visitor touch-points that locate someone at a place within the marketing funnel. It makes a difference, if a person seeks information, brand engagement, or price discounts. AI and the use of chatbots work better for some functions than others. Massey asks, "What is the experience once they click?"

> These devices can be used to manipulate rather than persuade. We want to persuade, not manipulate. So, the more people we have that take on experience experimentation culture, the more diversity we have. I think it will ensure that we have a higher ethical bar of people who are using this data.

Massey says the data trend should not "scare you away from getting excited about the creative part of the job." Social media marketers will need AI training to do the job five years from now, he adds. Consider an email subject line. Data scientists can help marketers improve results. "I've got to sit down and use it on a daily basis to answer questions." For now, email and Facebook continue to be the primary way to reach people. "Instagram is probably the next frontier," Massey says. Likewise, Pinterest can be effective. Increasingly, Facebook and YouTube video also are in the mix.

To some extent, the traditional marketing approach distinguishes use of social media from effective Instagram and Snapchat brand influencer campaigns. These sites, along with Twitter, started behind Facebook in offering targeted marketing data. Massey also is keeping an eye on Amazon and its integration of products and user data. "Every campaign is an experiment," he says. "If we can embrace that experimentation culture, we have the tools, we have the data. We just have to sit down and ask questions that we can answer with data."

Source: Lipschultz, J. H. (2017, November 13). Social Media Marketing Data Science and Brand Engagement. *Huffington Post*. www.huffingtonpost.com/entry/social-media-marketing-data-science-and-brand-engagement_us_5a09c6a0e4b00652392182c3

AS SEEN ON YOUTUBE

Assignment

Watch an interview with Internet pioneer Howard Rheingold. He was one of the first to understand in the mid-1990s and publish a book about virtual communities (Rheingold, 1993; Koh, et al., 2007). Consider why identity, interaction, and community remain important social media measurement and management concepts: https://youtube/661xiu6LidQ,

Questions

1. How can you learn to identify Rheingold's description of online "crap," such as "fake news" content, that may have a large reach on social media? How could you create an innovative product, process, or business model to respond as an entrepreneur to this problem of useless content?

2. Use Randa Zalman's example model in this chapter to develop a social PR campaign around a set of explicit goals, reporting requirements, and results for a local non-profit organization or event. What would be three specific opportunities and challenges of the campaign?

FIGURE 2.9 *Howard Rheingold. Photograph by Chris Michel, courtesy Howard Rheingold.*

USEFUL TOOLS

Social media managers must build media literacy skills to be able to quickly evaluate trending online content. Literacies and even social learning are possible (Greenhow & Robelia, 2009). This involves learning to critically think about what we read, see, and hear. As a social media manager develops these skills, it is very important to learn about a growing set of tools that can be added to your content measurement and management tool bag.

There are literally hundreds of free and paid tools for social media measurement and management. In fact, PostControlMarketing,com/links/ maintains a running list divided into: Social Media Monitoring & Metrics; Online Data Collection & Analytics; Social Content Scheduling & Automation; Social Media & Digital Media Research; Trade Associations, Awards, Conferences; Social Media News & Insights; Social Media/Marketing Podcasts; Social Media/Digital Marketing Training & Certification; and Social Media Channels. For our purposes, beginning with SEO and social media basics, students should gain competency in tools offered by Google, as well as tools native to Facebook, Twitter, and other popular social media platforms.

1. *Google Alerts* sends daily emails that offer data scraped from any keywords or search phrase. For example, the search "social media" generates daily fresh content from around the world. As with any Google search, personal brand and competitor keywords are important data.

2. *Google Trends* is a brainstorming tool that helps social media managers optimize content subjects and topics.

3. *Likealyzer* (https://likealyzer.com/) by Meltwater examines and ranks Facebook pages with a "LikeRank" score, tracks growth and engagement, lists top posts, and offers similar pages.

4. *Moz.com* (https://moz.com/free-seo-tools) offers a 30-day free trial for SEO search tools, such as keywords, volume, and difficulty.

5. *RetweetRank* (http://retweetrank.com) has a free dashboard to rank retweets. The Twitter Analytics dashboard (https://analytics.twitter.com/) also displays tweet impressions, profile visits, and mentions. A "top media tweet" feature offers insights into future best practices.

6. *SEO Analyzer* (https://neilpatel.com/seo-analyzer/) compares a website to competitors by offering a SEO, traffic, and speed score. Neil Patel's ad agency "cheat sheet" shows Google page rank for terms, such as "online marketing" and "SEO."

7. *Tweetdeck* (https://tweetdeck.twitter.com) by Twitter is a free, real-time tool for watching tweets by specific searches. This provides users with a sense of the volume of tweets at a given moment, while also archiving content by user columns.

8. *Twitter Assistant* by Union Metrics offers a real-time dashboard (https://app.unionmetrics.com/). Top tweet impressions along with characteristics, such as a photograph. Union Metrics also offers an Instagram Checkup that tracks engagement rate trends and top hashtags.

9. *UberSuggest* (https://neilpatel.com/ubersuggest/) is a keyword analyzer.

10. *Viral Video Chart by AdAge* (http://adage.com/results?search_phrase=viral%20 video%20chart) tracks the latest trending video.

11. *Website Grader* (https://website.grader.com/) provides a free overall score, as well as sub-scores for performance, mobile, SEO, and security. The site scores page size, page requests, and page speed, as well as other details.

In recent years, dozens of free or low-cost social media measurement and management tools have disappeared in the face of increased competition and movement toward larger, professional methods. There have been numerous mergers and partnerships between large firms. For example, Business Wire formed a partnership with Trend-Kite to connect news distribution with advanced analytics capabilities. The "Intelligent Communications Platform" was being marketed as one way to measure news release and PR campaign effectiveness. Similar to Cision's **Help a Reporter Out (HARO)** media relations data, PR people hope to pitch story ideas to journalists, bloggers, and other influencers within social media. Sprout Social Acquired Simply Measured with a goal of using social media branding "to build authentic, transparent, and personalized relationships with their audiences." At the heart of earned media work is the need for data-driven decisions about PR effectiveness to connect with larger business objectives. There is a delicate balance between the art and science of PR, as companies adopt machine learning AI tools and mesh them with existing human efforts. Paid tools offer social media managers the ability to explore data beyond a single platform.

Twitter influence measurement, for example, does not capture other platform or offline influence within complex social processes. Understanding the nature of social media engagement and how to develop reliable measures is central to current direction. Some systems do a better job than others at integrating potential content influence across all social and media spaces. While a tool such as Meltwater uses Google and social media search for data retrieval, automation comes with larger amounts of error. Social scientists treat this as the problem of "dirty data" that need to be "cleaned." Frequently, however, real-time social media analyses on deadline fail to address the limitation of poor data collection methods. For example, news site content behind pay-walls would require paid licensing to access complete data, but budget constraints may not allow for this. Budgeting and ongoing training are critical needs, if data collection and analysis are to become more rigorous.

The Hootsuite Platform Certification is training courseware for educational and enterprise settings that helps users learn effective use of the product. In general, free software is very limited. Data collection on Nuvi is a function of the cost of download-ing social media chunks or streams within a paid data plan model. Many companies offer clients a **social media dashboard**.

Adobe Marketing Cloud, for example, integrates social content management and analytics. The idea is to synthesize key insights on a screen to offer the user key data without needing to jump from screen to screen. Universal Information Services (@Universal_Info) is an international media tracking and news monitoring company that offers a dashboard product. President Todd Murphy (@Todder4News) says Universal examines keywords, performs indexing, and uses human coding of content instead of computer-ized, online coding with poor accuracy. Other companies, such as Cision (@cision) and Burell (@BurellPR) also combine computer tools with human coding. Dashboards track top hashtags, total word counts, top tweeters, top mentions, influence via social **network visualization**, top websites, impressions, top journalists, key topics, impressions by state, and other measures. The goal is to measure impact and publicity value for influencers.

A dashboard provides the client with the aggregate amount of social media conversa-tion, but it goes further in breaking down types of content across key platforms, which are each unique in terms of storytelling form (Vaynerchuk, 2013). Facebook and Twitter in this example are stronger social media spaces for an organic packaging of the mes-sage, but Facebook is much more active in a debate over mustard versus ketchup. At the same time, charity engagement appears stronger on blogs and YouTube. A user would need to drill down deeper into the data to examine specific content and posts to better understand how the results align or fail to measure up to strategic goals. Deep knowl-edge about social media marketing ultimately requires social science research skills to identify data variables, marketing channels, social networks, and meaningful online conversation (Miller, 2013; Sterne, 2010). Early in the development of social media, marketers began to list valuable metrics for understanding online behavior, such as:

- volume of consumer-created buzz for a brand based on number of posts;
- asset popularity (e.g., if several videos are available to embed, which is used more);
- growth rate of fans, followers, and friends;
- likes, favorites and comments.

(Sterne, 2010, pp. xx–xxi).

Social media measurement returns us to central issues of computer-mediated communication (CMC). These spaces allow us to develop online relations, explore interaction with new people, create identities and grow communities of interest. Early tools, such as Klout, attempt to measure influence across social media platforms. However, it quickly became clear that over-simplification of measurement lacked social science reliability and validity. Similarly, the early machine coding of conversation sentiment as positive or negative tended to be unreliable. We still see some social media dashboards that report sentiment data with showing reliability estimates or other statistical evidence. It takes time and human resources to accurately test for data quality. Social media impact assessment depends upon a deeper understanding of influence, trust, and engagement.

The measurement industry offers "deliverables" to clients, and social media metrics or analytics have become big business. The ongoing development of best practices for measuring communication tone, for example, should yield greater precision in the future. Whether or not social media engagement increases or decreases on specific sites over time, scientifically reliable and valid data will be needed.

PROJECT IDEAS

The Digital Analytics Association has identified new and active job titles that focus on data and analytics. Some of these are:

- Data analyst

- Digital strategist

- Business analyst

- Manager analytics

- Senior digital analyst

- Digital optimization strategist

Go to your LinkedIn account and search for one of these job titles, or one that is similar in focus. Read and evaluate the skills required. How many of these skills do you currently possess? How would you gain additional skill sets? Interview someone in your business market holding a job title. What do they suggest that students do to be prepared for the job market? Visit GlassDoor to answer this question: What is the current salary range for the job title "social media manager," and which specific experiences help predict entry-level versus senior manager status?

DISCUSSION QUESTIONS

1. Which basic concepts are most important in defining the future of social media measurement and management? Why?

2. How do quality content, coding, and SEO management impact the success or failure of your favorite websites? Why?

Social Network Sites (SNS) Measurement and Management

> *Set aside specific hours of the day for your social outreach. Perhaps twice during the day for responding and curating for your community! By having a set routine, you are less distracted and more conscious about your work.*

—Marsha Collier (@MarshaCollier, via Kim, 2018, para. 6)

> *In keeping with a more simplistic approach to understanding the application of social media planning, the Circular Model of SoMe for Social Communication . . . (recognizes that) social networks help people connect with others who share similar interests, passions, and beliefs.*

—Regina Luttrell (@GinaLuttrell, 2016, pp. 32–33)

Social networks help us think about how social media accounts cluster within groups and sub-groups of topical online conversation. The SoMe shorthand recognizes that strategic people within social networks build trust through sharing, listen for optimization opportunities for "authentic conversation," manage through real-time monitoring and replies, and influence via "audience" engagement (Luttrell, 2016, p. 33). Social media use dramatically grew between 2006 and 2018. In the U.S., about 73 percent of women and 65 percent of men in 2018 used sites (Kapoor, 2018). Social network users worldwide are expected to grow to more than three billion by 2021. In general, use is greatest among younger people, with nearly nine in ten of 18- to 29-year-olds in the U.S. regularly using at least one social media site (Kapoor, 2018). By far, Facebook and YouTube are the most regularly used U.S. sites (68 and 73 percent), but Instagram is the fastest growing (35 percent). Site use also varies by gender. For example, 41 percent of U.S. women use Pinterest. Further, a majority of users of Facebook (74 percent), Snapchat (63 percent), and Instagram (60 percent) report daily visits to the social network sites (Kapoor, 2018).

We also know that most marketers use social media to raise awareness of products and services through SNS reach, drive traffic to their websites by connecting links, cultivate loyalty, and even advance business goals. For example, social media tactics may generate new leads within the marketing process of moving from insights and thought leadership to sales.

These data highlight the need for social media measurement frameworks, as well as the nuts and bolts of website measurement. The Digital Analytics Association (DAA)

TABLE 3.1 *Total unique visitors by platform (000s)*

Property	2018	2017	2017 Rank
1. Google Sites	249,489	251,632	1
2. Oath (Verizon Yahoo!)	213,759	196.626	3
3. Microsoft Sites	213,504	184,072	4
4. Facebook	208,916	203,158	2
5. Amazon Sites	196,704	183,030	5
6. Comcast NBC Universal	169,801	165,596	6
7. CBS Interactive	164,492	162,827	7
8. Twitter	157,171	110,291	13
9. Disney	154,705	n/a	–
10. Apple	151,056	144,968	9

Sources: comScore, Latest rankings, Top 50 Multi-Platform Properties (Desktop and Mobile), April 2017: www.comscore.com/Insights/Rankings; comScore Ranks the Top 50 U.S. Digital Media Properties for March 2017, comScore, April 25, 2017, http://ir.comscore.com/releasedetail.cfm?releaseid=1022772. Other Top 25 media properties included AOL, Meredith, Turner Digital, PayPal, Wikimedia, Snapchat, Hearst, USA Today, The Weather Co., Conde Nast, Pinterest, Wal-Mart, Penske Media, CafeMedia, eBay, and Zillow.

has principles that can be used in exploring Google Analytics and optimization of sites. Internet World Stats estimated that China, India, and the United States were the largest three countries for Internet users in 2017, but accurate data are difficult to estimate. Countries such as Brazil, Indonesia, Japan, Russia, Nigeria, Mexico, and Bangladesh are all growing faster than the U.S. Internet and social media use are fragmented across dozens of highly popular sites, as well as millions of others (Lipschultz, 2019). While there is some alignment with the top iPhone app list mentioned earlier, the best estimate for total unique visitors shows Google ahead of Facebook in 2018, with Comcast NBC and CBS Interactive growing among the top media properties.

ᵗ𝕏 Thought Leader Deepti Ganapathy

Focus on Goal-Oriented Measurement to Derive Desirable Outcomes

"You know my methods, Watson," said Sherlock Holmes, as he put together the various pieces of the puzzle in his mind. Holmes had a remarkable power to detach his mind at will and go back to a case to pull the strands that lay scattered around and weave them back to present a convincing closure to a case.

For social media managers drowning in a world of data and hoping to navigate their ship in this ocean of data, critical thinking skills used by detectives like Sherlock Holmes, Miss Marple, Hercule Poirot, and Paul Drake from these all-time favorite detective novels can provide interesting starting points.

Social media measurement and management are similar to two oars

FIGURE 3.1 *Deepti Ganapathy (@ deeptiganapathy). Photograph courtesy Deepti Ganapathy,*

of an organization's boat in this ocean of data. Both these oars help balance the boat steering it forward. For businesses, using social media indicates confronting big data, analyzing situations, exploring options, and making managerial decisions. Scholars and researchers mining data use a variety of tools to obtain key insights. Content analyses, text mining, and semantic analysis are some of the popular methodologies. However, when understanding the data to be captured, scholars need to view data and data sources with a critical eye.

Social media measurement has the power to drive key policy decisions, mitigate natural and man-made crisis, provide behavioral patterns, and create massive digital awareness. The news industry is harnessing the power of social media to measure and manage its content and attract investments through advertisements. It is the algorithm that decides which news story we must read, pushing our news preferences towards a narrower narrative. Assuming the role of an editor, an algorithm decides to compile a list of most viewed and most shared news reports, prompting us to click on that particular headline. Most news organizations update their list of most-viewed stories at least once an hour. Scholars and consumers of news stories must be cognizant of the fact that data of one organization's pageviews may represent pageviews over the past hour, while data of another organization's pageviews may represent the same over the past day.[1]

On Twitter, the platform that I research extensively, 500 million tweets are sent every day, by 328 million users on Twitter with more than 54 percent of users earning more than $50,000 a year. Saudi Arabia has the highest percentage of Internet users active on Twitter.[2] These elites and influencers are logged into Twitter all over the globe comprising more than 79 percent accounts outside the United States.

Twitter is widely used to track and cover conferences. Climate change conferences such as COP21, 22, and 23 have become popular sources for journalists as well as policy makers and world leaders who use Twitter for digital diplomacy. The COP23 summit that was held in Bonn in November 2017 had an active Twitter account which simultaneously showed audiences the number of tweets generated, hashtags that were trending, geographical locations where maximum tweets were originating, key participants driving discussions through tweets, retweets, and replies, positive and negative sentiment analysis pie charts as well as gender specific ratios. A structured methodology of this manner helps in addressing key challenges involved in bridging the measurement gap between advocacy operations (outputs) and ultimate outcomes.

While measurement and management of social media data is critical for any campaign's successful outcome, knowing theories of communication and media consumption must serve as a backbone to this understanding. Behind the 'hashtag activism' or the 'like' and 'share' that amplifies a message sits a human being who is using the medium to express, gratify his needs, and feel powerful as a communicator. Hence, understanding of culture, communication, and behavior becomes necessary to complete this circle of measurement.

Business schools are launching specialized MBAs in analytics and big data due to the growing job market demands. Journalism schools have courses in data journalism. The biggest exposé of our times—the Panama Papers case—was a result of trails left behind by data. Governments across the globe are gaining insights about what their citizens want and feel through big data. A radio station in Bangladesh used measurement tools such as tone of voice, sentiments expressed, and words used to assess the success of a government program that was implemented in the developing country.

Technology is dynamically evolving, and its use need not be confined to social media platforms to obtain insights and gather critical information. Data can be collected and mapped in a plethora of unique ways. One such example is from the world's largest democracy, India.

The government in India conducted a massive data assignment that is yet to be replicated anywhere in the world. This Unique Identity Number (UID) project has, over the last eight years, assigned a unique 12-digit identity to India's 1.25 billion citizens, scanning millions of irises, capturing a staggering million pictures, collecting fingerprints, and recording a billion addresses. The scale and sheer volume of this data has been solely handled by the Indian government. Not surprisingly, this is the new oil, worth billions of dollars, facing the risk of being stolen and misused. The million-dollar UID project has run into controversy with cases related to data and identity theft filed in India's highest court.

Privacy is therefore a source of great concern that social media's rampant use has brought along with it. Cyber laws vary from region to region and the fine print is ignored by the user, resulting in a plethora of ethical violations. The scale, complexity, and speed with which data is getting updated on social networks is leading to the piling up of unstructured (80%) and structured (20%) data. The kind of value we are trying to elicit from analyzing various kinds and sizes of datasets to make better decisions will lead to pieces in this giant jigsaw puzzle falling into place. The missing gap that needs to be filled is to create digital literacy and awareness to enable the common citizen to understand the implications of making his identity a "free-for-all" that can be manipulated and misused on the World Wide Web.

References

Statista (2018). Number of Monthly Active Twitter Users Worldwide from 1st Quarter 2010 to 2nd Quarter 2018 (in Millions). www.statista.com/statistics/282087/number-of-monthly-active-twitter-users/

Zamith, R. (2018). A Computational Approach for Examining the Comparability of "Most-Viewed Lists" on Online News Sites. *Journalism & Mass Communication Quarterly, 95*(1), 122–141. DOI: 10.1177/1077699017714223.

Deepti Ganapathy, Ph.D, pursues a multidisciplinary interest in social media, seeking to explore the use of social media for strategic political and corporate communication, climate change communication, news coverage of human trafficking, and digital activism. Assistant Professor at NMIMS University's School of Business Management, Bangalore, she is a visiting faculty at the Indian Institute of Management Indore and the Indian Institute of Management Bangalore's Executive Education Program, where she conducts programs for senior bureaucrats and policy makers in the government of India. Her doctorate in social media and communication sparked work with scholars in Spain, New Zealand, Canada, UK, Italy, and the United States.

Social media networked data reflect connections between users and bridging between accounts located in neighboring sub-group clusters. In this regard, SEO marketing concepts help social media managers identify marketing journeys observed through data clicks.

HUB AND SPOKE MARKETING AND SEM AUDITS

Search engine marketing (SEM) begins with keywords and key phrases within a KPI marketing strategy mix to "leverage SEO" and "unleash" pay-per-click value (Kaushik, 2010, p. 343). Social marketers seek to develop an "optimal long-tail strategy" (p. 344), measure branding through conversion rates (search, bounce, time on site, visitor loyalty, and outcomes) within a campaign (p. 347) and relate all data to business ROI. In this model, social networks are seen as structure to observe individual user behavior within a larger social context. SNSs, such as Facebook, reveal the presence of interlocking relationships. There are networked conversations around influencers, words or phrases, hashtags, photographs, video, and website links.

SNS DATA OVERVIEW: SOCIAL NETWORK SITES (SNS)

Popular social network sites are used social media managers to launch and maintain a social media campaign. Each site has free organic, as well as paid, unique measurable data.

Facebook Insights

Facebook advertising has become increasingly important, but in order to demonstrate ROI there must be conversion **attribution**. Bucknell (2018) explains that Facebook and Instagram user interaction include watching videos, visiting a website, or even making a purchase. "When your ad leads to a conversion, Facebook will attribute (credit) the ad in Ads Manager" (para. 4). These data reflect effective or ineffective targeting. There is an "attribution window" of one to 30 days between and ad click and desired outcome (para, 5). Similar to Google, the Facebook process requires that a chunk of computer tracking code called a Facebook pixel is placed within the website. Possible tracking events include: purchase, lead generation, completed registration, saving payment information, placing an item in a virtual cart or on a wish list, checkout, searching, or content viewing. An attribution window can be added to a campaign report to show, for example, carousel or Messenger engagement. The idea is to link advertisement clicks to conversion for a purchase action. Facebook attributes, or credits, this within its Ads Manager. Facebook and sister platform Instagram measure highly successful stories that drive deeper user engagement through extended views.

Page summary data include pageviews, likes, post reach, and engagements. Top posts data show organic and paid reach and reaction.

FIGURE 3.2 *Facebook Insights. Facebook Insights courtesy UNO Social Media Lab.*

Instagram Insights

Instagram is a fast-growing social network site. Owner Facebook promotes use of Instagram Stories as a way to gain reach and engagement. *Social Media Examiner* offers strategy on the use of Instagram Stories for marketing (Stelzner, 2018a). "Among all the social platforms, Instagram is where people engage the most" (para. 19). Instagram rapidly approached one billion active monthly users, an estimated 500 million daily users, and about one-third of all accounts regularly viewing Instagram Stories (para. 20). The Instagram algorithm is known to emphasize individual user interest, as machine learned through previous behavior. Stelzner (2018a) suggests that the keys to success are found in Instagram data and the use of media storytelling skills that include structuring a beginning, middle, and end. In this sense, social media content have many of the attributes of traditionally successful media content. Interactivity and data, however, have fundamentally changed the nature of doing media.

Instagram business page managers benchmark number of followers, but also have free access to post data showing the number of hearts, comments, shares, saves, profile visits, and reach. Additionally, interactions may be a KPI for engagement. Profile visits also can be important in raising awareness. Reach can be assessed through the number of impressions—especially those driven by use of a specific hashtag.

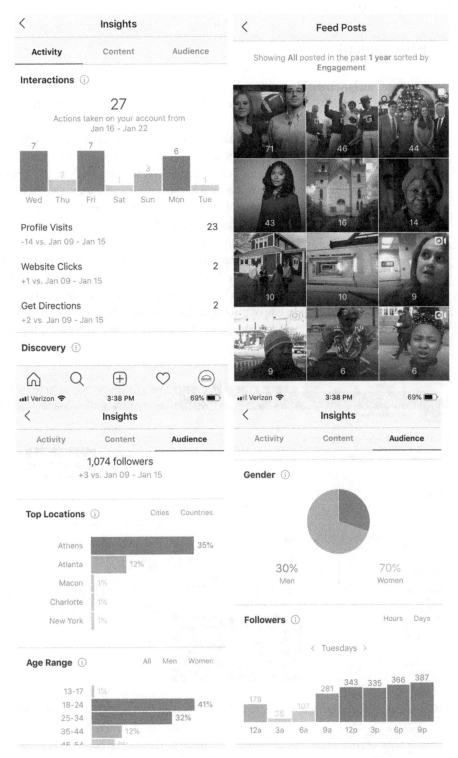

FIGURE 3.3 *Instagram Insights. Instagram Insights courtesy UNO Social Media Lab.*

Twitter Analytics

The Twitter Analytics dashboard is an extremely useful tool to benchmark and track KPIs over time. Once logged into an account, use https://analytics.twitter.com to see your data dashboard.

A 28-day overview includes the number of tweets and impressions, which can be used to calculate an average number of impressions per tweet. Additionally, social media managers may access the number of profile visits compared to the previous month. Profile views are extremely important on social network sites. On Twitter, for example, a profile may include a trackable hot link that drives new traffic to a landing page. Top mentions and engagements also may be a KPI for raising social media awareness. Total impressions and mentions are a raw measure of potential reach. A brand also may be interested in track the number of new followers each month or follower retention rates. At the post level, Twitter Analytics provides the top post, top follower and top mention. These are valuable data to refine management of future posts. The top media tweet offers insight into use of photographs or video in future content. Typically, these rich media elements increase engagement as much as ten times over simple text.

FIGURE 3.4 *Twitter Analytics dashboard. Twitter Analytics courtesy UNO Social Media Lab.*

Hosting a Live Twitter Chat

A valuable tactic within a social media campaign is the Twitter chat as one way to spark new engagement with followers and fans. Rob Mathison's (2017) excellent Hootsuite blog summary suggests that live Twitter discussion may "grow your social following, generate valuable discussions and feedback, and demonstrate thought leadership" (para. 2). This is important in gaining social influence, which may be the starting point for desired outcomes.

Twitter chats are moderated and scheduled public discussion that may have brand value. One possible structure involves use of scheduled question and answer periods. A Twitter chat reflects the value a brand places on transparency and open communication. Mathison (2017) identified six key elements:

1. A hashtag
2. A host
3. Topical content
4. Q & A
5. A scheduled date and time
6. A focus on participants

These elements suggest the need for planning and promotion through other thought leaders who can help raise awareness and spark event engagement. In other words, PR event planning skills are a necessary prerequisite for a successful Twitter chat. Key steps include: define purpose and goals; first research by participating in one; use strategic scheduling; create a catchy branded hashtag; plan for questions and answers; promote the event by leveraging existing brand relationships; and be a great host (Mathison, 2017).

Nothing is worse than creating an event that lacks energy. The interaction between an event host and brand ambassadors or well-known thought leaders helps raise interest and the likelihood of a successful outcome. Hootsuite suggests the use of memes or other ice breakers to get the conversation started. While planning is a key to any great social event, it also is important for hosts to remain flexible and ready to respond to unexpected developments.

Source: Mathison, R. (2017, September 19). A Step-by-Step Guide to Hosting a Successful Twitter Chat. Hootsuite Blog.
https://blog.hootsuite.com/a-step-by-step-guide-to-twitter-chats/

Live Twitter chats have been tactics, for example, used by rural communities in search of the secret sauce needed to engage with younger community members. Rural America is in a race for survival to leverage entrepreneurial online tools in order to compete for business against urban centers.

 ## Thought Leader Roberto Gallardo

Social Media, Intelligent Communities, and Management of Civic Engagement

As the digital age continues to unfold, multiple applications disrupt the socioeconomic landscape. Not only is it changing, but mindsets are, as well. Any community, individual, or business needs to update their approach, and better understand the unfolding digital age, maximize opportunities, and minimize threats.

My work defines "intelligent communities" as "those which have— whether through crisis or foresight— come to understand the enormous challenges of the broadband economy" (Bell, et al., 2014, p. 219). Once challenges of this new age are identified, opportunities also arise. The

FIGURE 3.5 *Roberto Gallardo (@ robertoge). Photograph by Andriy Zhalnin, courtesy Purdue University.*

Intelligent Community Forum identifies six indicators that define an intelligent community: broadband, innovation, knowledge workforce, digital equity, advocacy, and sustainability.

Due to their nature, intelligent communities strive to be responsive and effective with their citizens. For these reasons, civic engagement is augmented with digital platforms, including social media. Intelligent communities also pursue open data platforms not only to ensure accountability and transparency but also to provide the environment for residents to develop applications that further strengthen civic engagement.

Social media are digital age tools with a large impact. Not only do social media provide two-way communication channels in real time, but they allow us to expand a sense of belonging by joining virtual groups—blurring geographical boundaries prevalent before digital. Access to vast amounts of information empowers individuals and communities of all sizes and types (rural, urban, suburban), but also twists reality by reinforcing our echo chambers and filter bubbles (TED, 2011).

Understanding the pros and cons of social media may lead to a productive use of the technology. Urban and rural communities alike need to embrace social media to engage with their residents in an effort to boost civic engagement. While most of the hype has focused on urban communities (Crawford & Goldsmith, 2014), I believe rural communities have as much or more to gain by embracing social media and other digital platforms resulting in more responsive communities. Surely, you have heard of the small town and social media poster child example: the 3,500 resident Spanish town of Jun. This town has leveraged social media, specifically Twitter, to manage communication and engage with residents resulting in savings of up to $380,000 per year (Scott, 2016). Another great example were the Facebook groups that formed after an EF5 tornado hit Joplin, Missouri. The community very effectively coordinated information, needs, and offers. This resulted in what is now known as **social media emergency management (SMEM)**.

Another great potential of social media is the diverse base of users it has, especially age related. Many town halls and city meetings in small rural towns tend to have similar demographics. A non-diverse input from citizens will emphasize specific community issues while overlooking other equally important issues. Social media can help improve this valuable feedback providing more robust community information to policymakers allowing them to respond accordingly. Overall, the community becomes not only more responsive, but more effective as well increasing trust in local government.

As one example of a community that understand the intelligent community concept exercising effective management of civic engagement, the following data demonstrate return on investment (ROI) and key performance indicators (KPIs) such as top posters and sentiment scores.

Our Rural Futures Institute (RFI) funded project attempted to increase civic engagement in three rural Nebraska communities by leveraging digital

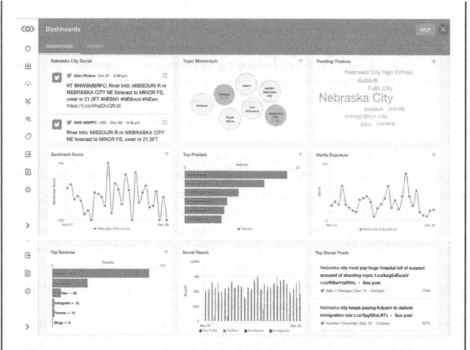

FIGURE 3.6 *Meltwater KPIs. Photograph courtesy Meltwater and the UNO Social Media Lab.*

platforms. What we have learned is that rural communities are eager to leverage this technology, but just need a bit more clarity on exactly how the technology can be leveraged. These communities have also come up with related processes and ideas that we hope to leverage across rural communities. Being able to measure and manage this powerful technology is necessary as more and more communities continue to transition and adapt to the digital age.

References

Bell, R., Jung, J., & Zacharilla, L. (2014). *Brain Gain: How Innovative Cities Create Job Growth in an Age of Disruption*. Intelligent Community Forum.

Crawford, S., & Goldsmith, S. (2014). *The Responsive City: Engaging Communities Through Data-Smart Governance*. San Francisco: Jossey-Bass.

Scott, M. (2016). The Spanish Town That Runs on Twitter. Retrieved from *The New York Times*: www.nytimes.com/2016/06/09/technology/the-spanish-town-that-runs-on-twitter.html

TED (2011). Eli Pariser: Beware Online "Filter Bubbles". Retrieved from TED: www.ted.com/talks/eli_pariser_beware_online_filter_bubbles

Roberto Gallardo is Purdue Center for Regional Development (PCRD) Assistant Director and Purdie Extension Community & Regional Economics Specialist. He holds a doctorate in public policy and administration, as well as a graduate degree in economic development and undergraduate degree in engineering. His focus is on use of technologies to spark local and regional economic development. He previously served as Director of the Mississippi State University Intelligent Community Institute. Contact him at: robertog@ purdue.edu.

Social media measurement and management is only as effective as available data. Some platforms are more responsive than others to the need for organic and paid data access tools. The increasing interest in data privacy is in conflict with the desire for access to measures of user behavior.

Snapchat Data

The initial popularity of Snapchat was built upon a perception that messages could be sent that would be deleted after being reviewed. However, cloud computing and screenshots meant that this was more hype than reality. Now that Snapchat has been transformed into a paid marketing space built upon a message app, brands want to see evidence of effectiveness. Snapchat has offered limited opportunities for free data, and paid advertisers spend large budgets for premium data. Celebrities such as DJ Khaled gained prominence and access to fans through increased numbers of subscriptions. These appear at the top of a "Discover" search. At the same time, Snapchat users are pushed "For You" stories that offer swipe data, repeat views, and other KPIs. Facebook and Instagram Stories effectively copied the Snapchat use of story placement within news feeds. Paid content resides alongside Friend Snaps—time-sensitive content that disappears. Friends may share location and private messages. Snap, Inc. has user data that allows for paid target marketing. Snapchat's story view data include viewers in a week. Its Insights dashboard includes year-to-date views and view time, daily reach, gender, and most popular age demographic group. Snaplytics was developed as a third-party content creation, distribution, and management tool. KPIs include open rates, views, average number of screenshots, and completion rates. Competitor Delmondo promotes the tool as a way to "surface" and benchmark top-performing Snaps. Snapchat traditional data include number of unique views over time, as well as views. Social media management tool Hootsuite has suggested that a raw number of photograph views can be used to manually calculate a "fall-off" rate within a story.

Pinterest

Pinterest boards tend to focus on individual interests. Brands in specific areas, such as clothing and home products, receive mentions through user sharing behavior. The site has been more popular with women, but it also has substantial numbers of men across age and other demographic groups. A board will have a number of pins, and each post may receive views. Like Snapchat, Pinterest data have been focused on paid KPIs rather than free organic data. A Pinterest business account for a brand opens the door to access in-depth analytics. The focus is on the people engaging with a business, demographics, and topic interests that may be related. A brand's audience is compared to the overall Pinterest community. A business account offers data on monthly views and engagement.

LinkedIn

LinkedIn is a growing professional social network site that offers an opportunity through the use of brief posts and in-depth articles to share branded content. Increasingly, it has become a content platform. By viewing your LinkedIn profile, free access is given to potential KPIs.

The number of post views may be tracked over time, as well as well as the number of search appearances. Importantly, a thought leader can learn qualitative data (location, companies, and job titles) about who viewed a profile. Blogging through extended articles is important because numbers of followers may be tracked over time. At the individual post level, LinkedIn reports number of views, likes, comments, and shares. Posts stats include how many people from your organization viewed the post, as well as the proportion of direct from LinkedIn views compared to those coming from other sites.

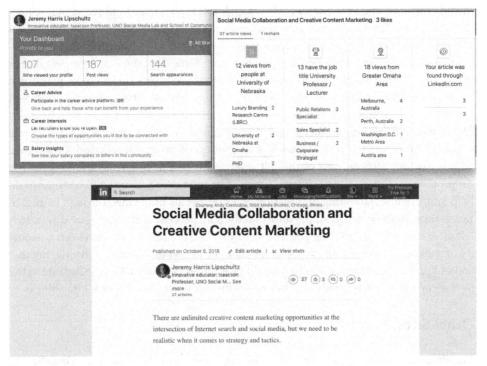

FIGURE 3.7 *LinkedIn audience data. LinkedIn data image courtesy UNO Social Media Lab.*

Reddit Votes

So-called Redditers spend relatively large amounts of time up-voting or down-voting items. The number of comments and shares also reflect engagement data. Reddit communities are important because the site cultivates a message board, pre-social media online community orientation. It tends to be less commercial. Still, users can personalize news feeds, search trending topics, and subscribe to communities, as well as vote in a democratic manner. A Reddit user will see popular content, as well as volume of voting and comments. Reddit users browse communities and popular Internet content.

YouTube

YouTube Studio remained in beta by Google at the end of 2018, but it shows the number of subscribers, monthly views and top video. Within a specific video, a social media manager may measure watch time, views, and average view duration. Lifetime audience retention is tracked, as well as likes and dislikes, and recent activity. Reach data include impressions, impression click-through rates, views, and unique views. A high external source for watch-time views may reflect social media effectiveness. For example, let us say 55.9 percent of a video audience was external, and within this 48.5 percent came from Facebook and 42.8 percent from LinkedIn. We can now benchmark what should happen when sharing a new video to these prime social media platforms. A social media manager now quickly sees and understands the connection between Google Analytics and social media measurement. There is still much work to be done. The YouTube marketing funnel shows that of 155 impressions, the click-through rate was only 2.6 percent. The 32 views had an average of three minutes and 40 seconds, which was only 19.6 percent of the full video. Perhaps the video was too long, or the drop-off happened because content became less interesting. Some A/B testing would help improve understanding for creation of better-performing video through increased watch time. In the video example under study, 53.1 percent of the audience driven to it left after only 22 seconds. The content simply lacked interest that would keep a majority of the audience watching. A social media manager would need to solve the organic content problems before developing a paid promotion campaign. Google has one of the best social media dashboards for filtering lifetime down to 30-, 60- or 90-day blocks.

Other Sites

Mobile social media apps continue to emerge, even as others such as Vine die. As mentioned earlier, TikTok has gained U.S. popularity. In response, Facebook launched Lasso. Both apps feature influencers lip-singing to songs, doing acrobatics, and attracting views, followers, and personal branding. Paid content is beginning to appear as promoted and boosted content. It is fair to assume that successful future apps will be mobile, fun, and innovative in terms of artificial intelligence and machine learning tools.

AS SEEN ON YOUTUBE

Assignment

Watch the following interview with Roberto Gallardo from Purdue University: www. youtube.com/watch?v=kt2zZo6KfN8

Questions

1. Why do rural communities have a need to use social media for business purposes? What are some of the challenges and opportunities?

2. What would be important KPIs for a local business trying to sell their products online?

USEFUL TOOLS

Klipfolio is a widget based custom dashboard tool that has been in use for about two decades. It began as a content aggregation tool, but it has grown into creating business value through data-driven decisions.

Social Media Marketing Entrepreneurs Should Listen to Customers

The typical definition of an entrepreneur frequently misses the mark by focusing on business risk instead of communication. Entrepreneurship works when it listens to customers and targets products or services toward growth. This deeper meaning has extended well beyond its nineteenth-century French origins. Klipfolio President and CEO Allan Wille reflects a growing interest in how entrepreneurs pivot by using data to make good decisions. "It's a story of perseverance and a lot of twists and turns," Wille says in reflecting on his company's launch in 2001 around a simple idea: "There's got to be a better way to monitor the information that matters to you."

Sixteen years ago, our email accounts were stored in what we now call "the cloud," but the Web was still new. "We approached it from a personal or consumer type angle," Wille says. Thousands of users built and shared widgets for making their personal dashboards better content aggregators, but it was so "massively popular" that Wille could not pay his hosting fees. There was no business model: news publishers didn't have money to pay the start-up to build them a desktop channel. Even though there were about 250,000 users, the company could not find "a repeatable, scalable business model," Wille says.

In 2004, Lufthansa recognized that large numbers of staffers were using the personal dashboard and asked a game-changing question: "Can we use it to push business data to our employees?" Wille's team worked through the night and responded with a successful pitch. The $35,000 annual contract "was like a huge windfall for us." More importantly, it was the first time they were paid well "to solve a real business problem using our product," Wille says. Intel, Staples, American Express, and other enterprise customers followed, as Klipfolio invested in developing business functions.

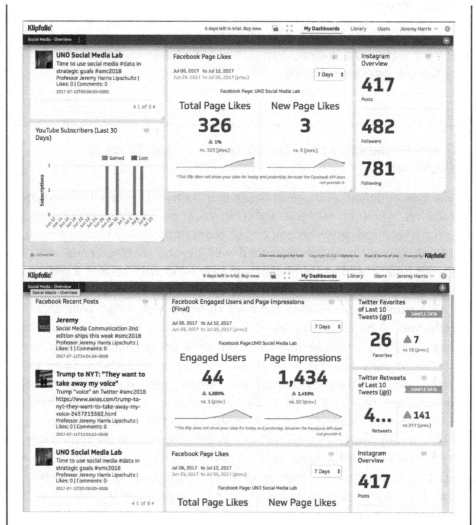

FIGURE 3.8 *Klipfolio Command Centre Dashboard. Images courtesy Klipfolio and the UNO Social Media Lab.*

@KLIPFOLIO

Even with more than 100 information technology customers at the time, Klipfolio had not yet found its space. "It felt like we were pushing string," Wille says. In 2010, an insurance company helped define three needs—mobile cloud-based, easier self-serve use, and less expensive. The new app grew from 350 business customers in 2012 to more than 9,000. "Here's the difference: that product felt like there was pull," Wille says. "When you have product market fit, you feel it; there's a fundamentally different feeling that you get throughout the company, and the way the company scales and asks questions." Klipfolio's current focus is on small and mid-sized business found through search engine optimization, content, and inbound marketing. "Truly, every company should be monitoring their metrics, if they want to grow, and scale, and be efficient," Wille says. "I think there has to be an authenticity or a genuine core belief that your company is doing something and is backing something that is important."

Klipfolio, for example, uses its dashboard to identify and measure key performance indicators for growth. One KPI metric is what it calls "true trials." Klipfolio defines it through the marketing funnel. "If we can get a trial user to come back, even a second day, their probability of turning into a customer is something like 50 percent," Wille says. "A true trial is somebody who comes back after one day of using the application, and we're optimizing around that." The metric can be combined with engagement rate, spending, and conversion data.

Klipfolio also serves broader business functions—monitoring warehouse and logistical data that include predictive models and alerts to avoid problems. Dashboards help users combine data sources and view real-time change from a control center. One important example is creating a ratio to compare social media activity and spending on advertising. Hootsuite or Buffer data can be combined with Quick Books data, Wille says. Current Klipfolio customers are combining as many as seven data sources into a single metric.

> *That's where things get really interesting . . . that ability to not only see everything in one screen, but then also be able to mash up and calculate more meaningful metrics, I think, is really important.*

—*Allan Wille, Klipfolio*

Most customers, though, are monitoring sales, finance, or social media data for the first time. "That's an infinite improvement in how they control and how they move forward, how they make changes," Wille says. He admits there is a learning curve for using Klipfolio, but the company emphasizes user support. The focus should be on a few metrics that change and spark conversation about why data are going up or down, and what can be done about it. The shift toward visual display of real-time data reflects a direction that now drives social media planning. We need to build flexible tools that allow for matching real-time, meaningful social media monitoring with employee and customer behaviors.

Social media are useful tools for businesses when the communication reflects relationship-building inside and outside companies. However, the emergence of artificial intelligence and chatbots represent challenges and opportunities for enlightened companies deploying meaningful and predictive social media data.

Source: Lipschultz, J.H. (2017, August 26). Social Media Marketing Entrepreneurs Should Listen to Customers. *Huffington Post*. www.huffingtonpost. com/entry/social-media-marketing-entrepreneurs-should-listen_us_59a09566e 4b0d0ef9f1c13c2

PROJECT IDEAS

Collaborate with your professor to gain access to a free or low-cost social network site measurement tool. For example, your campus may participate in a HootSuite, Meltwater, or other campus program. Determine the strengths and weaknesses of the data collected. Explore how to visualize the data in ways that make it easy to understand. Present your results to the class.

DISCUSSION QUESTIONS

1. Why is it difficult for us to collect and analyze relevant social media data? How could we innovate solutions that improve the experience for social media managers?

2. Which data are the most useful Facebook Insights for a public page? What does Facebook make available to page managers? What is missing? Why?

UNIT TWO
Strategic Social Media Measurement Tools

Social Media Metrics and Management Tools

> *Perhaps one of the most useful features of Twitter analytics is the ability to view data on recurring trends . . . valuable stats on Tweet volume for commonly used hashtags . . . As a brand, you want to create campaigns that spark conversation and increase your Tweet engagements . . . Twitter analytics breaks each trend down to the top gender, age, and location talking about it. This way, you can target your hashtag use based on your followers' demographics.*

—Lilach Bullock (@lilachbulloch, Bullock, 2017, paras. 1–2)

Native social media dashboard tools, such as Twitter Analytics (analytics.twitter.com), offer free real-time metrics that help social media managers think about KPIs. Consider the #MotivationMonday Twitter hashtag. Twitter found that males are 1.3 times more likely than females to use it, although it is most common among 18- to 24-year-old males and females. In 2016, 2.4 million tweets had a reach of 22 million and 125 million impressions (Bullock, 2017, paras. 4–5). The estimated volume of activity on this hashtag, though, may not be as unimportant as how it can be strategically used within a targeted social media campaign. There are hundreds of measures possible within social media. A foundations of website measurement can be applied to the context of social media sites. There are linkages, which include social media campaigns designed to drive site traffic. Still, social media managers must address the fundamental problem that different sites have measures that may not be comparable.

SIMPLE AND ADVANCED MEASURES

A discussion of social media data should begin with **vanity metrics**. The key question here is this: Does it matter how many followers you have on an account? It may not, if your personal brand or business brand lack strategies to leverage the numbers. However, celebrity Instagram accounts with millions of followers clearly have moved beyond vanity and to monetization of social media influence. Likewise, micro-influencers with a few thousand followers also may move beyond vanity. While cultivating important relationships may focus on qualitative research methods, the numbers matter for those organizations using social media to amplify messages and extend reach. Some brands have hired micro-influencers as paid promoters of products and services. As we will see later, the U.S. Federal Trade Commission (FTC) requires that there be disclosure of financial relationships in all commercial social media content.

SOCIAL MEDIA DASHBOARDS AND ADVANCED TOOLS

Social media plans are executed through the use of media monitoring and measurement. An owned media website may the core for integration of planning in an ongoing social media effort, as brands typically are interested in driving site traffic through a set of explicit strategic goals. A usability study must be conducted to determine if site visitors can find what they want and need.

 Thought Leader Jason Buzzell

Hompage Updating Focused on #TopTasks
The University of Nebraska at Omaha (@UNOmaha) updated its homepage five years before an eight-phase conversion project in 2018. The goals were simple:

1. Increase new student recruitment.
2. Provide more immediate information access.

Analytics were used to measure a breakdown of the changes by section, and why the campus made them.

Using tools such as Google Analytics, CrazyEgg, and usability tests as well as user surveys, the web team found top links such as My.UNOmaha.edu, Search, and Majors and Programs under the Academics menu *account for more than half of the clicks* on the homepage.

The hero image has become an industry standard in higher education. For the last five years, UNO used it for news and events—rotating three items throughout the week and updating the first slide almost every day. Yet, less than 2 percent of users click the first hero image for news and events, and users rarely see the second and third slide. Almost every user to the website takes one of two actions: use the search bar or log-in. Campus users tend to know where to find pages, but the web team was concerned that visitors, including valuable prospective students may find it difficult to navigate a search for university cost and application pages.

FIGURE 4.1 *Jason Buzzell (@ buzzilinear). Photograph by Ryan Henriksen, courtesy UNOmaha.*

Five Call to Action Buttons for Top Tasks and Goals

We live in a mobile world. Almost everyone has a phone or tablet. People want to find programs, people, jobs, and how to get to campus while on the go. Two main tasks the prospective student wants to accomplish when visiting our site are requesting more information and visiting campus. Many people who don't know our university also use the directory and contact us pages, as well as search for open job positions. The three website goals remain:

- Study and do research here
- Work here
- Visit or contact us to engage here

Facts, Figures, and #KnowTheO Information

Not everyone, even our faculty, staff, students, and alumni, #KnowTheO to the fullest. And this is most important to prospective students who start to scroll. By the way, people do scroll. This is documented by our research both at UNO and within other industries, especially new visitors or people who are engaged by the content. This focuses on four key facts or figures that build off our Advantage and Fact Books just like our other eight top-level pages on the website. These will be updated annually to reflect the work of the Advantage and the Fact Book, and aligned to strategic priorities focusing on:

- Value
- Engagement
- Culture or Events
- Recognition

Life at UNO

A second hero section focuses on campus life and things students could get involved in or get help with. Multiple calls to action will overlay a vibrant, engaging image to ensure a prospective student who may be interested gets more information on a potential program, service, or opportunity they may not have known about otherwise. Seasonally and during the semester, this image may change, but the calls to action will remain consistent.

News and Events

Most people are now using social media or searching for news on other sites, or have signed up to receive notifications or emails for things they are interested in from a variety of sources. With the focus on the prospective student, news and events were moved down the page. The design is changed to include up to four teasers for desktop users, so for those who still like to get their news via the homepage, one short scroll will take you there. The team continues to update news and calendar pages and encouraged the community to follow institutional social media channels and texting:

- Twitter
- Facebook

- Instagram
- LinkedIn
- YouTube
- Sign up for Emergency Text Alerts

Our Metropolitan University Mission and Global Footer

As an anchor to the homepage, the institution wanted to make the university mission clear with a call to action to our updated Mission and Vision page, as well as the Strategic Plan. This hero will remain static with occasional seasonal changes showing the great metropolitan cityscapes and our campuses embedded within it. Prospective students who reach this point should get the feeling of how many opportunities are at UNO, and why location matters. UNO updated the footers in early 2016 to expand the services and links, as well as add design re-enforcing the metropolitan university focus of Omaha and our region with the cityscape. Although some people often don't think the footer gets used, our research proves otherwise. Expanded opportunities for colleges and their departments to customize local footers was also added.

The team began to shift to look at the top navigation in all of the website. This includes how the navigation functions and accessibility upgrades, as well as again focusing on top tasks and which navigational items are not used as much being removed to help users focus. Homepages for the colleges were updated shortly after the main homepage, and in 2019, departments and centers planned a similar update. The campus social media team can take usability data as input for development of strategic content and links for posting on Facebook, Instagram, Twitter, and other platforms.

Jason Buzzell is Digital Communications Director at the University of Nebraska at Omaha. He previously was a digital content strategist at the University of Alberta in Canada. He began his career as a sports content creator and web analyst.

With a web team plan in place, the focus may return to social media influence. Data dashboards are useful for assessment and long-term evaluation. For example, data collected and analyzed over time allow for head-to-head comparison of influencers and their brands. Simple social media metrics may be augmented through the use of higher-level data analysis.

Social Media Marketing, Employee Sharing, and New Business

Businesses are learning that employee social networks have the power to raise awareness and increase audience engagement, and media companies have a need to measure and sell social sharing and reach. Splash Media Founder and Share Rocket CEO Chris Kraft built "a social media ratings company" that measures and compares company brands and employees within Facebook, Instagram, and Twitter.

The idea is "to measure social audiences in marketplaces" similar to television and radio ratings services. Local media markets offer unique opportunities and challenges. There is "a lot of entrenched thinking," Kraft says. "The type of media that we're measuring is a two-way conversation."

> *Broadcasters are used to having a tower, and sending a message out of that tower, and maybe seeing the audience at a special event a couple of times a year. Social's changed all of that. It's now a dialogue. It's now a conversation with your audience, and that's a hard concept.*

—*Chris Kraft*

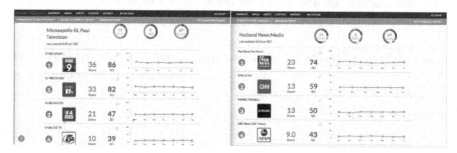

FIGURE 4.2 *Share Rocket network & Minneapolis data. Images courtesy ShareRocket and the UNO Social Media Lab.*

Federal Communications Commission (FCC) licensed broadcasters have been disrupted by mobile smartphone media that is "a finger push away," Kraft says. "And it's really changed the balance of that power equation, and now the audience has a lot more control." Academics have been writing about competition in "marketplace of attention," and data are increasingly important (Webster, 2014).

Share Rocket, in local television for example, measures the station brand, sub-brands (*i.e.* weather, sports, morning shows, etc.), and most recently individual journalists. "They're really a strong advocate for their station brands," Kraft says. "We've got some markets where as much as 30 percent of the social equity of a station rests in the talent as a whole." The goal is to engage in community conversation while promoting station brand. Share Rocket developed a **social equity index (SEI)** score that computes all activity, and it compares journalists within a local media market. "Our clients get to see a real-time index of how they're performing," Kraft says. "We teach our clients how to pull tactical insights," manage "strategic insights," and use an individual journalist "social scorecard," Kraft says. In other words, all journalists are compared to each other, as top social media performers are highlighted and benchmarked.

Journalists Rankings
The method can be used for other businesses beyond radio, television, and newspapers. Any company that understands the power of its owned media, would want to measure employees within social media.

Social Media Scoring
Facebook accounted for a whopping 95 to 97 percent of local TV market social media engagement, Kraft says. Organic reach of Facebook Live "is huge . . . is some of the most engaging content we measure across all of our clients' platforms," Kraft says. Shared content is "the holy grail" of "reach amplification." Share Rocket uses an advertisers' perspective to value social media engagement. Kraft says, "We think that local broadcasters, local publishers represent some of the safest harbors for advertising dollars" because of decades within communities.

It is clear that audience trust matters in an age of discussion about "fake news" and social media clutter. The valuation of social media sharing is at the forefront of social marketing efforts. Kaleida CEO Matt McAllister measures news and information flow and consumer sharing habits: "sharing and referral traffic have a significant and reliable relationship." This places employee advocacy promoted by Dynamic Signal, Edelman PR, and others within a new context. Journalists, and all employees for that matter, will face new corporate pressures to not only be a "brand ambassador," but also to be social media influencers driving clicks and future business.

Source: Lipschultz, J. H. (2017, May 23). Social Media Marketing: Employee Sharing and New Business. *Huffington Post*. www.huffingtonpost.com/entry/social-media-marketing-employee-sharing-and-new-business_us_59246dafe4b07617ae4cbfef

ShareRocket was one of many data tools impacted by the aftermath of the 2018 Facebook data scandal. The social media ranking tool lost Instagram data access, but this was regained for 2019. The company was able to develop, rebuild, and test an application to scrape data from Instagram business profiles in use since 2015. For television news social media managers, ShareRocket warned in an email, "talent using Personal Profiles will need to upgrade to Business Profiles in order to be tracked going forward" (ShareRocket, 2018, para. 4). One limitation of social media data is that non-business personal users may not be measured as market influencers. There is an Instagram process for converting from a personal to business profile (https://help.instagram.com/502981923235522). Obviously, attempts to aggregate and rank social media influence within an organization and across competitors should account for Instagram, as well as Facebook, Twitter, LinkedIn, and other important sites.

SOCIAL MEDIA MONITORING AND SOCIAL NETWORK ANALYSIS (SNA)

Beginning in the 1960s, rural sociologists studied diffusion of new ideas, processes, and products through network structure and collaboration (Rogers, 1995). "Direct collaboration between individuals in a pair of cliques" was distinguished from "indirect collaboration" through solid and broken lines on a graph (p. 57). The mapping of network structure is a powerful construct because it places individuals in relative position to others within a grouped conversation:

> The *innovative-decision process* is the process through which an individual (or other decision-making unit) passes from first knowledge of an innovation, to forming an attitude toward the innovation, to a decision to adopt of reject, to implementation of the idea, and to confirmation of this decision.
>
> (pp. 201–202)

The value of social media is obvious in raising awareness through sharing new information, persuading others through the voice of influencers, driving urgency of decisions, offering feedback during change cycles, and reinforcing through "confirmation" (p. 202). We would expect social media conversation and engagement to have some impact on the rate of adoption. "Innovators," in this way, are thought leaders driving "early adopters," as well as the early and late majorities moving toward change (p. 262). Rogers (1995) viewed "opinion leaders" as important because they have "followers" of change (p. 293). For example, a relatively small group of academic scientists in the late 1980s and early 1990s were innovators driving social and technological change toward the Bitnet and later the larger Internet as "interactive communication technologies" (p. 315). Here we might think about "technology clusters" as innovation "boundaries (Rogers, 2003, p. 14). While the example of what researchers called an "invisible college of diffusion researchers" was more simply "a highly interconnected network of scholars in 1973" (p. 56), the study of social networks within contemporary popular social media platforms offers a peer-reviewed framework for understanding influence. The central characteristics of "innovativeness" include frequent travel, rejection of "dogmatism and fatalism," and inclination toward opinion leadership (p. 292). We have just painted a picture of a social media thought leader likely to be found at or near the center of a social network map. She or he may have strong "ties" to other influencers, as well as weak ones to a social media audience (p. 339). In other words, network structure pictures through social network analysis tools offer one important way to understand how, where and why influence is shared by thought leaders. Social networks reflect linkages created and maintained based upon trusted relationships. This is one reason the PR industry is concerned about the loss of global trust in institutions and leaders over recent decades. Social network analysis (SNA) developed from small group communication and creation of transparent algorithms that were adapted for social media research using the NodeXL academic license along with traditional content analyses techniques (Hansen, et al., 2011; Himelboim, et al., 2013).

PR Trust and the Social Media Marketing "Echo Chamber"

The growth of social media sites is happening at the same time trust for social institutions, such as the media business, continues to decline. From National Opinion Research Center (NORC) data over several decades to the more recent Edelman trust Barometer, it is clear that we are in search of new paths for finding credible online information. It appears that global public trust in institutions—government, business, and mass media—is at historical lows.

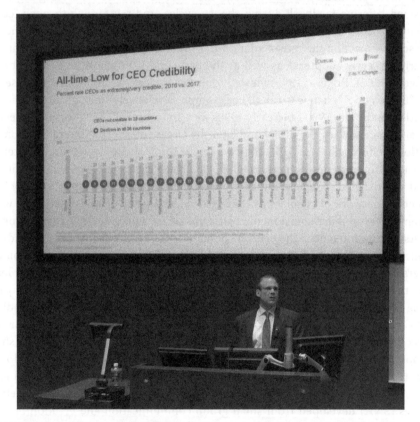

FIGURE 4.3 *Kevin Cook (@EdelmanPR). Photograph by Jeremy Harris Lipschultz, courtesy Edelman Digital, Chicago.*

"This notion of media being the Fourth Estate, we've come to believe, is eroding," Edelman Chicago Chief Operating Officer Kevin L. Cook says. "We're also in an age where technology allows us to completely manipulate our news feeds and tailor what we read to only want we want, only to what suits our sensibilities," Cook says. "Peers, and 'people like you' are the most trusted sources of information" within an 'echo chamber.' People trust friends, family members and colleagues more than a CEO, media organization or others in power. "It's a horizontal world now . . . It's peer-to-peer," Cook says.

Businesses now start inside with employees to promote positive messages. Edelman urges companies to focus on how they recruit and retain talent. The world's largest public relations (PR) firm has added an engagement practice to address how companies use social media. For example, Dynamic Signal offers a mobile app that helps companies share positive news through employees' influential social networks.

> *Employees often times are an un-tapped resource for brands and organizations. They're highly trusted. They're highly credible, and because . . . they're sharing information in their newsfeeds, there's a huge opportunity for brands and organizations.*

—David Armano, Edelman global strategy director

Employees can leverage their social networks within companies, and also outside, to help advocate through directed communication and channels. It takes a reset of employee culture and a clear collective understanding of company vision, mission, and values. It also takes a leadership shift away from social media policies that tell employees what *not* to do, and toward guidelines promoting effective engagement. Facebook Workplace is among the enterprise tools that were explored to help identify organization thought leaders. The need for employee engagement ranges from conditions during a business restructuring to the more mundane company celebration. Media storytelling, though, backed by social media measurement offers new opportunities for branding and marketing. It is clear that this new emphasis will demand that employers not only improve their PR efforts, but also hire professionals with skills to evaluate and apply consistent and credible social network analysis. An ongoing challenge is that people now take the view that, "I trust my media, and I trust my newsfeeds," but not content outside of the "filter bubble." Academics are increasingly making the case that we need a rekindling of free expression on controversial issues.

Social media marketers, of course, use homogeneous groups and like-mindedness to their economic advantage by targeting messages to those most receptive. Jim Sterne, author of *Social Media Metrics* and president of eMetrics, contends that traditional media and PR are being replaced by relationship building, customer reviews and branding based upon keeping promises.

Still, given the trust data, it may be an overstatement that PR and advertising no longer have important roles. Credibility remains important social capital that must be earned and retained in order to advance business goals and objectives. "That's why we feel so strongly that every company needs to be a media company, and (they) need to have a strong presence where people can go and get the facts," Cook said. The convergence and integration of PR, advertising, and social marketing will continue, even as skepticism remains high for those abusing power. Too often, companies offer lip service to customer engagement without building meaningful long-term relationships. As we look to the future of social media trust, there is a need to focus on the newest innovation wave AI.

Source: Lipschultz, J. H. (2017, March 15). PR Trust and the Social Media "Echo Chamber." *Huffington Post*. www.huffingtonpost.com/entry/pr-trust-and-the-social-media-marketing-echo-chamber_us_58c95cbae4b01d0d473bcfce

The trust problem frequently was seen within social media conversation on Twitter, which often is politically polarized and divisive. Polarized social media data can be visualized, but research accuracy may be a problem. With so much data on Twitter, for example, any use of the search box tends to collect valuable data along with extraneous uses of words and phrases that may be connected to unrelated conversation.

Entrepreneurial tools were developed to innovatively scrape Twitter data, clean searches for non-relevant ("dirty") social research data, prior to performing analyses that would be considered scientifically reliable and valid.

ᵗ⧽Ѧ⧼ Thought Leader Stu Shulman

Text Analytics for Mining Twitter Data
New tools allow social media managers to build custom machine classifiers for sifting Twitter data. The topics covered include how to:

- construct precise social data fetch queries;
- use Boolean search on resulting archives;
- filter on metadata or other project attributes;
- tabulate, explore, and set aside duplicates, cluster near-duplicates;
- crowd source human coding;
- measure inter-rater reliability;
- adjudicate coder disagreements;
- build high quality word sense and topic disambiguation engines.

FIGURE 4.4 *Stu Shulman (@StuartWShulman). Photograph courtesy Stu Shulman.*

DiscoverText was designed specifically for collecting and cleaning up messy Twitter and other text data streams. Use basic research measurement tools to improve human and machine performance classifying data over time. The tool helps reach and substantiate inferences using a theoretical and applied model informed by a decade of interdisciplinary, National Science Foundation-funded research into the text classification problem.

The key breakthrough led to a patent (US No. 9,275,291) being issued on March 1, 2016. We built a tool for adjudicating the work of coders. For example, if I ask 10 students to look at 100 Tweets that mention "penguins" and code whether or not they are about the NHL's Pittsburgh Penguins, there will be imperfect agreement. Some coders will have deeper knowledge of the subject and some tweets will be inscrutably ambiguous. Adjudication allows an expert to review the way the group labeled the tweets and decide who was right and wrong. This method of validation creates a "gold standard" and it allows us to score over time the likelihood that an individual coder will create a valid observation. Participants will learn how to apply "CoderRank" in machine-learning. The major idea of the workshop is that when training machines for text analysis, greater reliance should be placed on the input of those humans most likely to create a valid observation. Texifter proposed a unique way to recursively validate, measure, and rank humans on trust and knowledge vectors, and called it CoderRank.

Stuart W. Shulman, Ph.D. is founder & CEO of Texifter. He was a Research Associate Professor of Political Science at the University of Massachusetts Amherst and the founding Director of the Qualitative Data Analysis Program (QDAP) at the University of Pittsburgh and at UMass Amherst. He is Editor Emeritus of the Journal of Information Technology & Politics, *the official journal of Information Technology & Politics section of the American Political Science Association.*

ELECTRONIC WORD-OF-MOUTH (EWOM) IN MARKETING COMMUNICATION

Successful social media content is a function of sharing across social networks. Electronic word-of-mouth (eWOM) may spread based upon content or argument quality, source, and message credibility (Hwang, 2013), relevance, and other factors help explain the diffusion and adoption (Chu & Choi, 2011; Doh & Hwang, 2009; Lu & Keng, 2014; Sandes & Urdan, 2013). One way to conceptualize measurement is through foundational communication and marketing theories, such as eWOM. Academic research findings about social media demonstrate the conceptual value of eWOM and its models. Miller (2013) studied consumer paths of learning through engagement and listening, as it was found that brand advocacy represents important validation of information through community conversation. The use of social media to stimulate new conversation within a social network appears to be important. The eWOM research studies impressions, social comparison, and message sentiment. Lu and Keng (2014) connected eWOM to cognitive dissonance and other traditional psychological concepts and constructs to explore untruthful and negative truthful messages. Social media content sharing of news is a rich psychological and sociological process that may begin with awareness and engagement. Individuals may collect social capital and use personal influence, as they spread ideas across their social networks.

BEST PRACTICES: SOCIAL CAPITAL, DIFFUSION, PERSONAL INFLUENCE, AND SOCIAL NETWORKS

Social capital may be seen as a way to express the value of networked influence. Social network analysis (SNA) focuses on systematic study of interpersonal social interaction, popularity, participation, and isolation. Network structure can be seen through online connection, linkages, and bridging behavior (Hansen, et al., 2011). Online communities may be clustered within social space. Each Twitter account of "vertices" or "nodes," for example, has connected "ties" or "edges" with others (Hansen, et al., 2011, p. 33). SNA is easiest to observe within Twitter map visualization data. Tight networks and "role relationships" allow researchers to observe online communication behavior (Garton, Haythornthwaite, & Wellman, 1997, para. 3). Mapping of opinion leadership, social stratification, and influence indicates visual structure value in understanding communication within an event, such as news or a PR event. Social network structure based upon the concept of betweeness centrality may offer an estimate of communication influence (Smith, et al., 2014). Such data attempt to measure centrality and prestige (Russo & Koesten, 2005). The collection of SNA data over time reflect "big data" and present challenges and opportunities for understanding the use of social media (Guo, et al., 2016, p. 332). The current SNA fits within a broader context of social media communication research (Brandtzaeg, 2012). Popular public relations can be seen as a media framework to understand the differences between types of media. Each type requires different approaches to developing an effective social media campaign. This book argues for an integrated model for utilizing all four media types—owned, earned, paid, and social, as well as more recent models.

PAID, EARNED, SOCIAL, AND OWNED (PESO) MEDIA

The use of Google Analytics to optimize SEO of owned landing pages typically is a starting point for development of social media strategies that complement traditional online marketing efforts. Social media began about two decades ago as organic computer-mediated communication (CMC). The development of online identities, interest in human interaction, and cultivation of communities with shared values made participants obvious targets for later paid marketing. It was not long before the fields of journalism, public relations, and advertising recognized the value of earned and paid media efforts.

Cision (2018) created an earned media management (EMM) model to reflect the changing nature of PR. The paradigm underscores that nearly three-fourths (73%) of marketers connect "positive earned media" to growth in brand awareness and sustained health (p. 2). This is curious because a whopping 95 percent of budgets go to paid advertising (p. 3), and surveys suggest a lack of useful data. The Cision EMM model calls for:

1. A systematic approach to PR and comms job functions

2. The strategic combination of technology, data, processes, and analyses

3. Proving business impact

(p. 5)

Yet, Cision (2018) found than only about half of the teams surveyed (52%) "use end-customer data to inform how to strategically communicate to influencers and journalists" (p. 5). Thus, EMM requires, 1) mapping "the influencer graph" of "an influencer, their content, and the actual audience that consumes it;" 2) "smart engagement" that mixes "reach and relevance;" 3) "true measurement" of communication "efficacy," and connection to outcomes; and 4) "comms transformation" through integration of owned, earned, and paid media (pp. 6–7). Social media managers need this type of workflow in creation of social media.

SOCIAL MEDIA AUDITS AND THOUGHT LEADERS

Social media managers should regularly perform systematic audits of owned media properties and those that compete with her or his organization for share of branded voice. A common tactic is to use a CEO or other organizational thought leader to build followers through blogging and micro-blogging, social media interaction and engagement, online community building, and even customer support. We all encounter problems with products and services, but the willingness of a leader to engage, express empathy, and find a solution can have a large impact within a community of brand fans and followers. Social media auditing data over time reveal the impact and ROI of thought leader efforts.

AS SEEN ON YOUTUBE

Assignment

Watch Stu Shulman's explanation about the use of Sifter filtering to clean social media search data: www.youtube.com/watch?v=6G_YG6MBleg

Questions

1. Why is it important to filter data collected from social media before conducting an analysis?

2. What is a specific example of a search word that needs to be filtered before a social media manager analyzes the data? Why would failure to filter lead to measurement error?

USEFUL TOOLS

Many have attempted to compile a comprehensive list of social media measurement and management tools. We should distinguish between free or low-cost academic tools and expensive business tools. There are many tools mentioned throughout this book, and here it is suggested that a better approach may be to identify the most frequently used and mentioned:

Adobe Analytics—Adobe's goal is move "way beyond vanity metrics" by addressing digital marketing data complexity of "channels and interactions." Data focus on why website visitors have interest. Adobe attempts to go beyond Google Analytics.

Ahrefs—a competitor site analysis tool (https://ahrefs.com/) that helps a brand understand relative rankings.

Alexa—offers global web page rank data. A site information search (www.alexa.com/siteinfo/unomaha.edu) offers free data about web popularity, global region of visitors, percent of search engine traffic, keywords, upstream sites of visitors immediately before, downstream sites after, top sites linking to a URL, audience overlap with similar sites, and page load time. Alexa charges for demographic data access.

Bitly—The Bit.ly tool creates a unique URL for real-time tracking. OneView tracks site visitors across channels with macro and micro-level data on the customer journey. The company also offers a paid dashboard tool.

Brandwatch—This tool focuses on customer conversation. The company merged with Crimson Hexagon. A dashboard offers real-time data analytics and word clouds for social media listening.

Buffer—This is a social media content scheduling tool that shows post reach, impressions, link clicks, comments and social shares. A Buffer team may have more than two dozen members within an organization, and each may have different levels of tool access.

Buzzsumo—This content analysis program collects data across social media channels. Views and shares are tracked and analyzed.

Chartbeat—This real-time online publishing tool links site visitor data to webpage heat maps focused on exactly which items trend higher or lower for clicks at a given moment.

Cision—The tool focuses on earned media management through media relations. It connects social media data to influencers using the Help A Reporter Out (HARO) database.

comScore—These data estimate trust used in planning, transacting, and evaluating social media data. These data are treated as "transformative currency" designed to prove ROI.

CoSchedule—This tool integrates email and content scheduling and marketing. Project management tools include individual team member publishing progress assessment.

Dynamic Signal—This enterprise +5,000 employee company tool leverages employee social media content, sharing, and influence through a mobile app. A PR office can send to key influencers approved social media content consistent with company policies.

Facebook Insights—Native Facebook free data allows page managers to track overall metrics and top performing posts. The data allow for benchmarking and tracking performance on KPIs over time. Valuable demographic data may be accessed for free, and Facebook also offers granular psychographic and behavioral data within paid boosted campaigns.

Google Advanced Search—The tool (www.google.com/advanced_search) offers free and powerful search filtering methods for words, numbers, language, region, time, site location, file format, and licensing. Free and paid dashboard tools have been built upon search window APIs:

- Find pages with: all these words; this exact word or phrase; any of these words; none of these words; or numbers ranging from ___ to ___.

- Then narrow your results by: language; region; last update; site or domain; terms appearing; or file type.

- Find pages with similar links, visited search pages; or customized search settings.

Google Analytics—Social media managers typically have access to real-time webpage analytics. These foundational data track site visits and great detail. GA data include demographics, geodemographic location, psychographic lifestyle, and device type. Direct, organic, social, and referral data track visitors to websites. GA also offers site flow data once on pages.

Google Trends—(https://trends.google.com/trends/) is a search tool by interest and region. To tap into questions people are asking, try Answer the Public (https://answerthepublic.com/). Combined, these tools contextualize branding and marketing.

Hootsuite—This tool is considered a leading paid social media management tool. Student, professional, and enterprise versions help social media managers with the scheduling of content across networks, customer engagement, and branding.

HowSociable—This tool scores a user or topic across social media channels by "social media brand magnitude," but the simple measure algorithm is proprietary. These type of scores essentially aggregate and weight data across sites.

Hubspot—This customer relations management (CRM) tool addresses marketing, sales, and service functions. Hubspot boasted more than 52,000 companies across more than 100 nations using the tool that integrates contacts, companies, deals, tasks, notes, calls, emails, teams, and meetings.

IFTTT—offers free customized tools that link functions. For example, one tool saves a screenshot to a Dropbox folder. Another tool automatically saves tagged photos.

Instagram Post Insights—User post numbers, followers, and number of followers are found within profiles. Post-level tools include photo views, video plays, likes, and comments. Instagram's sister IGTV app tracks video view time, swipes, and other data.

Keyword Tool—The search tool (https://keywordtool.io/) scrapes important data from Google, YouTube, Bing, Amazon, eBay, App Store, and Instagram. Beyond keywords, it also searches for questions and prepositions. The tool searches prominent and important Instagram hashtags. For example, #socialmedia had 11,848,345 million posts, #socialmediaqueen with less than 205,732, and #socialmediaexpert with 159,638.

Keywords Everywhere—This is a Chrome and Firefox extension (https://keywordseverywhere.com/) for identifying words and phrases that should be used in SEO.

Klipfolio—This widget-based dashboard tool allows managers to connect social media data to KPIs through important business goal data.

LinkedIn Profile Dashboard—The LinkedIn dashboard offers free native insights about personal branding through profile view data and qualitative viewer information. Data are collected an organized in weekly snapshots about user professional networks.

Meltwater—The dashboard scrapes social media, news, and other content across online channels. The Meltwater tool offers social media data about top content, posters and sources, media exposure, social reach, and machine-coded sentiment. Meltwater purchased Sysomos, which offers brand marketing insights on customer experiences.

Moz—This SEO optimization tool focuses on website customer data. Mozt is the world's largest SEO professional community responding to constant Google algorithm and other industry changes.

Nielsen—Traditional media radio and television ratings data have been augmented with consumer and marketing analysis. Advertisers, media owners, agencies, retailers, and manufactures have an industry in these global estimates.

NodeXL—This open source, open data, and open science social network analysis (SNA) data tool maps conversation clusters on Twitter, Facebook-owned pages, and other sites. Twitter output lists include top influencers, top hashtags, top replies, and top mentions.

Nuvi—This sophisticated paid dashboard tool collects and presents social media listening data for use in campaign management. The real-time social media listening tool by Brickfish measures sentiment and segments over time. Social mention growth, for example, can be tracked over time and across network conversation. Brickfish also operates the enterprise version tool Groundspark.

Pew Internet—Survey and other social data are collected and publicly reported over time. Pew Internet has published dozens of studies about social media, and academics may receive access to data files for further secondary analysis.

Salesforce—This popular customer relations management (CRM) tool is popular with small and large businesses interested in connecting social media marketing to sales data.

ShareRocket—This is a social media ratings data platform for competing businesses and their employee influencers. They are ranked in real time across key social media channels by market and market share. The propriety social equity index (SEI) score estimates share value on a 100-point standardized score.

Slack—This internal messaging tool allows organizations and social groups to privately share content within threads organized by topics and hashtags.

Social Bakers—This AI-powered social media marketing suite monitors and measures audience and influencers, content, and community management.

Social Mention—This tool scores strength, sentiment, passion, and reach across blogs and other sources. Searches can be organized and downloaded to Excel data files for further analysis.

Sprout Social (Simply Measured)—This social media management software focuses on finding, forming, and deepening brand connections.

Trendkite Union Metrics Insightpool—Union Metrics offers free Twitter Assistant (formerly TweetReach) and Instagram Checkup dashboards. Mentions, retweets, top followers, and contributors can be viewed for Twitter data. On Instagram, average number of posts, time of day, post engagement, and hashtags offer social media managers meaningful insights.

Twitter Analytics—The native Twitter dashboard (http://analytics.twitter.com) offers a free 28-day account summary, tweets, impressions, profile visits, mentions, and followers. It highlights top performing text, photos, and video.

Twitter Tweetdeck—This free native platform tool (http://Tweetdeck.Twitter.com) allows users to create columns of saved searches to view new posts in real time. Organizations may use Tweetdeck to broadcast public displays of key topic activity.

Universal Alpha Clips—This media monitoring company has access to traditional media, such a local television news content, as well as online and social media data. The app is targeted at PR professionals seeking to demonstrate ROI of their work to the C-suite.

YouTube Studio—The innovative YouTube dashboard offers social media managers views, view time, and average duration data. There is a video analytics page for each published video. Watch time, views, subscribers, and revenue data are displayed over time. Audience retention is measured by during in minutes and seconds across the percent of total content length. Sentiment may be estimate through channel likes.

PROJECT IDEAS

Form a three- or four-member class team and select a free social media measurement dashboard tool. For example, Union Metrics has a Twitter Assistant and Instagram Checkup. Use these tools to track the social media of your group's most active member. Use the data to identify some KPIs. Write and present to the class a proposal for managing the accounts during the next month, quarter, and year.

DISCUSSION QUESTIONS

1. Why is social media brand management challenging for Instagram accounts? How do data help focus goals and objectives?

2. How can we determine which KPIs are useful within a social media dashboard? Why would this be helpful over time?

Academic Social Media Research

> *In the race to understand social media behavior, researchers have often mistakenly equated social media usage with the more cognitive and emotional involvement of social media engagement.*

—Brian G. Smith & Tiffany Derville Gallicano (@LambSchool & @Gallicano 2015, p. 82)

A solid foundation in social science research is important, not only for academics. Social media managers must strive for accurate and reliable measurement. The future of social media measurement demands that academics and practitioners use rigorous social scientific methods for quantitative and qualitative data collection, management, and analysis. At the heart of exploratory research is the need to develop strong conceptualization of exactly what we seek to measure. Routine social media use may be distinguished from cognitive and effective engagement that "refers to the absorption and immersive state of social media usage" (Smith & Gallicano, 2015, p. 82). In this view, typical interactivity, such as liking and sharing, "may not be sufficient" to claim engagement, which may happen at a much deeper level (p. 82). Within a public relations social media management paradigm, for example, engagement would need to be understood by relating it to relationship-building, trust, satisfaction: "evaluating the link between social media engagement and the organization—public relationship is of theoretical and practical importance to public relations and strategic communication" (pp. 82–83). More research is needed to explore use cases in which engagement may be more important for consumers than their satisfaction (Mersey, et al., 2012). For example, a deep level of engagement may be associated with a "sense of presence" in younger social media behavior: "Millennials considered themselves engaged with organizations based on their investment of time and attention, and they expected organizations to invest consistent interest in them" (p. 86). This view aligns with a practical view that best practices of social media management include a commitment to transparency and authentic relationships. Presence, virality, and utility also are dimensions of a blog engagement scale (Hopp & Gallicano, 2016). Presence was measured as, "the extent to which audiences believe the blog is involving, absorbing, agreeable, and personable" (p. 139). This appears to contribute to positive perception along with content utility and sharing attributes. Rigorous conceptual data help us to understand social media measurement and management at a deeper level.

The highest academic research standards also must be applied to media entrepreneurship because start-up projects may be rushed to market without appropriate concern for the practical value of theory and research. Research on women entrepreneurs, for example, has found that a firm may benefit from human capital (education level, management skills, and age) added through women participation, but did not find an association with social capital, as measured through social network or family support (Welsh, et al., 2018). As a company quickly grows, there may be hostile conditions the deter performance and an interest in embracing transparency. Within an organization, size has been found to be an important variable in barriers to adopting social media as part of internal and external communication strategy:

> factors most frequently named as hampering the adoption process of social media are factors related to blocked access (significantly more prevalent in large organizations), a lack of knowledge and skills as well as tangible (e.g. money) and intangible (time, effort) resources. From our data we can therefore confirm our initial hypothesis that company size does matter . . . and that companies mostly focus their efforts on a few popular platforms like LinkedIn, Twitter and Facebook to reach out to stakeholders. However, once adopted both large organizations and SMEs [small to medium-sized enterprises] seem to perceive important benefits.
>
> (Verheyden & Goeman 2013, p. 13)

When it comes to the study of social media management, lessons learned in PR should recognize the dangers of potential public manipulation (Grunig, 1989). These include the temptation to disseminate propaganda, to withhold from the public "negative information," or to use "sophisticated manipulation methods" instead of a "two-way symmetrical" approach that benefits an organization, as well as the public" (p. 29). In contrast, an elitist organization would favor its interests instead of the broader public interest in open, accurate, and honest communication. Unfortunately, SNSs, such as Facebook and Twitter, have been corrupted by posts that go beyond a lack of authenticity and deceive viewers. This needs to be addressed when we marvel at viral social media distribution data or become overly excited about the success found within social media campaign numbers.

Some viral posts happen in real time because people jump to incorrect outrage. For example, a game video of a young Chicago Cubs fan dropping a baseball that was picked up by a celebrating older man quick demonized the celebrant on Twitter and other social media channels. However, the video lacked important context (Simon, 2018). "What the Cubs discovered from people nearby was that the man in question wound up with four balls during the game, and gave three to children, including the young man who had appeared to be swindled. He also gave one to his wife; it was their anniversary" (para. 6). The Cubs social media team had quickly responded to negative sentiment by giving the boy a signed baseball and tweeting before learning to fuller context. "Unfortunately," a Cubs spokesman later said, "a video that was quickly posted and unverified has made a national villain out of an innocent man." The unidentified man also issued a statement: "Man foul balls came our way that day and were happily shared among children . . . I am not 'that guy' that the media and social media made me out to be" (para. 8). Whether through confusion or outright manipulation, viral social media distribution needs authentication methods.

An alternative is to identify key constructs, such as perceived relationship investment (PRI), and its relationship to trust, commitment, and satisfaction (Cho & Auger, 2013). Authentic relationship-building within social media measurement and management should assist social marketers and media consumers in making judgments and acting upon information, entertainment, or other types of postings. As is the case with traditional face-to-face relationship-building, context matters when interpreting the shared meaning of communication. If a balance is tilted toward reputation management of personal and corporate brands, then consumers are left with the responsibility for exercising critical thinking skills about all social media content.

Increasingly, there is concern about the use of social science, especially behavioral psychology, to drive effective social media campaigns. Simply put, the ability to collect granular data and then use it to manipulate people raises serious legal and ethical issues. For example, children's advocate groups suggested that the technology industry has a widespread "practice of using persuasive psychological techniques to keep kids glued to their screens" (Tanner & O'Brien, 2018, para. 1). The condemnation was based upon "research that links excessive use of social media and video games with depression and academic troubles" (para. 2). The fear of missing out (FOMO) has been found to have some psychological basis in terms of addiction and withdrawal symptoms (Baumer, et al., 2015). In general, CMC tends to follow interpersonal communication research findings within a mediated context (Berger, 2005; Chen & Persson, 2002).

Media effects research historically have concluded that negative outcomes depend upon many variables, including parental and other mediation and intervention. The American Psychological Association has not prohibited its members from working on new media technologies projects with technology entrepreneurs focused on business success rather than ethical boundaries. These goals may not be mutually exclusive, but self-regulation does not always protect consumers. In the aftermath of the Cambridge Analytica scandal, industry interest in **predictive analytics** does not appear to have slowed. Edelman Singapore and the Singapore Economic Development Board (EDB), for example, launched the Edelman Predictive Intelligence Centre (EPIC):

> a three-year strategic collaboration to research and develop new approaches to communications marketing planning using predictive and intelligent technologies. The partnership . . . will address a gap in the data analytics market, deploying behavioral science to help brands improve their understanding of human behavior and the motivations that influence and inform people's decision-making.
>
> The Centre's vision is to change the way organizations build relationships and trust with consumers and stakeholders through scientific analysis of what matters to people and drives their behavior. EPIC is committed to ethical practices in the collection and management of data and will ensure that its standards are in compliance with GDPR and other regulations.
>
> (Edelman Singapore, 2018, para 1)

The difficulty is that industry-funded research, in contrast with peer-reviewed academic and publicly funded studies, tends to be proprietary and secretive. Further, a center located in Asia is far removed from European Union and U.S. pressures to comply with data privacy protection. Lee (2018) was leading the new center and noted the potential power of predictive analytics:

> The potential power that predictive intelligence will put in our hands as communicators is enormous. The Internet of Things enabled consumer electronics, smart city initiatives, blockchain-enhanced business processes and AI augmented apps to rocket us toward a wired and connected society, resulting in better quality data being generated in bigger volumes. Similar to when social networks, tweeting and blogging first became mainstream, we suddenly have access to information that was previously very difficult and costly to acquire.
>
> (para, 5)

The question remains as to whether or not the industry on its own can cultivate trusted relationships with all stakeholders that is based upon *their* behavioral data. It would seem that this will require higher levels of transparency than is the norm for competitive business people with a personal set of economic interests and values. The EU right to be forgotten law (RTBF), for example, is considered by scholars as "entrenched" law. "It is conceptually derived from an individual's sense of dignity that encompasses his self-determination of what information to share with others and how and when to share it" (Youm & Park, 2016, p. 289).

In this context, Google search and SEO driven by voice and other natural language technologies are likely to be increasingly important and invasive. Keyword tracking that may begin within social media sites, such as Instagram, allow brands to monitor conversation, offer targeted free content, participate as influencers, use engagement to move consumers through a marketing journey and experience, and occupy enormous amounts of personal time and attention. The technology itself has few bandwidth limits when it comes to video and other rich media. The line between organic and paid content is not always clear, and the involvement of Alexa and other AI may make disclosure more complicated. Brands still want to be convinced that paid media have ROI based upon traditional media **cost per thousand (CPM) models**. The use of website analytics for tracking is an important measurement piece within the larger social media measurement and management context. From share of voice to time on site, brands would like complete control over user information and entertainment experiences—a captive audience to sell to and build loyal customers and fans. It is not that traditional media use has disappeared, rather that multi-screens splinter attention. Social media content continue to offer the potential for interactive engagement at a deeper level of user commitment.

QUANTITATIVE AND QUALITATIVE SOCIAL SCIENCE RESEARCH

The use of social media by political campaigns sparked a strong interest in academic research following to 2016 U.S. election. Predictably, there are theoretical and methodological issues in conducting reliable and valid social research (Dimitrova & Matthes, 2018): "comprehensive aggregate studies offer evidence that the effects of social media consumption and use are hardly uniform across different contexts and groups" (p. 333). There remains a need for theory building and precise models that go beyond data description and are "more nuanced" and explanation of "political and civic engagement" (p. 338). For example, within the political context partisan social media use follow traditional relationships and discord (Chan, 2018). In one study, Facebook page likes "had a modest but significant positive effect on personal votes," which suggested a two-step personal influence model of "candidates' messages mediated by . . . friends" (Bene, 2018, p. 374).

Beginning with the 2012 U.S. presidential election, big data research methods were more likely in the evaluation of social media data analytics. Guo, et al. (2016) examined computer-assisted text analysis in millions of tweets, and the research team found "some valuable information" in "summary statistics" (p. 350). However, research methods appeared to have an impact on results: "Understanding why certain algorithms perform better than others is crucial to externally valid results" (p. 352).

Within the U.S. 2016 presidential election context, research has begun to demonstrate that President Donald Trump may have benefited from higher levels of social media volume and intensity than Hillary Clinton. Hale and Grabe (2018) found gender and bandwagon potential effects with Reddit content: "the Trump subreddit attracted more activity than the Clinton subreddit," and "the Trump subreddit accumulated a significantly higher score and a greater number of comments" (pp. 464–465). A "perceived bandwagon of support for Trump" may have been driven by the conclusion that, "Trump was portrayed as a multifaceted leader . . . scoring positively in masculine, feminine, and gender-neutral leadership characteristics" (p. 465). These data align with initial and exploratory social network analyses of Twitter conversation about the candidates and election.

TESTING AND REPLICATION OF DATA

Rapid social network site structural innovation to respond to user interests and market competition present a primary challenge for academic researchers seeking to replicate research results (Bossetta, 2018). From digital architecture to functions, integration of data may be challenging. Snapchat in 2016 "offered only rudimentary analytics," but then added email access: *Digital architectures are subject to rapid and transformational change*" (p. 492). As is discussed throughout this book, social media managers, therefore, must be innovative entrepreneurs when it comes to data collection and new tools to analyze findings. Moreover, use of A/B testing and other applied research techniques are subject to constant reevaluation. One scholar, for example, attempted to compare "most-viewed" online news lists and concluded that there were two problematic dimensions—change rate and time to reach a list: "scholars should not assume that such data are comparable and should instead ensure such comparability through empirical analysis" (Zamith, 2018, p. 134). Research suggests that perceived trust and satisfaction are related to evaluation of content quality (Shen, 2017). Use of online content appears to have great variability in terms of audience motivation and intensity of interest (Jarraeu & Porter, 2018). "Super users" may also be considered opinion leaders within social media, as they seek communities to share "unique information," entertainment and experiences within highly specialized areas (p. 153). For academics using professional social sites that archive their scholarship, such as BePress Digital Commons, readership data are a new form of interest. KPIs may include total number of downloads, number of new monthly downloads, and number of papers. However, these raw data offer no clues into the quality of academic readership and highlight the problem of using large numbers that have no scientific meaning or value.

For journalists on social media sites, such as Twitter, credibility appears to be influenced by interaction with other site users (Jahng & Littau, 2016). Additionally, research suggests that message credibility in a social media era can be explained by perception of content as "accurate, authentic, and believable" (Appelman & Sundar, 2016, p. 73). "Together, these three adjectives reflect the concept of message credibility" (p. 73). However, the degree to which these findings apply across global cultural and political contexts is unknown. Social media uses are known to vary when political conditions are less stable, and gratifications obtained from new media tend to be complex (Sundar & Limperos, 2013).

Chan (2017) explored roles of online news and social media sites in stimulating protest participation in Hong Kong. A "social identity model" examined "injustice," "identity," and "efficacy" (p. 669). Social media and alternative media use may combine as variables among many others in contributing to feelings of "anger" (p. 673). Chan (2017) noted that younger social media users also are more likely to be within an age group participating in social movements and protests about inequality and democracy: "alternative media rely heavily on social media to disseminate content, given their lack of financial resources to do any promotion" (p. 674). Application of social media models also has been limited by the lack of development within communication research of concepts, such as social capital, "social cohesion," and structural social network analysis (Lee & Sohn, 2016, p. 741). SNA theory and methods continue to develop across a global network of scholars (Butts, 2008).

Identification of existing social networks allows academic researcher to study longitudinal interaction (Yang, et al., 2018). On study observed social media health forum conversation over five years—9,369 patients and 90,965 messages (p. 1033). Social networks sometimes exhibit social support structure, which can be "directional" through a reply or "reciprocated" (p.1041). A key finding was that, "those who received more social support from others in the community were motivated to provide significantly more social support in the following year" (p. 1047). Consistent with decades of computer-mediated communication studies, social media online communities are an important context for understanding identity presentation, interactive engagement, and other dimensions of behavior.

Social media educators use research entrepreneurship to address dramatic change brought by new technologies. This involves "removing the disconnect between theory and practice," developing communities of practice (CoP) to spark "collective learning," and "creating critical distance" for "perspective" (Mulrennan, 2018, pp. 324–329). Surveys, though, tend to rely on industry leaders to determine student needs, such as:

- Content creation skills

- Marketing and public relations principles

- Writing abilities

- Crisis training.

(Freberg & Kim, 2018, pp. 384–387)

Media educators face similar challenges of experienced professionals within organizations that expect them to keep pace with the newest technologies, mentor younger colleagues, and be a role model for those with less social media experience.

ᴛ📡 Thought Leaders Roma Subramanian and Andrea Weare

#NotOkay—Using Information Science Tools to Investigate Disclosure about a Concealable Stigmatized Identity on Twitter

In October 2016, a leaked tape from a 2005 television interview between then presidential candidate Donald Trump and *Access Hollywood* host Billy Bush revealed Trump seemingly bragging off-screen about routinely sexually assaulting women (Bullock, 2016). In response to the leak, on October 7, 2016, writer Kelly Oxford publicly tweeted her first experience of sexual assault and encouraged women to do the same. By the next day, one million women tweeted in response to Oxford—most marking their experiences with the hashtag #notokay (Domonoske, 2016).

FIGURE 5.1 *Roma Subramanian (@romasubramanian). Photograph by Cassidy Conrad, courtesy UNOmaha.*

Given the rampant stigma of sexual assault, this was unprecedented Twitter participation by a marginalized population. Twitter, among other social media platforms, affords users the ability to organize politically by using their collective tweets as a "tool by which to challenge the failed mechanism of institutional politics" (Jenkins, et al., 2016, p. 3). And with enough "stick," social media-based activist campaigns can reach beyond their marginal grassroots and into mainstream sociopolitical con-

FIGURE 5.2 *Andrea Weare (@ amweare). Photograph by Cassidy Conrad, courtesy UNOmaha.*

versations (Jenkins, et al., 2013; Penney, 2015). As researchers, we wanted to better understand how #notokay users tweeted their sexual assaults. We asked ourselves, who were the key players and what were the key themes in the first 24 hours of #notokay, and what were the key tweets and additional hashtags used? Finally, what was the pattern of the #notokay conversation and how did it evolve over time?

Method and Findings

To answer these questions, we developed a two-part research study. First, we used the text analytics software tool DiscoverText, specifically its Gnip Historical Power Track tool, to search and retrieve tweets from the first 24 hours of the #notokay campaign by using the query term "notokay" (Schulman, 2011). Using the Historical Power Track tool made it possible to access the full archive of public Twitter data ("Custom historical tweet collections," 2018). We retrieved an archive of 43,688 tweets from the first 24 hours of #notokay. The archive contained the text of each tweet, the metadata for each tweet (e.g., username, user bio summary, posted time), as well as the live display of each tweet. The archive was made up of 1,331 groups of duplicate tweets and 14,851 unique tweets.

To remove duplicate items and create a more heterogeneous sample of the first 24 hours of #notokay tweets, we selected one item each from the

1,331 groups of duplicate items and combined them with the 14,851 unique items to create a "seeds and singles" bucket (or a specialized subset of a raw data archive) of 16,182 unique items. Since Oxford asked women to tweet at her, to capture these tweets, from the seeds and singles bucket, we used "search query" in "Advanced filters" to search for the term "@kellyoxford" and created another bucket of 3,535 tweets. Of the 43,688 tweets analyzed using the software, the top three most retweeted or viral tweets were two tweets by Kelly Oxford (6,345 times) and one by *TeenVogue* (1,565 times).

Using the "filter by meta" option in "Advanced filters," we filtered by hashtag and found that the main hashtags associated with #notokay (26,349) included #TrumpTapes (4,261), #NeverTrump (647), #RapeCulture (537), and #BillClintonIsRapist (226). Also, using the "filter by meta" option in "Advanced filters," we filtered by user-location and found that most #notokay Tweeters were from the United States, but 325 tweets originated from countries like Pakistan, Australia, Canada, and the United Kingdom.

We also used the social network analysis tool NodeXL, which stands for Network Overview, Discovery, and Exploration, to investigate Twitter user patterns like their influence level on Twitter. Using NodeXL, we were able to create maps of the hashtag in the first 24 hours of the campaign, highlighting "key people, groups, and topics," as other scholars have done (Smith,

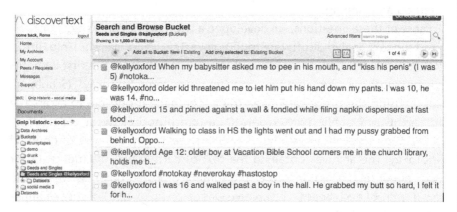

FIGURE 5.3 *DiscoverText Data Collection. Image courtesy DiscoverText and the UNO Social Media Lab.*

et al., 2014, p.5). A NodeXL map of a dataset of 3,535 tweets containing the hashtag "notokay" and "@kellyoxford" revealed a broadcast network structure.

In the second part of our study, we were interested in how users crafted their disclosure of assault to followers amidst the harsh stigma of sexual assault. The word "stigma" can be traced to the Greeks who used brands to mark the skin of criminals and slaves as tainted or immoral (Bos, et al., 2013). Today, it is more broadly defined as an undesirable visible or invisible attribute that indicates a spoiled social identity and results in social disapproval (Bos, et al., 2013).

Those with concealable stigmas, such as individuals who have experienced sexual assault, are often faced with the decision of when to disclose that identity, which can have implications for their physical and mental wellbeing. Considering the stigma sexual assault survivors face and how rape-supportive culture at large keeps many from ever disclosing, we hoped to glean common themes in disclosures made online (Brownmiller, 1975).

To do so, we applied the Disclosure Processes Model (DPM) to a random sample of 1,000 tweets from the bucket of 3,535 tweets (described above) that was collected using DiscoverText (Chaudoir & Fisher, 2011). The DPM indicates that disclosing a stigma, such as sexual assault, has many parts to the process including goals (e.g., self-expression), the disclosure event itself (e.g., how much you reveal), factors/processes that help or hinder disclosure (e.g., social support), and a feedback loop (e.g., how the disclosure event influences the likelihood of disclosing again).

By focusing on someone's #notokay tweet as the disclosure event itself, we discovered five themes, including "Sexual assault happens to women of all ages in a variety of locations" and "Women who are sexually assaulted do not receive support from those around them and, thus, feel obligated to label their experience as 'fact,' "proof,' 'evidence,' or 'truth.' "

Conclusion

Using social media software like DiscoverText and NodeXL, we were able to show how online audiences use social media platforms like Twitter to disclose stigmatizing identities, like sexual assault. This study shows how these tools can be used to study historical online health events, which is important considering the half-life of a tweet is a mere 24 minutes (Rey, 2014). We also hoped to showcase how the DPM can be applied to online environments like Twitter even though it was originally created to explain disclosures made face-to-face. Finally, we hoped to prompt a discussion about how measurably small Twitter activist campaigns—like #notokay—may have the ability to prime an audience to participate in larger ones—like #metoo—that possess professional and celebrity endorsements, as we saw with the #metoo watershed firings in media organizations in 2017.

Next, we are interviewing #notokay tweeters to better understand their disclosure in their own words. Overall, we hope to shed light on the stigma of sexual assault and how individuals are using their social networks, like Twitter, to share their stories with their followers.

References

Bos, A. E. R., Pryor, J. B., Reeder, G. D., & Stutterheim, S. E. (2013). Stigma: Advances in Theory and Research, *Basic and Applied Social Psychology*, 35:1, 1–9, DOI: 10.1080/01973533.2012.746147

Brownmiller, S. (1975). *Against Our Will: Men, Women, and Rape*. New York: Ballantine Publishing Group.

Bullock, P. (2016, October 8). Transcript: Donald Trump's taped comments about women. *The New York Times*. Retrieved from www.nytimes.com/2016/10/08/us/donald-trump-tape-transcript.html

Chaudoir, S. & Fisher, J. (2010). The Disclosure Processes Model: Understanding Disclosure Decision Making and Post-Disclosure Outcomes among People Living with a Concealable Stigmatized Identity. *Psychological Bulletin*, *136*(2), 256–236. doi: 0.1037/a0018193

Custom historical tweet collections. (2018). Retrieved from https://discovertext.com/sifter/

Domonoske, C. (2016, October 11). One Tweet Unleashes a Torrent of Stories of Sexual Assault. *NPR*. Retrieved from www.npr.org/sections/thetwo-way/2016/10/11/497530709/one-tweet-unleashes-a-torrent-of-stories-of-sexual-assault

Jenkins, H., Ford, S., & Green, J. (2013). *Spreadable Media: Creating Value and Meaning in A Networked Culture*. New York: NYU Press.

Rey, B. (2014, March 5). Your tweet Half-Life Is 1 Billion Times Shorter than Carbon-14's.

Wiselytics. Retrieved from http://blog.wisemetrics.com/tweet-isbillion-time-shorter-than-carbon14/

Shulman, S. (2011). DiscoverText: Software Training to Unlock the Power of Text. Paper presented at the 12th Annual International Digital Government Research Conference: Digital Government Innovation in Challenging Times. College Park, MD.

Smith, M.A., Rainie, L., Schneiderman, B., & Himelboim, I. (2014, February 20). Mapping Twitter Topic Networks: From Polarized Crowds to Community Clusters. *Pew Research Center*. Retrieved from www.pewinternet.org/2014/02/20/mapping-twitter-topic-networks-from-polarized-crowds-to-community-clusters/

Roma Subramanian (Ph.D., Missouri) and Andrea Weare (Ph.D., Iowa) are Assistant Professors of public relations and advertising, School of Communication, University of Nebraska at Omaha. Subramanian's science editing and PR relate to research focus on health communication, news about stigmatized disorders, impact of social and mobile media on health, and physician–patient communication dynamics. Weare teaches strategic communication, media, and qualitative research methods. Her research focuses on digital and strategic communication, gender and the body. Areas of interest include popular culture, health, philanthropy, and entrepreneurial communication.

An obvious focus for academic social media research (Khang, et al., 2012) would be the concerns about polarized social networks, the impact of echo chambers, and filter bubbles that magnify political division, and the lack of editorial gatekeeping in wide open platforms (Allcott & Gentzkow, 2017):

We define "fake news" to be news articles that are intentionally and verifiably false and could mislead readers. We focus on fake news articles that have political implications,

> . . . Our definition includes intentionally fabricated news articles, . . . It also includes many articles that originate on satirical websites but could be misunderstood as factual, especially when viewed in isolation on Twitter or Facebook feeds.
>
> (p. 213)

Particularly on Twitter, researchers have been able to document through visualization the existence of polarized crowds. It can be argued that social media re-created a false news problem that can be traced to at least nineteenth-century news content. The findings also align with traditional persuasion theory and its research emphasis on reinforcement of existing views through consonant media content, as well as twentieth-century "conspiracy theories" (p. 215). During the 2016 election, social media represented an estimated 13.8 percent of "most important source" for election news, and this share is rapidly growing (p. 224). Attempts to model potential impact of social media posts have been problematic, but this is a rich research area for future study. News content dissemination, for example, happens before it is received, shared, and discussed (Weeks & Holbert, 2013). Social media managers should be aware of the most recent academic research findings and the implications on their ongoing work.

Applied academic research data indicate that the established market shares of Facebook and YouTube are being challenged by Instagram and other social media apps (Smith & Anderson, 2018). For example, "Some 78% of 18- to 24-year-olds use Snapchat, and a sizeable majority of these users (71%) visit the platform multiple times per day" (para. 2). For the first time in 2018, more Americans used social media than read print newspapers for news:

> Social media sites have surpassed print newspapers as a news source for Americans: One-in-five U.S. adults say they often get news via social media, slightly higher than the share who often do so from print newspapers (16%) for the first time since Pew Research Center began asking these questions. In 2017, the portion who got news via social media was about equal to the portion who got news from print newspapers.
>
> (Shearer, 2018, para. 1)

Television news also showed a declining trend line, although nearly half (49%) report using it. It remained ahead of news websites (33%), radio (26%), social media (20%), and print newspapers (16%) for getting news often.

Academic researchers, including graduate students, have swarmed social media as an area of study. At recent international meetings of the Association for Education in Journalism and Mass Communication (AEJMC), for example, social media research topics went from a novelty a decade ago to one of the largest research areas. An AEJMC interest group was being formed, and the Social Media Professors group on Facebook grew from a handful of members to hundreds in its first two years. At the doctoral, master's, and undergraduate levels, students are intrigued to understand how and why social media have become some important in the lives of much of the world's population.

Thought Leader Sam Petto

A Social Media Use Research Project

As we start to explore research on organizations' social media use, one quickly discovers that effects research has dominated the agenda. These kinds of studies test the impact of a specific message or strategy using conversation starters in posts, for example, or frequently retweeting followers. That research is valuable, but it leaves a large gap: what if the people you are trying to reach are looking for something not measuring?

In a 2018 M.A. thesis, my focus was on why social media users initiate interaction with organizational accounts. I was curious about the motivations that lead us to direct message brand accounts, post on brand profiles, or tag brand accounts. There was little previous research. I knew effects research was not right for

FIGURE 5.4 *Sam Petto (@sampetto). Photograph courtesy UNOmaha.*

this study. Testing social media users' reactions to organizations' responses would be complicated and drastically inefficient. Interviews might lead to interesting findings, but would participants really be representative of other social media users? How would I know if a focus group member's opinion was an outlier? I knew I wanted a comprehensive approach, something that could show significant trends, so I developed an exploratory online survey. I was inspired by other social media studies that leveraged uses and gratifications theory—a framework suggesting that we know enough about our own media habits to explain why we are making specific choices. Or in other words, the best way to understand why someone created a Pinterest board with 34 different photos of rain jackets is simply to ask.

Method

Amazon's Mechanical Turk service was utilized to recruit 200 social media users who had used their accounts to direct message an organization's account, tag an organization's account, or post on its profile. Most of them had used all three methods. The social media users ranked their level of agreement with a series of statements about what motivated them to post, tag, or direct message. As an example: "I direct message an organization to get useful information about products/services." The statements came from prior studies investigating motivations behind why Facebook users like corporate accounts. Each statement linked back to one of four key factors: 1) socializing, 2) entertainment, 3) self-status seeking, and 4) information seeking. Why these factors? A lack of time and resources limited my ability to develop reliable new scales for measuring use, and previous research demonstrated reliability. Even if respondents disagreed with every single factor, the goal was to add valuable knowledge: namely that motivations for initiating interaction with accounts were apparently wildly different than motivations for liking accounts.

After running the survey, data were imported into the Statistical Package for the Social Sciences (SPSS) Statistics, and these generated descriptive statistics. Averages of all the responses showed that across all methods of outreach information seeking was the strongest motivation for initiating interaction with organizations, followed by socializing, entertainment, and self-status seeking. In fact, self-status seeking was the only factor where respondents leaned toward disagreeing that the motivation played a role in their outreach to an organization.

Would these motivations also differ based on method? To find out, I ran paired sample T-tests with respondents who had used all three methods of initiating interaction. This statistical test offers researchers an opportunity to compare means between the same subjects under different conditions. For example, was I acting on the same motivations when I direct messaged Nike as compared to when I tagged them? The tests showed responses significantly differed by method of interaction. In other words, how someone is reaching out to an organization might indicate gratification obtained.

Results

- Direct Messaging: People who direct message an organization are more likely to be seeking information than those who tag or post on a profile.
- Tagging: People who tag organizations are more likely to be acting on a desire for increasing self-status than those who direct message or post on profiles.
- Posting: People who post on public profiles are more likely to be interested in socializing than those who send direct messages. (No significant difference in socializing was found with SNS users who tag organizations.)

While my sample size was small compared to most published studies, these results helped me feel more confident in my data. After all, nothing here defies expectations. It makes sense that tagging is more likely to involve some attempt to boost self-status. These kinds of messages are blasted out to a personal social network, while direct messages are entirely private and

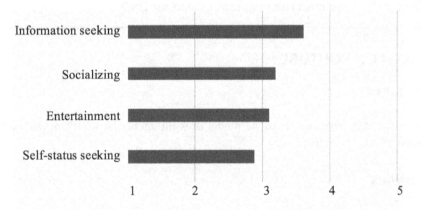

1= Strong Disagreement, 5 = Strong Agreement

FIGURE 5.5 *Media use motivation data. Chart courtesy Sam Petto: Information Seeking (3.61), Socializing (3.19), Entertainment (3.10), and Self-status Seeking (2.88).*

posts on public profiles may not be shared with friends depending on the network. Likewise, it stands to reason that people who are going to an organization's page to post something might be interested in interacting with other customers or fans of a specific brand.

All studies have limitations and mine is no exception. A friend who works in customer service for a major wholesale company was able to spot what may be a missing factor right away. There was nothing measuring the motivation of wanting a company to do something. For example, what if someone wants a poor customer experience addressed or is calling on a company to reduce plastic waste? The four factors I examined don't speak to an action-seeking motivation. Or are there several different types of action-seeking motivations? If so, do they differ too? As you progress in your academic journey, you'll find these kinds of questions are nothing new. Any good study won't just offer new answers; it will also raise many new questions.

Sam Petto is Associate Director of Editorial and Media Relations at the University of Nebraska at Omaha. A public relations professional and former television journalist, Petto is also a FEMA-certified Public Information Officer (PIO) and crisis communications lead for UNO.

AS SEEN ON YOUTUBE

Assignment

Watch Sam Petto explain his social media user interaction research project: https://youtube/BSNhvquMFfo

Questions

1. If you were developing a follow-up study, which theories and concepts would drive research questions (RQs)? Which methods would be appropriate to answer the RQs?

2. Based upon previous research in this area, what results would you expect? How would you likely interpret these? What research limitations might require development of future questions?

USEFUL TOOLS

Amazon Mechanical Turk—MTurk is called a "crowdsourcing marketplace" and out-sourcing tool. It is used for data collection, survey participation, content moderation, collective intelligence insights from data analysis, and machine learning (www.mturk.com/).

PROJECT IDEAS

Use your campus library search tools to find a recent peer-reviewed academic article about some aspect of social media measurement and management. Consult with your professor for a desired paper structure and write a one-page abstract of the findings. Post a PDF of the abstract and the original article on a discussion thread for your course online site, such as Canvas or Blackboard. Discuss with peers the value of academic research.

DISCUSSION QUESTIONS

1. How does the peer-review process offer an opportunity to improve the quality of social media research? Why do a lot of professionals tend to read blogs and white papers rather than academic journal articles?

2. What could be done to better apply academic research findings to the daily lives of social media managers? How could an entrepreneur develop a tool to help?

UNIT THREE
Best Practices in Social Media Measurement

Integration of PR, Advertising, and Marketing Plans

> *You likely don't have just one target audience, or persona . . . Build these out and support your personas with social data from a listening solution, so you have real-time intel on what each demographic likely to buy your product is talking about and cares about.*

—Lucy Hitz (@LLHitz, 2018, para. 3)

Increasingly, social media management best practices require a broad and deep set of skills that cut across public relations, advertising, and marketing. Target marketing within social media begins with planning and development of a process. Simple social media marketing plans start by exploring and focusing on a target audience, specific social channels, ROI metrics, and available resources: "What pain points will you solve?" (Chen, 2018, para. 4). MarketingCharts.com (2018) survey data from a relatively small sample (N = 224) of influencers suggested that email (82%), social media (54%), as well as websites and blogs (51%) were the "most effective channels they use for marketing content to prospective customers" (para. 3). While these data may not be generalizable, the mix of email, social media sites, and owned media websites is very common and effective. The measurement tool Sprout Social has developed a lean process for utilizing social media data: track personas and target demographics, read a metrics map (awareness → consideration → decision → adoption → advocacy → label content and track progress), learn recent approaches, and incorporate paid content (Hitz, 2018, paras. 3–20). Other similar and common models include customer acquisition → service → loyalty (Chen, 2018, para. 24). At each step, there are granular data points, including key demographics (Fontein, 2016). Descriptive data, however, should be enriched by examining concepts that link to behavior.

Awareness may include a series of information-seeking steps, numerous brand "touch points," and a range of organizational departments—from marketing to legal (BrightVessel.com, 2018, para. 1). The idea is to identify content on sites, such as Instagram, that simply work best to achieve explicit goals within organizational boundaries, policies, and governance. Lipman Hearne in Chicago, for example, has helped more than 700 institutions raise more than $31 billion in a half century of work that includes re-branding major universities across all media.

Any organization, including nonprofits, may utilize social media strategy and tactics within a broader development fundraising campaign. Brand and philanthropic marketing are growing areas. Social media measurement, as with any form of social measurement, requires that we understand exactly what we are trying to quantify. Influencer marketing, for example, is a popular way to extend the reach of messages and seek

FIGURE 6.1 *Peter Barber is Executive Vice President at Lipman Hearne (@LipmanHearne). Photograph by Jeremy Harris Lipschultz, courtesy Peter Barber.*

credibility within trusted social networks. Too often, however, social media managers reach for tools to accomplish this task before asking fundamental questions, such as:

1. Type of influencers (celebrities, bloggers, micro-influencers, etc.)?
2. Specific channels (SNSs, blogs, etc.)?
3. Goals, objectives and KPIs?
4. Influencer guidelines and boundaries?

(Bullock, 2018)

Use of Email to Micro-Target Qualitative Relationships

The UNO Social Media Lab (@unosml) used a campus email list (N = 138) to distribute a holiday newsletter in December 2018. Within the list there were micro-influencers and potential donors. The content focused on student projects, faculty research, and community engagement. It featured

TABLE 6.1 *Mailchimp data*

1. **Successful Deliveries 137 (99.3%)**
2. **Bounced 1 (0.007%)**
3. **Unsubscribed 1 (0.007%)**
4. **Total Opens 70 (51.1%)**
5. **Reach: Unique Opened 42 (30.7%)**
6. **Clicked 5 (3.6%)**
7. **Awareness: Clicks Per Unique Opens (11.9%)**

Top Links Clicked	*Total Clicks*	*Unique*
1. Google Drive PDF Research Abstract	6 (27%)	2 (20%)
2. Lab Twitter Moments of Spring Semester Guest Speaker	4 (18%)	2 (20%)
3. Instagram Account Profile	3 (14%)	1 (10%)
4. Social Media Lab Website	3 (14%)	1 (10%)
5. College Faculty Profile Website	3 (14%)	1 (10%)
6. Student Lab Tech Twitter Profile	2 (9 %)	2 (20%)
7. Project Funding External Website	1 (5%)	1 (10%)

links to owned media websites, social media content on Facebook, Instagram, and Twitter, as well as a video. Email is sometimes forgotten, but it has the potential to grow social media followers, increase awareness and reach, and achieve specific campaign goals. The Mailchimp data dashboard three days after the distribution offered insights for the direction of future email campaigns.

Click map data showed where readers clicked and engaged with content—perhaps wanting more information, such as about the external institute that was funding a lab project and the faculty research abstract. Follow-up experimental eye-tracking data could provide additional user information. A key finding from the mailing data was the effectiveness of the Twitter Moment summary, which also had been the most effective content during a lab event that featured live tweeting with a hashtag. The data also measured effectiveness of social media posts of the newsletter page and showed that five clicks came from two Facebook posts, and two from LinkedIn. Newsletter opens came from campus mail servers, as well as others:

TABLE 6.2 *Email domain performance*

Domain	Email	Bounces	Opens
Unomaha.edu	115 (83%)	1 (1%)	32 (28%)
Gmail	12 (9%)	0 (0%)	7 (58%)
Unl.edu	2 (1%)	0 (0%)	0 (0%)
Cox.net	2 (1%)	0 (0%)	1 (50%)
Purdue.edu	1 (1%)	0 (0%)	1 (100%)
Other	6 (4%)	1 (17%)	2 (40%)

Newsletter opens move us a step closer to understanding the human behavior behind a decision to read and process information. The exploratory pilot email offered data that are useful in planning and executing future content distribution, as well as scaling it to a larger external audience.

Social marketers must follow a strategic path that: *defines* goals and metrics; *audits* current content; and *maps* a customer journey (Chen, 2018). Increasingly, however, the cost for Twitter, Facebook, Instagram, and other data is rising with monetization of social network sites, such as Twitter. Academic efforts to improve reliability and validity of data have been thwarted by higher pricing and limited access. For example, "It's not possible to use Twitter's advanced search function to pull all tweets related to a certain subject within a date range" (Alaimo, 2018b, para. 3). The rising cost for historical data has driven Texifter's Sifter program to end part of its operation and focus on historical data already collected for academic use. The tool was designed to filter and clean social media data prior to analysis and presentation. Twitter is a publicly held company that has a fiduciary responsibility to shareholders and charging more for academic data may create a new revenue stream. If academics cannot find adequate funding, though, data reliability and validity may take a back seat. With this in mind, social media managers must critically evaluate the use of all data and metrics, as they innovate PR, advertising, and marketing practices. Too often, social media content decisions have been made without regard for available data. An exploration of industry best practices begins with an assumption that data offer insights that have the potential to produce better long-term results.

BEST PRACTICES IN SOCIAL MEDIA MEASUREMENT

Best practices originate with data-driven decision making, and one survey suggested that 80 percent of marketers use metrics (Trendkite, 2018, p. 1). Public relations, meanwhile, is rapidly transforming into what is known as "digital PR," as 87 percent of public relations executives responded that the digital shift will redefine their work by 2022 (p. 2). Some digital PR teams have adopted a marketing funnel mindset that moves audiences from brand impact, based upon the Trendkite model:

Brand Impact → Digital Impact → Bottom-line Impact

We should be able to accurately measure through social media how a particular brand is "perceived in the marketplace" (p. 4). Most social media campaigns start with a measure of awareness, which can be benchmarked against future change. We can use many social media measurement tools to track mentions. The Meltwater dashboard, for example, has a widget that scrapes social media public Facebook posts and tweets. Combined with creation of a set of Google Alerts focused on brand keywords, it is possible to monitor the real-time conversations that mention a brand.

It is important to note that the interest is in monitoring *relevant* mentions over time to identify trends. If brand mentions happen within a context of competing brand mentions, then share of voice (SoV) may be a KPI. Not all mentions are equal. We would like to be able to categorize by sentiment—positive, neutral, or negative. However, machine-coded sentiment historically lacks reliability and consistency. Even human coders of sentiment have disagreement over content context. If the goal is to raise awareness through increasing numbers of positive mentions, then we need to be able to accurately code and measure sentiment. Machine learning is improving on this front, but social research suggests that all data have error. So, the long-term goal is to measure and reduce unexplained variance in mentions and other social media data.

Digital impact, according to the Trendkite (2018) framework, links social media activity to owned website traffic, SEO, and "social amplification" (p. 9). As mentioned earlier in this book, links from other websites to a brand's owned media offer what Google calls authority, which can have a positive impact on page rank and search. It may be the case that search is far more important than social media mentions in terms of driving visitors to important clicks on a page that move a person to act. Trendkite (2018) points to the Moz domain authority 100-point scale to estimate site importance: "A well-established publication with quality traffic, informative content, and strong audience interaction will generally have higher Domain Authority" (p. 12). Likewise, a brand can establish authority of its own, as others backlink to its site. In this regard, social media mentions help amplify brands and their messages—especially when engagement features tagging of another. The bottom line for most brands is to be able to measure, at least indirectly, ROI through website conversions, increased revenue, or other positive outcomes for a business or non-profit. For example, non-profits use social media to raise awareness about fundraising campaigns or volunteer opportunities. Even when we cannot establish direct measures, social media managers suggest that "mindshare" and "reputation" management have long-term benefits for more concrete business objectives (p. 19).

INTEGRATION OF PR, ADVERTISING, AND MARKETING PLANS

Social media management planning application can be learned through examples within the fields of public relations, advertising, and marketing. There are challenges and opportunities, as these industries converge on established goals and tactics integrated across the traditional interests of the three fields. Specifically, PR was built upon the value of earned media placement in traditional news and other media, as well as cultivation of media relationships over time and reputation management. Advertising historically created a value proposition around control of message content and placement. Marketing identified the importance of the brand, demographic and psychographic targeting, and direct communication opportunities, such as through an email list. The MailChimp tool is one of the most popular "fremium" services, which allows free distribution for up to 2,000 targeted addresses, and paid for larger lists. Digital is a term that expresses how our measurement and management tools offer overlap between PR content, such as blogs, paid media post boosting and advertising, and branding targeted through social media influencers. Amazon, for example, rapidly dominated the struggling U.S. retail sector in recent years by leveraging user data, product reviews, and an emphasis on customer convenience.

Freberg (2019) frames a "performance and decision action audit" around an "inventory + benchmark audit," an "evaluation" of KPIs and brand "mission and business objectives," and "decision + action steps" that keep ROI and platform "health" in mind (p. 18). She distinguishes social media monitoring as "a systematic and sustainable" long-term process from real-time "monitoring and listening" (p. 97). Her strategic planning "components" include organizational mission and vision statements, environmental scans of social, political, technological, and economic factors, communication audits, budgeting, and social media calendar development (pp. 115–135). Likewise, Quesenberry (2019) uses marketing techniques to establish a calendar, metrics, and budget. The calendar establishes "persona" and targeting within specific channels, a "theme," "assets," "tags/keywords," and content scheduling (p. 266). In this view, KPI's begin with platform data—Facebook and Instagram Insights, as well as Twitter, LinkedIn, and Pinterest Analytics. Instagram Story Insights, for example, measure "story impressions, reach, replies, and exits" (p. 270). A "social media metrics template," then, should identify specific social media channels and objectives, measuring each with a KPI (p. 271).

The integration of numerous digital skills is central to understanding why ambitious employers now ask so much of their interns and future employees. Valmont (2018), a global leader in water irrigation management systems, hired a Social & Digital Marketing Intern and listed these "essential functions" that included a wide range of specific tactics:

- Schedule content across social channels

- Monitor comments, draft responses

- Assist copywriter with content creation

- Compile reporting and analysis of social platforms

- Assist with social media strategy and maintain editorial calendar for assigned divisions

- Recommend strategies to increase participation

- Assist dealer network with social media strategies

- Assign blog posts to writers and follow-up

- Put edited blog posts into layout

- Schedule blog for production on social media

- Perform website audits

- Update web page content

- Create marketing emails, using copy provided by Copywriter

- Schedule and implement email creative into HubSpot

- Flag articles/ads online and in print

- Participate in brainstorming sessions

- Assist with company meetings and events

- Digital marketing testing and QA

(para. 4)

Students must prepare by learning and applying traditional PR, advertising, and marketing skills. Typically, journalism and media communication undergraduates will be competing with marketing, business administration and even MBA graduate students. Employers want deep skills in writing, editing, content production, data science, and more general office functions.

STEP-BY-STEP

At the most fundamental level, we need to consider the value for an organization or community of building trust through transparency and social media engagement. A social media audit of existing conversation allows social media managers to consider stakeholder perception, competing social media, and the most important location for messages.

Owned media websites should be at the heart of social media strategy. An optimized landing page offers a social media manager continuous Google Analytics data and other insights about effectiveness in achieving short- and long-term goals. On Facebook, for example, a social media manager might start with determining the impact of number of monthly posts, as well as content elements that spark engagement. Social media community members expect response to comments and answers to questions in near real time. If a community is attacked by a troll or ongoing negativity, then it is the social media manager's responsibility to respond and then cultivate positivity for a brand. Comments and shares can be key metrics for benchmarking and tracking success over time.

A strong branding effort on Facebook can be boosted through paid posts that have organic success, and A/B testing of two forms of a message are an important way to determine future direction. Social media community members love contests or challenges, and a community manager can experiment to find sweet spots. Best practices include use of timely photographs and video keyed to holidays and other seasonal events that produce social media traffic spikes. We want to further amplify branded messages to extend reach. Positive Facebook reactions are one useful tool used to measure sentiment of community members. However, care should be used in evaluating sentiment. An angry face reaction, for example, may have multiple meanings. A community member may or may not be angry with a brand. It depends upon the object of the perceived anger.

On the other hand, thumbs-up likes and heart loves may be a rough measure of the intensity of support for a piece of social media content. An interest in sharing the content is a brand opportunity to extend reach to other communities. Key influencers may intersect between your core social network and an overlapping one. Over a six-month period, one approach would be for a social media manager to identify the top five Facebook posts in terms of reactions, shares, and comments.

Consider the example of a small, suburban community on the outskirts of a larger city. To spark local business, the town creates a series of weekend events designed to keep residents nearby and attract visitors. One such branded event could be supported with Facebook paid posts. The effort generates important metrics.

These data points also can be connected to SEO website analytics for the community, as well as individual businesses. Each store can track the effectiveness of this social media campaign against sales data during the period compared to previous events. Ideally, A/B testing of social media posts and refined event planning should result in lower costs per engagement over time, as we connect these data to increases in event attendance and resulting revenue. In this sense, social media expenses must be compared to other business expenses, such as traditional media advertising or marketing budgets.

TABLE 6.3 *Paid Facebook reach and engagement*

Facebook Budget	$150
Two Sponsored Posts	32,293 impressions
No. of Likes, Shares and Comments	281 engagements
Reach	5,356
Cost Per Engagement (CPE)	$0.18

If Google Analytics reveals that Facebook is a top source for driving visitors to website traffic, then paid and boosted social may prove ROI. If not, other social media and media channels need to be considered.

At a deeper level, a social media manager should consider the value of influencer marketing. Every community has influencers, and these should be leveraged via organic and paid methods. The Meltwater dashboard allows users to track social reach across media and social media channels. The NodeXL tool identifies influencers at the center of each social media topic. On Twitter, for example, new followers may generate profile views. These in turn can take new viewers to a link to a website. It is at this point that the social media manager again should review the website to make sure there are no dead links or other issues that would confuse visitors. Too often, a customer journey ends in frustration because the website has coding, content, or optimization problems. For example, if the website is not mobile-friendly, then it is about a decade out of step with current best practices. Likewise, a search window must have the functionality to answer visitor questions. State-of-the-art is use of artificial intelligence, such as chat-bots that engage and assist a visitor. This keeps the newcomer on the page longer, as machine-learning guides her or him through a customer journey on the marketing funnel. For management to be effective and efficient, best practices include use of a social media calendar. Begin it with a spreadsheet that includes content organization:

Month	Date	Topic	Content Post	Photos	Links	Hashtags	Target

As a social media campaign develops, we can add KPI metrics for each site. For example, LinkedIn increasingly is being used to brand and leverage social media influence through posts and articles. As with other sites, posts may receive likes, comments and shares. On LinkedIn, a post also may be saved, which is an indicator of deeper engagement. Individual influencers, such as a CEO, may track LinkedIn profile views, number of searches, and information about who by occupation is searching and viewing. Over time, a LinkedIn influencer should be growing followers and views of original articles that promote a brand and its events. Articles also offer data about number of views, likes, comments and shares. As LinkedIn grows as an established social media content platform, articles with hot links have a great opportunity to drive website traffic and campaign ROI. It is likely that a growing social media program across platforms will need more than an Excel spreadsheet. Hootsuite is one popular paid social media management system that continues to innovate the process.

While a lot of brands spent a majority of resources on developing Facebook, it is likely that current efforts are shifting to LinkedIn and Instagram, as well as other fast-growing platforms. Instagram, for example, allows a brand to focus on showing its products or services. Top Instagram influencers have millions of followers. That said, it is worth recognizing that the pressure to compete within the influencer comes with potential dangers. Gritters (2018) highlights the psychological impact upon some young women. In the words of one influencer: "I felt a certain pressure to brand myself, and there was so much anxiety in that" (para. 2). She is not alone. Academic research has documented the connection between excessive social media use and depression—including negative social comparison with ideal body types (Lup, et al., 2015). Frequency of Instagram use was associated with percent of strangers followed, a social comparison score, and depressive symptoms. Research results "supported moderated mediation, with strangers followed significantly moderating the indirect association of Instagram use with depressive symptoms through social comparison" (p. 250). The clearest finding was that "more frequent Instagram use has a marginally significant direct association with greater depressive symptoms" (p. 250). The implication for social media influencers and managers is that they must "anticipate, understand, and maintain greater control over the consequences of social networking for their well-being" (p. 251). As Gritters (2018) noted, the Instagram influence business now generates billions of dollars (Mediakix, 2017). Beyond Instagram, YouTube is also a social media platform that thrives on influencer persona and potential negative aspects of excessive monetization, but it contributes to social networking through digital communication (Kurylo & Dumova, 2016). While YouTube engagement can be limited, some tight online communities are successful by posting comments, questions, and links that provide important details. For example, "do it yourself" (DIY) projects shown in set-by-step video frequently require special tools or other products sold online.

Likewise, YouTubers command significant influence. YouTube Studio offers post and channel analytics, such as monthly watch time and views. A YouTube video can been seen natively on the platform, but it also can be embedded into a LinkedIn article, a tweet, a Facebook post, a WordPress blog, or other site. A top YouTube video offers important analytics: watch time in minutes, views, number of subscribers, and estimated revenue for monetized content. The data can be compared to a previous video or typical channel performance. The average duration of views in minutes and second can help determine if a video format is hitting or missing the mark.

Using social media within public relations, advertising, and marketing involves giving up a degree of control to online communities and audiences. The more PR goals and tactics align with community member needs, the more likely it is that a campaign will be effective over time. Proactive strategy, content, and distribution are essential to increasing the likelihood for success. Some large agencies charge clients about half of fees for the value of strategy creation and maintenance. The other half involves the cost of creating and distributing engaging content across social media channels. The key is to create and maintain an important presence on key social media channels. For example, a brand targeting teens and young adults may decide it is worth spending on

Snapchat to develop user filters that help them create branded content that is fun and engaging.

Still, a social media manager must always be listening for opportunities to answer questions, share needed information and cultivate a brand fan and potential influencer. Obviously, best practices suggest that a brand should try to remain positive in social media content and responses. A larger sense of community makes it easier to exhibit compassion within a brand voice. These are key points of context, as a brand builds trust through engagement over time. This, in turn, creates a foundation for addressing any future crisis communication that may play out on social media and other channels. Daily monitoring, interaction and engagement, data evaluation, and community collaboration help a social media manager to not be alone during difficult times. In fact, a social media community may transform itself into a support network during times of crisis. Of course, proactive tactical planning is always a good idea. We develop the best response ideas outside the heat of the moment—ones that take into account online and offline community context. It is in this space that a social media manager may thoughtfully address the nature of community engagement within each social media platform, as well as value of photographs, images, memes, video, and other reach media.

The most effective social media planning happens when coordinated with larger PR, advertising, and marketing goals and tactics. The blending of traditionally separate functions is creating a complex convergence of perspectives and approaches. Traditional PR media relations has transformed through social media planning, execution, and evaluation.

MEASURABLE OUTCOMES AND MONITORING

The social media measurement field may be connected to the older **Integrated Marketing Communication (IMC)** field of research and practice through PR influence and structure (Smith & Place, 2013). We understand the importance of integrating available tools in the targeting of audiences. Traditionally, marketing has emphasized the value of promoting branded products and services through a set of situational goals and objectives, strategies and tactics. One of the challenges is to integrate big data across the various functions of an organization. For example, if ROI is partially judged by leads, conversion, and sales, then finance department data will need to be connected to social media spending. An IMC model urges vertical and horizontal integration within a business, but also between an organization and others. Large PR, advertising, and marketing agencies attempt to serve client needs, but tools and data create a complex IMC landscape that will only become more complex with the diffusion of AI machine learning. IMC may use traditional media, online, and social networks: "Each approach may be slightly different for the specific medium. But they'll all direct the audience to the same message" (Lake, 2018, para. 1):

> Integrated marketing strategies help pull all of a brand's message points together into one cohesive whole to ensure that the message is not disjointed and confusing. Especially today, when customers are bombarded right and left with news and information of every ilk, integrated marketing relays one clear message, regardless of the channel.
>
> (para. 11)

IMC involves target marketing based upon purposes, internal and external organizational structure, and relationship to overall strategic planning, mission, and vision statements.

SWOT ANALYSIS

The social media planning process often begins with a popular business analysis framework. Social media managers need to spend time critically examining the competitive landscape before applying the results of website and social media auditing. A SWOT analysis can be used as an overarching framework for social media management, as well as a check on various aspects of a particular campaign. For example, a campus social media lab may use a SWOT analysis to inform an upcoming campaign to raise awareness, increase engagement and drive positive outcomes.

Strengths: Assets, Competitive Advantages, and Processes

The example campus social media lab may identify faculty knowledge assets in the area of social media. As early adopters of popular social media platforms, there may be a competitive advantage in teaching smart, enthusiastic students about social media measurement and management through the learning and use of new data tools.

Weaknesses: Assets, Competitive Disadvantages, Gaps, and Processes

The same campus lab, however, may be limited in funding to purchase and use paid tools. This would result in knowledge gaps in comparison to other, well-funded labs. Without state-of-the-art paid tools access, lab faculty, staff and students may not produce the strongest possible client or community work and published research.

Opportunities: Innovation, Entrepreneurship, Growth, and Markets

In this example, the lab may use available free or low-cost tools to demonstrate ROI to campus leadership in a position to assist with funding. An entrepreneurial mind-set would lead the team to develop social media management and measurement projects that raise awareness about the opportunities to harness social media management tools in campaigns that raise awareness about the lab and its stakeholders. Increased engagement may offer opportunities for fundraising, grants, or creation of sustainable endowments.

Threats: Competitors

Social media obliterated traditional media gatekeeping models and opened the door to anyone or any organization effectively becoming their own media organization. While this opens the door to direct communication by lowering the barriers to entry, it also means that our example lab is in competition with a lot of other knowledgeable academics and social media professionals. Development of a social media campaign, then, must take into account the noisy reality of Facebook, Instagram, Twitter, Snapchat, YouTube, LinkedIn, and other clutter. Objectives must take into account the SWOT analysis results in development of realistic and measurable objectives.

SMART OBJECTIVES

We need to take audits and analyses and develop realistic and measurable objectives. The popular SMART objectives model offers a framework for examining a campus radio station social media footprint. This in-depth case study uses real data from the University of Nebraska at Omaha MavRadio.fm (@MavRadioUNO) owned website and radio station, earned media, paid media promotion, and shared social media.

Specific

MavRadio.fm is a streaming college radio station focused on music and campus sports programming. A visit to the owned website reflects a desire to increase listener. The "LISTEN LIVE!" button is prominently found in the upper-right-hand corner. A KPI is the number of listeners at any given time. Most listeners find the content through the website or its Tunein.com channel, which is second on this list. Social media have been used to raise awareness about the station, its personalities, and radio programming.

Measurable

Initial measurement begins with website Google Analytics. During the first week of December 2018, for example, the website had 142 users in 171 session. Average time on site was less than two minutes with a very high bounce rate of 74.85 percent, which increased 5.9 percent from the previous week. These data can be used to benchmark what is measurable over time. A lack of current active users suggests that a plan needs to be formulated to address this through creation of more current and engaging website content. Once created, the content can be shared across the station's social media accounts at Facebook, Instagram, and Twitter. Google Analytics data show that current traffic comes from all four major sources—referral (39.86%), direct (28.67%), organic search (16.78%), and social media (14.69%). Clearly, there are measurable opportunities to optimize website SEO and social media that drive traffic. Facebook is the seventh largest source of traffic, and the other social media channels do not appear among the top ten.

Most listeners are from within the United States, but growth also is seen from Brazil and Norway. The station had a relatively large desktop audience (57.3%), followed by mobile (41.5%) and tablets (4.9%). Measurement suggests an opportunity to develop a campaign that would grow mobile audiences to the website and Tunin app. A growing number of visits (18 in the week under study) landed on the podcasts page. Again, the station has an opportunity to grow a listener fan base through creation and promotion of podcasts. Data also show that site user retention is a problem, again indicating a lack of timely and fresh content that brings fans back. In terms of demographics, the largest target markets are 25 to 34 and 18- to 24-year-olds. There is an opportunity to grow the student audience as the station's main target. The website audience is 54.15 percent male, and sports occupy two of the top three interest areas. The psychographic data also indicate a strong interest in computers and technology, but the station lacks programming in this area. Surprisingly, slightly less than half of the audience (49.3%) visited from inside the United States, and this is another potential target for audience growth.

Achievable

Social media accounted for only 23 website sessions during the week under study. Thirteen (56.52%) of the social media visitors came from Facebook and 10 (43.48%) from Twitter. There are opportunities here to set goals and develop conversions to loyal listeners. It would be achievable to grow social media visitors to the site at the same rate of overall site visits. All but three of the social media visitors to the website left and bounced after landing on the home page, and the three taking a second step all came from a Facebook post.

Realistic

The website data suggest setting realistic grow goals by taking a deeper look at Facebook Insights. The UNO MavRadio – KVNO 90.7 HD2 page had 26 views during the week under study. Post reach was 494 (down 12%) despite 28 video views (up 180%). There were five new page likes, 126 post engagements, and a 60 percent response rate within an average of one hour, 17 minutes. The station developed a campaign around promoting its radio personalities. A recent paid post ran for seven days at a cost of $11. It reached 143 Facebook users resulting in six post engagements. The total spend was 83 cents to reach the highest percentage of 18- to 24-year-olds (50.3% male). Over time, these branding campaigns may help to grow younger and more female website visitors and radio station listeners.

Timed

The top Facebook post during the week was organic. It focused on the end of the university semester, stress, depression, and sleep. The post had a reach of 362, with engagement of 40. This included 12 likes, two loves, four shares and two comments about the station's bake sale. Four station personalities were shown with the bake sale goodies. The post originated at an associated academic unit, and this demonstrates the potential value of strategically time collaboration with others' social channels. There was no negative feedback, so the post achieved a positive branding goal. These are important seasonal data which could be collected, combined in an Excel spreadsheet and compared over the years.

Timed campaigns should utilize video about the radio personalities. Facebook Insights data revealed that the top two videos were about a personality winning a state broadcasting award, and a preview interview about the college volleyball team's successful season. During the week under study, though, only seven minutes of video were viewed (up 133%), and there were a whopping 28 three-second video views (up 180%). The Facebook data suggest the need for strategic and well-timed engaging media storytelling through video that quickly attracts and retains viewers. The station needs to use A/B testing of two different forms of an engaging story to determine which version should be boosted in the paid budget. Ongoing data analysis can integrate website and social media data.

REPORTING RESULTS

Regular reporting of outcomes is an essential function within the planning and execution process. While clients or the C-suite may ask a social media manager only for a quarterly, semi-annual, or annual report, individuals should plan to build daily or weekly infrastructure for monitoring and evaluating. The personal value of writing down a to-do list within a strategic framework provides a social media manager with an honest assessment of effectiveness in time to make important corrections before a report to higher management.

Social media managers should not be shy about demonstrating a value proposition within the work. We cannot assume that others will recognize our value within the larger organizational mission, vision, and plan. The focus must be on measuring objectives. The Alexa.com blog offers a free, downloadable reporting template. Alexa Marketing Director Kim Kosaka urges contextualizing the numbers, explaining the story behind marketing results, and direct connection to goals. "Clients want to see results that show you're advancing toward the foals you set," she wrote in her blog. Reporting should include assigned tasks, campaign goals, and stakeholder preferences. Outcome-based reporting must happen within the context of a budget. For social media managers, time spent measuring and managing must be considered a key expense. Higher management wants to know if there was ROI that can be shown through the data. A business, for example, typically seeks to generate leads, identify new customers, and convert their social media behavior to sales and company revenue.

Email metrics and Google Analytics remain the starting point for demonstrating digital media ROI. Beyond these data, a success story can be built upon SEO rank, and paid click metrics such as click-through rates. Email open rates and CTRs may be effectively used to drive traffic. Tools such as Mailchimp offer free and paid dashboards to track success. Once these are established, a social media manager may provide context to social media measures, such as mentions or comments. Ideally, an integrated plan has all of these working in the same direction and toward common goals. Honest evaluation and reporting address failure and learns from it. An entrepreneurial mindset leads social media managers to embrace failure and not hide it. When an organization recognizes what it does not do well, leaders can strategically decide on priorities. While social media managers embrace strategic planning, they should not ignore opportunities to take advantage of unplanned trends, social media mentions, and engagement. These also are opportunities to use innovation and pivot toward more successful goals. The faster that a social media manager and her organization recognize failure and change plans, the more likely that measurable ROI happens.

t📡 Thought Leader Amanda Bright

Why You Should Stop Worrying about Disparate Audiences and Focus on the Universal Gap

We throw a bevy of social media posts and products into the world each day, and although we have metrics to gauge the effectiveness of content (including demographic analytics), the precise nature of the audience is often elusive. This is especially true when an organization's social audience is diverse or, more precisely, when subgroups within that audience are disparate. For three different, small organizations I've worked with on social media management, this has been the case. Although there was one primary audience for

FIGURE 6.2 *Amanda Bright (@ amandacbright). Photograph courtesy University of Georgia.*

each social media strategy, that audience was not the most engaged or communicative, or even the largest by metrics. Content may have been targeted toward one conceptual demographic, but it was seemingly several auxiliary subgroups who spent the most time or consumed the most content.

Dealing with Audience Disparity

For the Illinois Journalism Education Association, we meant to target scholastic journalism advisers in our state, but often it was student journalists, school administrators, parents, and even professional and academic media stakeholders who engaged with us on Facebook or Twitter.

For Indiana State Online's social media presence, a stated goal was outreach to current and prospective online students, but on-campus students (taking perhaps one online course), online professors, and distance learning professionals seemed more interested and active on our social accounts such as LinkedIn or Instagram.

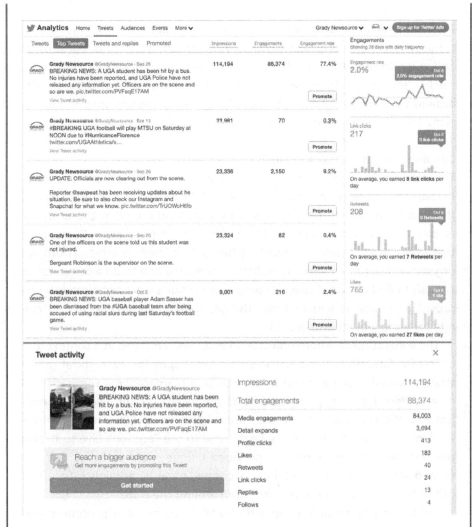

FIGURE 6.3 *Twitter Analytics data. Image courtesy Amanda Bright.*

For Grady Newsource, a capstone course that is a working newsroom meant to serve the communities of northeast Georgia, UGA students, alumni, and other journalism academics are the most common voices and eyes, not to mention the personal connections of the student journalists themselves.

Given this reality: Do we alter our strategy to capture better metrics for those who we are supposed to be serving? Or do we change our mission and vision to orient toward those who we engage with organically? Then, the larger question: How many masters can we serve? Each of these smaller organizations do not want to forsake the audience already built, but at the same time it is important to fulfill purposes and plans, too.

Building Bridges with Commonality
The solution in each of the three organizations' social media strategies became the intersection of the universal and the gap. First, we had to locate, through focus groups, feedback, and experimentation, what the universal or common interest(s) between the audience subgroups were. Sometimes, these were broad categories, but they had to be of high interest to both our organic and target audience members. Second, we had to do a comparative analysis to find out what specific content or products were not already being provided to these audiences. It was this gap that would provide an opportunity for engagement and growth.

The social content where universal interest was engaged in a context that otherwise lacked coverage became the sweet spot for each social media strategy, whether it was a state-level non-profit, an academic outreach tool or a student laboratory for local news reporting. For the Illinois Journalism Education Association, we went from between 20–50 views for a Facebook post to more than 1.2K, as we decided to use Facebook Live to stream our state awards ceremony. This provided unique video coverage but also tapped into the desire of advisers, students, parents, administrators, and others to see the best of journalism from around the state.

For Indiana State Online, an intentional focus on both procedure and strategy for positive online learning outcomes brought in our various subgroups without duplicating what other university social accounts were producing. This led to a 45 percent increase in Facebook likes, a 181 percent increase in Twitter followers, a 372 percent increase in Instagram favorites and a (rather astounding) 2,226 percent increase in LinkedIn connections over a one-year period.

For Grady Newsource, although we are only weeks into reflecting on our strategy, the analytics are bearing out that breaking local news is our crucial crossroads. Instagram's IGTV, Stories, and regular coverage of three break-ing events in a week took an average impression number from 450 to more than 9,600. On Twitter, 650–800 impressions is standard, but breaking news heralded 87K engagements, leading to 405 profile clicks, 14 replies, and four follows in a day. Therefore, the social strategy is pivoting toward filling the widening local news hole as a perceived gap, especially as all subgroups are responding positively to such coverage.

Pursuing the Universal Gap

There are still inroads to be made in order to craft daily content for these types of smaller organizations. The gender divide for all three tends to lean female (all at 65%+), and the age demographic falls a bit younger than the strategy would prefer (most playing best in the 18–24 range). However, for smaller organizations that do not want to compromise any existing audi-ence segment, but still grow and engage their intended audience, some reflection and analysis for this point of intersection is worthwhile. Instead of targeting subgroups separately, look for what content needs or wants that they have in common, as well as what is left up for grabs by the negative space of other social strategies.

Amanda Bright is an academic professional specializing in digital journal-ism at the Grady College of Journalism and Mass Communication at the University of Georgia. Formerly, Bright was a professional journalist, a scho-lastic journalism adviser, the education editor for MediaShift, a journalism instructor, and adviser at Eastern Illinois University and the media content coordinator for Indiana State University Online. She also served as the social media director and web administrator for the Illinois Journalism Education Association.

AS SEEN ON YOUTUBE

Assignment

Watch Chicago Public Square Publisher Charlie Meyerson (@Meyerson) explain the low cost of launching a local news website promoted through an email list and his social media accounts. The challenge is taking a project from a hobby to a profitable business model by scaling to a larger audience: www.youtube.com/watch?v=R9aO48qTK7Q

Questions

1. Identify a personal or professional interest area you have that may have entrepreneurial potential using Meyerson's model. Answer SWOT analysis questions: What are your strengths and weaknesses?

2. Assuming you would go forward with the project on a limited budget, which specific SMART goals would be key at the launch phase of the site and email list? How might these evolve, as your business grows and matures?

USEFUL TOOLS

Social Bond (social-bond.com) connects brands with social media influencers, and helps with campaign monitoring, measurement, and management (Bullock, 2018). Each influencer network is an audience described by their demographic and psychographic characteristics. For example, Social Bond blogged about 18 "famous beauty influencers" and their "must have" makeup. Some tools combine large databases of social media influencers, but context of influence is very important. The connection of influencers and advertisers typically happen through tool dashboards and face-to-face meetings, as relationships are built.

PROJECT IDEAS

Select a local nonprofit and study the social media footprint for this agency. Review all available social media accounts. Conduct a brief interview with the social media manager to determine if a SWOT analysis has ever been conducted: Are there indications that the organization has articulated SMART goals?

DISCUSSION QUESTIONS

1. How would behaving as an entrepreneur impact work as a social media manager in an existing business or nonprofit organization? Which organizational stakeholders may make this difficult? Why or why not?

2. How is the convergence of advertising, public relations, and marketing affecting the job responsibilities of social media managers? Are you optimistic about the future of the profession? Why or why not?

Social Media Data Law and Ethics

The widespread use of social media by journalists has triggered most news compa-nies and professional organizations to develop guidelines for best practices, either in their codes of ethics or in stand-alone social media policies.

—Daxton R. "Chip" Stewart (@MediaLawProf, 2017, pp. 224–225)

The maturing of social media includes a significant shift from a "Wild West" open space to one now dominated by concerns about law and ethics. From data privacy to jour-nalism norms, social media data carry with them important responsibilities. Emerg-ing themes within major social media policies emphasize transparency, friending and following "appearance of independence and neutrality," content review standards, sourcing, separation of personal and professional, maintenance of confidentiality, and intellectual property protection (Stewart, 2017, pp. 226–230). New technologies, such as social media, regularly challenge existing law and ethics. For example, decades of state public records laws exist to protect access to government records by news media and the public. The goal is to promote an informed electorate. However, messaging apps designed to disappear may be used by public officials to thwart public access to information (Foley, 2018):

> The proliferation of digital tools that make text and email messages vanish may be welcome to Americans seeking to guard their privacy. But open government advocates fear they are being misused by public officials to conduct business in secret and evade transparency laws.
>
> (para. 3)

Social media are paradoxical in that individuals value privacy at the same time as seeking very public forms of communication.

States have moved in different directions—some offering government employees legal privacy protection, while others demand use of official email and social media with government-issued computers and mobile devices. Two mobile apps, Confide and Signal, were designed to operate similarly to the original Snapchat by deleting all messages once read. In cases where public employees use the tools to skirt open records and open meetings laws, it can be argued that they are acting in defiance of existing law. Behind these issues are the complexities of data.

Social media campaigns happen within a regulated environment. Policies, law, and ethics provide social and legal boundaries for behavior within the planning and measurement process. At the same time, social media users frequently behave in an unethical manner. For example, #PlaneBae was a viral hashtag after a woman switched airplane seats and talked with a male model throughout the flight (Lorenz, 2018a, July 13). The woman later complained:

> Without my knowledge or consent, other passengers photographed me and recorded my conversation with a seatmate. They posted images and recording to social media, and speculated unfairly about my private conduct . . . Since then, my personal information has been widely distributed . . . I have been doxxed, shamed, insulted and harassed. Voyeurs have come looking for me online and in the real world.
>
> (paras. 4–6)

The case raises serious legal and ethical issues about privacy when the subject of social media content was not seeking any attention. At the same time, #PlaneBae continued as a meme that strangers used for selfies during airplane flights. Brands such as Alaska Airlines and T-Mobile also interjected real-time social media within the #PlaneBae hashtag. Clearly, big data were generated by the case, but laws and ethics attempt to establish boundaries. Recent case law suggests that the courts wrestle with a balance between First Amendment freedom and a right to data privacy.

Big data within ubiquitous mobile media have triggered legal privacy concerns and global calls for individual data protection. In cloud computing sites, such as DropBox, Google Drive, and Apple, the remote storage and sharing of personal and identifiable data present property ownership questions. Social media sites ask users to guard privacy at the same time as they monetize data for advertising and other purposes consistent with **terms of service (ToS) end-user agreements**. These contracts between sites and users offer little U.S. federal protection. The California Consumer Privacy Act of 2018 (AB-375) was approved to build upon a state constitutional amendment in 1972 that treats privacy as an "inalienable" right: "Fundamental to this right of privacy is the ability of individuals to control the use, including the sale, of their personal information" (Section 2).

> (a) A consumer shall have the right to request that a business that collects a consumer's personal information disclose to that consumer the categories and specific pieces of personal information the business has collected.

> (b) A business that collects a consumer's personal information shall, at or before the point of collection, inform consumers as to the categories of personal information to be collected and the purposes for which the categories of personal information shall be used. A business shall not collect additional categories of personal information or use personal information collected for additional purposes without providing the consumer

The language is model legislation that did not go quite as far as the General Data Protection Regulation (GDPR) in Europe. In *California v. TWC* (2019), the state claimed that The Weather Channel app, owned by IBM, continuously tracked and sold user location data. The lawsuit alleged that, "The permission prompt does *not* disclose that TWC will share geolocation data with third parties, nor that geolocation information will be used for advertising or other commercial purposes unrelated to weather or to the services the app provides" (p. 8, count 28). *The New York Times* reported that the app has 45 million active users, and that at least 75 companies harvested individual location data—in some cases up to 14,000 times per day (Valentino-DeVries & Singer 2019, paras. 2, 5). A city attorney was quoted: "If the price of getting a weather report is going to be the sacrifice of your most personal information about where you spend your time day and night, . . . you sure as heck ought to be told clearly in advance" (para. 6). The company claimed it disclosed the practice, but user agreements use complex legal language that users typically click without reading.

U.S. federal privacy legislation was under consideration in Congress, and most global social media sites have adopted GDPR as a standard in order to avoid international legal problems. International law is building these privacy rights upon the fundamental value of human dignity (Mills, 2015).

FIGURE 7.1 *Jon Mills (@UFLaw). Photograph by Jeremy Harris Lipschultz, courtesy Jon Mills.*

GDPR defines "personal data" as "any information relating to an identified or identifiable natural person . . . who can be identified, directly or indirectly, in particular by reference to an identifier." Following the Cambridge Analytica 2016 presidential election data breach and manipulation, Facebook was forced to re-examine its policies. Third-party apps had been granted broad and deep social network data. Facebook CEO Mark Zuckerberg told Congress in 2018 testimony that "it's now clear we didn't do enough to prevent these tools from being used for harm."

FEDERAL TRADE COMMISSION (FTC) REGULATION

The FTC has the legal responsibility for policing commercial fraud in the S.S., and the regulatory agency applies **administrative law** to warn bloggers to disclose financial interests when endorsing products or services. The FTC also reminded Instagram celebrities about disclosure rules. The agency found that the hashtags #ad, #sp, and #sponsored are not clear paid promotional disclosure of financial interests to followers and fans. In one letter, the FTC wrote: "if you are endorsing a brand and have a 'material connection' with the marketer (that is, a connection or relationship that might affect the weight or credibility that your followers give the endorsement), then your connection should be clearly and conspicuously disclosed, unless the connection is already clear from the context of the endorsement" (FTC, 2017). The FTC has the power to fine violators, require them to stop deceptive practices, and take corrective action for failure to deliver on promises.

Confessore and Kang (2018) investigated the lack of basic U.S. privacy law, and the failure of the FTC to provide adequate oversight of Facebook, Google, and other social media companies that collect vast amounts of personal data. Of particular concern is the merging of message data from Facebook Messenger and WhatsApp with user location, search, and site visit data that create a profile for targeted advertising purposes. The FTC has a relatively small staff that was cut decades ago over a television regulation dispute with Congress:

> Critics said a greater problem was cultural. The F.T.C. is haunted, for example, by a clash with Congress in the 1980s over an attempt by the agency to ban television ads for junk food directed at children, known as "KidVid." Lawmakers pulled funding and severely weakened the F.T.C.'s power to issue new regulations.
>
> (para. 18)

It remains to be seen, however, whether or not the U.S. will alter its media industry self-regulation emphasis. The U.S. is in conflict with European and other global approaches. While U.S. social media users have a lot of freedom, errors in judgment may spark litigation. At the same time, the U.S. Supreme Court has begun through recent cases to articulate First Amendment rights.

Uber and Lyft Passengers Were Secretly Live-Streamed

In St. Louis, Uber and Lyft passengers were apparently not told by their driver that he was live-streaming their ride chatter on Twitch. A 32-year-old told news reporters that he had $3,000 in camera equipment—earning $3,500 from live-streaming views, subscriptions, and donations. *The New York Times* reported that there were about 4,500 followers and 100 subscribers paying $5 per month to view the rides.

Jason Gargac claimed that he quit informing passengers because the video did not feel authentic. He appeared to monetize communication during the rides, much in the way reality television attracts viewers. However, Gargac allegedly failed to receive consent from his subjects to record or broadcast the content. Uber and Lyft quickly ended relationships with the driver after the news stories. Some riders who earlier complained apparently had received small ride credits. The *St. Louis Post-Dispatch* first reported that Gargac had used video on about 700 rides. The "creepy" ride video gave Twitch viewers the opportunity to comment, such as "She doesn't sit like a lady though" (Heffernan, 2018, para. 6).

Under Missouri law, consent is not required to record someone, but passengers could file invasion of privacy lawsuits. The legal question focuses on the expectation of privacy during a paid ride. Interestingly, though, Gargac had eventually posted on a passenger widow notice that they were giving consent by entering the Chevrolet Silverado, which had recording devices. A four-inch sign, though, did not mention Twitch live-streaming, according to the *Post-Dispatch* story: "Notice: For security this vehicle is equipped with audio and visual recording devices. Consent given by entering vehicle." The *Post-Dispatch* reported that the newspaper has watched the Twitch channel before conducting interviews.

Clearly, Gargac was operating as a digital entrepreneur. However, his action may have legal consequences. Beyond the law, one can make the case that his behavior was unethical by failing to be fully transparent and disclose all of his financial interests. If Uber and Lyft were aware of the broadcasts, then the companies could face liability. Gargac's defense is that the cameras were primarily for his safety, and the monetized broadcasts were secondary to his purpose. Still, most passengers were unaware that people online were making sexual and other comments about them, and even able to learn the location of their homes.

Sources: Heffernan, E. (2018, July 20). St. Louis Uber Driver Has Put Video of Hundreds of Passengers Online. Most Have No Idea. www.stltoday.com/news/local/metro/st-louis-uber-driver-has-put-video-of-hundreds-of/article_9060fd2f-f683-5321–8c67-ebba5559c753.html

Zaveri, M. (2018, July 22). St. Louis Uber and Lyft Driver Secretly Live-Streamed Passengers, Report Says. *The New York Times*. www.nytimes.com/2018/07/22/technology/uber-lyft-driver-live-stream-passengers-nyt.html

The rapid and ubiquitous adoption of mobile smartphones created opportunities for technology companies because the computers in our pockets also are tracking devices. The continuous stream of location data offers marketers what they long desired: a way to target consumers at the right time and place. An Associated Press investigation in 2018 found that Google tracked movements—even when users had opted out in privacy settings (Nakashima, 2018). While Google told its users, they could turn off location history, this was found to be an issue: "That isn't true. Even with Location History paused, some Google apps automatically store time-stamped location data without asking" (para. 7). The linkage of Google searches to location is valuable to marketers, as well as police investigating crimes. The fact that U.S. law and policy lags far behind technological innovation suggests that individual privacy is not being protected by entrepreneurs monetizing valuable personal data.

Digital Data Trails, Brand Insights, and Mobile Users

Phunware Data CEO Alan Knitowski

Consumers using branded mobile apps leave a digital trail, and this simple fact is changing business, advertising, and social experiences. Phunware Data CEO Alan Knitowski focused on the value of audience behavioral insights. The mobile software in 2018 "touched" more than 625 million devices through 5,000 applications. Phunware big data offered brands "more than 40 billion actionable insights" per month. Audiences can be targeted and engaged based upon data showing how and where consumers use apps, Knitowski says,

FIGURE 7.2 *Alan Knitowski (@alanknit). Photograph courtesy Phunware, Inc., NASDAQ: PHUN.*

"and being a horizontal slice through all of the vertical walled gardens—not

just Facebook and Twitter, but groups like Apple and Google and Microsoft, and others."

In an airport, shopping mall, sports stadium, or during a live event, the Phunware IDs translate into 650 million monthly active users. As we shift from the Internet Google and social media Facebook waves to a mobile wave, Knitowski says Phunware data will change the way the Internet of things develops through global business to consumer targeting at inside or outside venues. "You get into contextual awareness, you get into interests of what users like or don't like, what they want to be engaged with [and] what they don't, what brands they care about [and] which ones they don't," Knitowski says.

> *It's like having a global, real-time focus group indoors and out with contextual and location-aware applications that not only know all the things about what you're doing and who you are, but they dynamically can change the value that you present to a brand, depending upon where you are at.*

—Alan Knitowski

At Starbucks, for example, brand value depends upon how much a consumer buys, but his or her value changes when they are at the airport. Knitowski says that for most brands 20 percent of their audience represents 80 percent of revenue. Phunware wants to "enable brands in the virtual and physical world . . . to know who was there, what they were doing, what they liked, *and* what their value was to that brand." It's about "most appropriate engagement," Knitowski says.

What is less clear is how individual users will evolve to keep up with the mobile shift. Chad Hill, co-founder and CEO of digital marketer HubShout, found in a survey that adults do not realize they can be fired for what they post on social media. Many incorrectly claim First Amendment protection while working for a private business, he says. Drinking, drug use, and other inappropriate photographs may be problem content. "I think companies can decide that they're not going to hire based upon some of these comments or some of the things you're doing," Hill says, "people put a lot of information up on the Web, or up on Facebook that may come back to bite them down the road."

Imagine future privacy and professional implications when a user agrees to share her or his every move of mobile data in exchange for brand offers. The media literacy problem is even more daunting for high school and college students, Social Assurity CEO Alan Katzman says. Social Assurity teaches best practices for students that focus on effective use of LinkedIn, Twitter, Facebook, and other sites. The curriculum "emphasizes the value of networking, active community engagement and developing a unique and authentic personal narrative to best tell their own 'self-story'"—important in college admission decisions, scholarship awards and the job search.

"For most teens and most college students, their social media is an amplification of a very small sliver of their life," Katzman says. "What we want to do is . . . counter-balance that, not to tell them 'don't post the social part of your lives,' they should have fun with it." While students may begin to understand the value of personal branding, the next 12 months are likely to bring dramatic business access to their mobile data. "We're getting about 70 user event records per user, per month," Knitowski says. "This is just what you're naturally doing with what you engage and like, and we capture that information, always based upon what the user wants us to know."

It will take media literacy skills for users to make smart decisions about location sharing or participating in a brand loyalty program. Free Starbucks or airport Wi-Fi, for example, is traded for Phunware ID data tracking. "We get to know more about you," Knitowski says. Brands gain granular, targeted consumer data, which may increase sales conversions. In theory and practice, ever more personalized data filter media content, product and service offers, and loyalty perks. The rich, real-time data are "natural because we're not forcing anything, we're just letting people be who they are, use what they like," Knitowski says, "and they're walking around with a device in their pocket everywhere they go."

Phunware also is moving to convince media buyers to increase their share of budget spending on mobile data and reduce "imperfect" traditional advertising spending. Knitowski wants to "blow up the $100 billion media buying industry so that (the company) can be an alternative when people think about Google, Facebook, then there's Phunware." There is no disputing that the intersection of mobile apps, favorite brands, and frequent places will help define the future of social media business and data. Nobody forces users to download apps, agree to service terms, or share location and other personal data. However, it is likely that a significant slice of consumers do not stop to think about the long-term sharing of our most personal data within a network of global corporations.

Note: In late 2018, Stellar Acquisition III, Inc. announced in an Athens, Greece press release the merger with Phunware, a company valued at $301 million with a January 2019 initial public offering (IPO). One estimate suggested that location-targeted mobile ad revenue will be more than $18 billion. Stock prices for PHUN soared to $145, fell almost 50 percent in one day and then rose again. Phunware continues to use a four-phase model: 1) strategize mobile ecosystem, timeline, and budget; 2) create custom mobile app; 3) launch by targeting and acquiring high-value users; and 4) engage, monetize, and optimize in brand-appropriate ways. IBM partnered with Phunware as one of ten start-ups at the center of blockchain business networks, funding a new IBM Blockchain Accelerator program. Multiscreen as a Service (Maas) and Security Token Offering (STO) PhunCoin loyalty programs push incentives to consumers. IBM predicted that blockchain will create $3 trillion in economic value by 2030.

References

IBM (2019, January 21). Announcements: 10 Startups in the Next Wave of Enterprise Blockchain Business Networks. www.ibm.com/blogs/blockchain/2019/01/10-startups-in-the-next-wave-of-enterprise-blockchain-business-networks/

Lipschultz, J. H. (2017, May 22). Digital Data Trails, Brand Insights and Mobile Users. *Huffington Post*. hwww.huffingtonpost.com/entry/digital-data-trails-brand-insights-and-mobile-users_us_57f27bbbe4b095bd896a14c9

In *Carpenter v. United States* (2018), the U.S. Supreme Court considered Fourth Amendment data privacy in criminal law. Timothy Ivory Carpenter's mobile phone data placed him possibly nearby a series of robberies in 2011. During his trial, he sought to suppress the digital evidence because police did not have a warrant or prove to a judge that there was probable cause to collect the data. In particular, historical mobile data have the potential to present a summary of movement over time, and the Court found Fourth Amendment search and seizure privacy concerns. The law is designed to protect people. Chief Justice John Roberts, a conservative on the Court, was joined by its four liberal justices in a narrow split five to four decision that the police search of mobile data was illegal. In doing so, the majority found an "expectation of privacy in the record of his physical movement." The four dissenting justices found that such data are no different from access to conventional business records. Earlier, in *Ontario v. Quon* (2010), the Supreme Court supported a police department's monitoring of officer text messages when using city-issued equipment.

CASE LAW

Beginning in the late 1990s, the U.S. Supreme Court began to address Internet law. The foundational *Reno v. ACLU* (1997) case established online publishing First Amendment rights. The Court found unconstitutional portions of the Communications Decency Act, which was part of the Telecommunications Act of 1996 and found the language too vague. The Court rejected the idea of mandating zoning of adult "indecent" Internet content away from children. Later, in *Ashcroft v. ACLU* (2002), the Court voted eight to one to return the Child Online Protection Act of 1998 (COPA) to lower courts to reconsider application of the obscenity law in standing behind a 1973 legal test. By 2007, District Judge Lowell Reed found that software filters "are far more effective than COPA would be at protecting children from sexually explicit material," and he struck down the law as "not narrowly tailored to Congress' compelling interest."

In *Ashcroft v. Free Speech Coalition* (2002), the Court, by a six to three vote, rejected a ban on "virtual" child pornography, as defined in the Child Pornography Prevention Act of 1996, as violating the First Amendment. Later, in *United States v. American Library Association* (2003), a lower court decision was reversed. The Children's Internet Protection Act of 2000, which requires libraries supported by federal funds to install filtering software on computers, was found to be a constitutional and effective measure to block pornographic images that are deemed harmful to children.

Reno v. ACLU (1997) established a strong First Amendment Internet right, but the shift of communication to social media and social networking sites presents new issues.

Facebook users, for example, agree to a ToS agreement based upon their set of community standards. Most other sites and computer software also require user agreements. The U.S. Supreme Court ruled in *Packingham v. North Carolina* (2017) that a state statute making it a felony for registered sex offenders to use personal Web pages was unconstitutional. Packingham more than a decade earlier had been age 21 and convicted of having sex with a 13-year-old girl. He was listed as a registered sex offender. Eight years later, he posted on Facebook under the identity "J.R. Gerrard" about his joy at having a traffic ticket tossed out of court. In a sweeping First Amendment decision, the Supreme Court found that it "must exercise extreme caution before suggesting that the First Amendment provides scant protection for access to vast networks in that medium." The Court called social media "principal sources for knowing current events, checking ads for employment, speaking and listening in the modern public square, and otherwise exploring the vast realms of human thought and knowledge." As such, a state could not permanently bar someone from exercising online First Amendment speech rights. The legal principle of state action protects social media communication when a public forum can be established.

In *Elonis v. United States* (2015), the Supreme Court reversed Anthony Elonis' federal convictions in a case of Facebook threats against his ex-wife, former employer, and others. Elonis has used the pseudonym "Tone Dougie" on Facebook "to post self-styled rap lyrics containing graphically violent language and imagery concerning his wife, co-workers, a kindergarten class, and state and federal law enforcement." He used disclaimers that the posts were fictitious and an exercise of his First Amendment rights. The FBI began monitoring the posts and later charged Elonis under the federal statute with a "threat . . . to injure the person of another."

At trial, a judge rejected government proof of a "true threat," and instead instructed jurors that Elonis "could be found guilty if a reasonable person would foresee that his statements would be interpreted as a threat." Chief Justice John Roberts wrote the opinion that reversed the conviction. In a "Halloween Haunt" post of a photograph, Elonis had held a toy knife to a co-worker's neck with a caption that said, "I wish"—leading to his firing and a new post: "Y'all think it's too dark and foggy to secure your facility from a man as mad as me? . . . I'm still the main attraction. Whoever thought the Halloween Haunt could be so f***in' scary?" After the firing, Elonis adapted a sketch about killing the president and substituted his wife, explaining that while it is illegal to threaten to kill someone, it is not illegal to explain the law. "Did you know that it's illegal for me to say I want to kill my wife?" Elonis went on to ask about the protection order, "Is it thick enough to stop a bullet?" Among what he called rap lyrics were "Pull my knife, flick my wrist, and slit her throat . . . Leave her bleedin' from her jugular in the arms of her partner [laughter]." The Court, though, concluded from precedent that, "'the crucial element separating legal innocence from wrongful conduct' is the threatening nature of the communication . . . The mental state requirement must therefore apply to the fact that the communication contains a threat."

One of the earliest social media cases involved a mortuary science student who posted satire on Facebook about a body in a University of Minnesota lab (*Minnesota v. Tatro*, 2012). The school won the case because students agreed in writing to professional conduct policies. While the family of a dead person may not generally claim invasion of privacy, educators may require students to adhere to classroom rules.

The study of media law and policy is complex, but social media boundaries exist. While the Federal Communications Commission (FCC) exercised its regulatory authority to repeal network neutrality rules aimed at Internet service provider (ISP) fairness of data bandwidth use and pricing, the courts have raised concerns about the impact of data throttling. Self-regulation in the U.S. norm, as in the case of Facebook (2018) community standards aimed at deleting "hate speech" that "directly attacks people" (para. 7). As already noted, the First Amendment allows for some forms of speech that may be offensive to some individuals or groups. The mobile data environment is challenging because three regional bell operating companies (RBOCs)—AT&T, CenturyLink, and Verizon—exercise control of most of the business. While, mobile devices offer users instant access to information, they also are uniquely suited to track location over time. Such surveillance may be valuable to businesses and governments. Further, the use of smart televisions and other home devices, as well as Google YouTube searches and viewing, create individual and identifiable data records.

Social media users engage in communication that may have legal implications. In the area of libel, for example, the spread of false and defamatory content about individuals may result in litigation. Particularly with the subject of a social media story is a private individual, mere negligence may be the standard of proof to win a large judgment against a media defendant.

The use of **digital rights management** (**DRM**), such as watermarking content creator identities, has had limited effectiveness in stopping illegal file sharing over the years. For social media communication, music, photographs, and video are targets for theft of intellectual property (IP) rights. The Digital Millennium Copyright Act (DMCA) in some cases has led to large settlements for content owners. Social media managers must be careful to not infringe on others' rights, and also protect their own original content from theft. On the global front, however, it has been very difficult to protect U.S. copyright in other countries that do not value the concept.

European countries have advanced the idea of a **right to be forgotten** in Internet search. Google and other large players have negotiated rules for protecting individual privacy at the same time that the technologies need to remain useful, effective, and valuable. Similarly, hate speech and racism definitions vary around the world. The spread of revenge porn content on social media sites also is leading to new case law and concerns.

Likewise, the law has begun to address a right to require consent for someone to be photographed or videotaped in social media content. In some cases, commercial, government, and military personnel have utilized blocking technologies to stop creation and spread of live video during events, and this raises new First Amendment and other legal issues. In an era of big data, the scale of the legal issues has become enormous.

THE FUTURE OF GENERAL DATA PROTECTION REGULATION (GDPR)

Global social media publicly held companies, such as Facebook, must operate at an international level. It is expensive and difficult to create national limits or freedom from others' boundaries. When the EU established tighter social media data protection regulation, and the state of California followed, it became increasingly difficult to skirt international law. U.S. users benefited from data protection that called for personal user privacy. While this limited social media manager access to non-public data, it was an example of balancing interests under the GDPR framework. It always is dangerous to predict the future, but the trend appears to be toward safeguarding social media user data and limiting measurement and management to publicly available social media pages. This seems to be a fair balance between individual privacy and business needs. The tracking of individuals on Facebook, in Google searches, and even within messaging apps for targeted advertising purposes, however, appeared to be the battleground for U.S. regulators. The Federal Trade Commission (FTC), for example, had reached a data privacy agreement ("consent decree") with Facebook in 2011, but the social media giant may have violated the law (Singer, 2018, para. 4). Facebook Beacon in 2007 had broadcast user purchases to friends, and the Electronic Privacy Information Center pushed in 2009 for an investigation. The heart of the complaint was that Facebook had "shared users' personal details with advertisers even though the company had promised not to do so" (para. 11). A Facebook settlement with the FTC finalized in 2012 appeared to protect user data:

> The settlement requires Facebook to take several steps to make sure it lives up to its promises in the future, including by giving consumers clear and prominent notice and obtaining their express consent before sharing their information beyond their privacy settings, by maintaining a comprehensive privacy program to protect consumers' information, and by obtaining biennial privacy audits from an independent third party.
> (FTC, 2012, para. 2)

The FTC agreement with Facebook required semi-annual audits of third-party apps, which might abuse data protection rules. Cambridge Analytica, however, was one such company that appeared to get away with violating rules before and during the 2016 presidential election. Facebook has claimed it is transparent about data use, and the company rejected *The New York Times* investigative conclusion that Amazon, Microsoft Netflix, Spotify, and other online companies accessed and utilized personal data. Google search data suffers from similar issues when it is paired with other social media and purchasing data. When large corporations form partnerships around online user data, there are legal and ethical concerns. By one estimate, more than ten terabytes of big data flow each day on Facebook: "the techniques mist be available both to process these data and to use them for descriptive, prescriptive, and predictive analytics" (Lerbinger, 2019, p. 113). The field of corporate communication has been transformed by social media, and all of us face personal concerns about use.

MEDIA ETHICS

While law attempts to create enforced boundaries and limits on social media content, ethics introduces the more subjective and individual self-regulation based upon beliefs and values. Normative ethics ask us to act upon what is right or wrong based upon what should or ought to be done (Ward, 2019). Professional organizations often guide individuals through the development of codes of ethics.

PRSA Code of Ethics

The Public Relations Society of America (PRSA) has been at the forefront of urging members to work within an ethical framework. In their Code of Ethics preamble, PRSA speaks about "ethical responsibilities," including anticipation of "ethical challenges that may arise" (para. 1). PRSA members make a commitment to "serve the public good" (para. 2). While PRSA no longer attempts enforcement of ethics, a member may be expelled when convicted of a crime.

PRSA's Member Statement of Professional Values expresses "core values," and "the industry standard for the professional practice of public relations" that are "vital to the integrity of the profession as a whole" (para. 1). These include responsible "advocacy" (para. 2), "honesty" through "accuracy and truth" (para. 2), and "expertise" in "specialized knowledge and experience" (para. 3). When it comes to social media measurement and management, we may interpret this as addressing the need for SEO, social measurement, and marketing knowledge and skills. PRSA also calls for "independence" by providing "objective counsel" (para. 4), a balance between "loyalty" to clients or stakeholders and an "obligation to serve the public interest" (para. 5), and a general sense of "fairness" in work: "We deal fairly with clients, employers, competitors, peers, vendors, the media, and the general public . . . [and] . . . respect all opinions and support the right of free expression" (para. 6).

The PRSA Code of Provisions of Conduct values a "free flow of information" as a "core principle" in "contributing to informed decision making in a democratic society" (para. 1). The guidelines are intended to emphasize integrity within all professional relationships—including "the process of communication," correction of errors, and limiting conflicts of interest "when giving or receiving gifts by ensuring that gifts are nominal, legal, and infrequent" (para. 2). By allowing for exchange of some gifts, PRSA is less rigorous than journalism ethics that generally require complete independence and no perks. PRSA also promotes "healthy and fair competition," while preserving "an ethical climate" and "fostering a robust business environment" (para. 4). The principles also value respect, trust, responsibility, disclosure of financial interests, and avoidance of deception. By urging disclosure of sponsorship arrangements, PRSA aligns with FTC guidelines. At the same time, PRSA recognizes that client privacy, confidentiality, and trust are important. This can sometimes place PR practitioners in a difficult ethical situation. For social media managers, transparency and disclosure of interests should be core values because conflicts of interest tend to extend to public perception of conflicts of interest. Incoming PRSA members take a pledge:

I pledge:

To conduct myself professionally, with truth, accuracy, fairness, and responsibility to the public; To improve my individual competence and advance the knowledge and proficiency of the profession through continuing research and education; And to adhere to the articles of the Member Code of Ethics 2000 for the practice of public relations as adopted by the governing Assembly of the Public Relations Society of America.

I understand and accept that there is a consequence for misconduct, up to and including membership revocation.

And, I understand that those who have been or are sanctioned by a government agency or convicted in a court of law of an action that fails to comply with the Code may be barred from membership or expelled from the Society.

_____

Signature

_____

Date

www.prsa.org/ethics/code-of-ethics/ethics-pledge/

PRSA's decision to emphasize best practices over sanctions has been somewhat controversial, as the organization prefers education over enforcement. For example, the MyPRSA site Code of Conduct articulates a set of Community Rules & Etiquette and Privacy Guidelines. As an open forum online community, rule violators receive warnings prior to 90-day suspensions and revocation of membership. The online rules specify that members may not "attack others," but should "stimulate conversation not create contention" (para. 5).

Source: https://connect.prsa.org/codeofconduct

A RETURN TO TRANSPARENCY, INDEPENDENCE, AND AUTHENTICITY

Social media companies face continued scrutiny over their profiting from private user data. Entrepreneurial business models include targeting consumers through the use of app data that track location, movement, purchasing behavior, and indicators of intent. It is clear that Facebook and Google have lacked transparency in communication with users, as well as government regulators. The profit motive hinders independence because the desire to serve clients and partners may supersede mission statements claiming online community interests come first. Ward (2019) explored a shift in journalistic ethics from traditional norms to questions about "identity," "scope," "community engagement," and "global impact" on other issues (p. 5).

> Engagement is about goals. Objectivity is about means and methods. Objectivity is a means to certain goals, such as truthful interpretation of unbiased decisions. Objectivity is a method that requires interpreters to adopt a certain stance and honor rational norms of evaluation. Objectivity and engagement are compatible because they are different aspects of agency . . . The value of objectivity is that it helps us to be intelligently and fairly engaged.
>
> (p. 24)

Ward (2019) argues for "impartiality" over "neutrality" (p. 25). In this view, disruption through new technologies altered "a global public sphere" (p. 34), which has a need for individual, social and political "dignity" (p. 67). He adds "dignity of justice" as a way of emphasizing that we ought to live "among persons and institutions of ethical character" and reason (p. 67). Online communities should use "holistic ethics" that require rejection of "extremism" (p. 89). Instead, "a discipline of mind that distinguishes between reason and unreason" must be based upon "evidence" and "being informed" (p. 95). An ethical social media manager would benefit from a classical ethical distinction of reason over desire. From social media content creation to ROI analysis, impartial online community engagement focused on reasonable communication should lead us to reject extreme conclusions. Just as a social scientist respects the ongoing research process, a social media manager may constrain a conclusion by understanding the idea of limitation and the need for more study.

The first decade of social media business suggests a general lack of authenticity—technology companies tend to express online community ideals, yet funding and profit must be considered when evaluating any successful social media company, as it moves from start-up to mature business. At the same time that personal social media data should be private, a substantial chunk of our public-facing footprint is not only available for collection and analysis, it can be contextualized. Social network analysis (SNA) is a method that visualizes our individual posts on Twitter, and positions these within network graphs. Hidden data illuminated by network structure goes well beyond the current legal and ethical discussion about data privacy. SNA validates that social groups play an active role in content sharing and interpretation. This is an important larger context to understand that human digital behavior can be tracked and analyzed. No amount of regulation or professional ethics can take away a reasonable truth: the fundamental nature of digital data is that users can be tracked across the Internet, and social beings tend to cluster within networks. If individuals are to practice normative ethics, then they will need to cluster with others seeking reason over tyranny. This is no easy task because the data reveal polarized political engagement.

t📡 Thought Leader Marc A. Smith

Cultivating Creative Connections in a Networked World—#ThinkLink

We were among the first to discover the existence of polarized crowds on Twitter and have published descriptions of six common social network structures. You can learn more about this in our Pew Internet (2014) article.

NodeXL is a visualization tool built as a Microsoft Excel template to collect, organize and analyze social media "big data." It is a way to identify top social media influencers, as measured through their betweeness centrality. If you can make a pie chart, then you can make a network chart. I'm a sociologist interested in studying online crowds because these seem very important to me. In 2008 and 2016, crowds changed history. Crowds matter.

FIGURE 7.3 *Marc A. Smith (@marc_smith). Photograph courtesy Social Media Research Foundation.*

When crowds fill a public space, photo journalists rush to the scene to take pictures. Out NodeXL tool allows researchers all over the word to grab photos of cyber crowds. These structural images have been published in thousands of peer-reviewed research articles over the past decade.

It is annoying to me when news media report that something "went viral" on social media. That phrase does not help us understand the nature of the crowd behavior. NodeXL is a tool that provides us with information about the crowd, the words and hashtags they use, their links to other sites, and even sentiment.

So, the NodeXL tool is like a camera that snaps real-time pictures of crowds, but it also captions the photos with granular data about the conversation. My organization, the Social Media Research Foundation, has been giving away at cost these cyber cameras that build lines between people when they reply or mention one another. The structural features that emerge from our open source, open data, and open science algorithm document empirical evidence about clusters of accounts. The most frequently used words help us understand why the shape of the crowd is important.

We have applied to virtual crowds nearly one century of network theory knowledge and now have more than 50,000 maps available to search, view, and download at NodeXLGraphGallery.org.

From politics to marketing brands, the maps help tell a larger story about the development of social crowds on sites, such as Twitter and Facebook. We now study billions of social media users and can identify what I call "the mayor" of each network. This is the person at the center of a graph. Our ability to study through data search words over time means that we can observe change.

Online community connection is not a metaphor, or poetry. We see communities through their structures, which may be used to broadcast messages, support members, or do something else. We are interested in the people who serve as bridges within a cluster because people may be connected or isolated. Edges are the unit of analysis within the networked paradigm. Two entities may be connected by edges.

Social network analysis helps us assess the true nature of a social media crowd, but we face new limitations. Facebook has further limited researcher access to those pages managed by the user. While Twitter offers limited free access to about 18,000 tweets per search and 50,000 tweets per day, their cost of larger data collection is now beyond the reach of researchers. We can use NodeXL to aggregate slices of data over time, but this limits what we can see in large, rapidly developing online conversation.

Our two-dimensional NodeXL maps also are limited, and we have begun to develop three-dimensional images that show more context. We can see the shape of conversation through the six archetypes of network structures. You do not need to be a computer programmer to use NodeXL. It is a tool that employs scientific method to collect, organize, and analyze meaningful social media crowd data.

Marc A. Smith (Ph.D. in sociology from UCLA) is an entrepreneur and data scientist, and directs the Social Media Research Foundation and Connected Action. He has spoken around the world about NodeXL and social network analysis.

AS SEEN ON YOUTUBE

Assignment

Watch the interview with media ethicist Stephen J. A. Ward about the unprecedent media revolution: www.youtube.com/watch?v=6CaDPqOFIaE

Questions

1. How would you address toxic elements of the social media public sphere? Do you think there should be more regulation or less? What role should a free press play?

2. How would you strike a balance between individual data privacy and the needs of social media managers to collect and analyze relevant data?

USEFUL TOOLS

PRSA resources:

Study and discuss ethics case studies: see how colleagues handled issues in PRSA Ethics Case Studies (www.prsa.org/ethics/resources/ethics-case-studies/).

Watch an ethics webinar: "Ethical Public Relations: Everyday Expectations" (http://apps.prsa.org/learning/calendar/display/6776/Ethical_Public_Relations#.XCPp389KgWp).

Take an ethics quiz: ethics knowledge can be scored (www.proprofs.com/quiz-school/story.php?title=eq-prsa-ethics-quotient-quiz-2011).

Read about current ethical issues: blogs and news articles offer recent trends in social media practices and ethics (http://prsay.prsa.org/).

PROJECT IDEAS

Use your campus library Lexis or Westlaw account to search recent law review articles using the terms "social media" *and* "data" *and* "privacy." If you do not have access, try Google Advanced Search (www.google.com/advanced_search) to find a law review site or other relevant information. How are legal scholars developing innovative ideas about data privacy, big data, and GDPR?

DISCUSSION QUESTIONS

1. Search the end user terms of service and privacy agreement for your favorite social media site. How does this contract language benefit or limit you and the site? What should be done to make these agreements fairer?

2. Think about data privacy as an entrepreneur: What type of new social media site could be created to offer users data privacy rights? How could content ownership be managed in innovative ways?

Customer Relationships and Content

> *Thus, if you want to increase your share of voice, don't just give your customers something to talk about, give them SOMEBODY to talk about, too.*

—Jay Baer (@JayBaer, 2018 a, para. 10)

Not that long ago, marketers called social media content the "king" of the process. Now, however, content is seen as serving the deeper goal of building relationships. Social media communication "conversation listening," or "share of voice," appears to be a measure of user-generated content by business customers or other stakeholders (Baer, 2018a, para. 1). Businesses compete for happy customers expressing positive sentiment across their social channels and networks. Baer (2018a) urges that brands remain top-of-mind through repetitive customer engagement, help and delight customers, emphasize a person and face of the brand, and "recognize people for taking the time to create content about your company, whether that content is satisfaction-driven or dissatisfaction-driven" (para. 12).

Organizations need to cultivate relationships and loyalty. Businesses leverage brand loyalty, as we have seen in this book, because individual influencers can be much more effective than paid advertising. Similarly, nonprofits rely upon donors and volunteers to survive. Social media are managed to share content that sparks fresh engagement. Social media marketers have offered specific tactics for shifting from a model of content as broadcast to one that emphasizes authentic engagement:

1. Quickly respond to comments and messages.

2. Develop a personality that aligns with branded content.

3. Seek product and service feedback and reviews.

4. Relevant content and images should drive a **call to action (CTA)**.

5. Develop plans that activate fans and their content.

(Tay, 2018)

Organic social media content, most notably user-generated content, is a lifeblood for branded social media campaigns. Tay (2018) noted that Burger King's InstaWhopper tag, for example, sparked 34,675 coupons in just three hours (para. 49).

CUSTOMER RELATIONSHIPS, CONTENT, AND SERVICE

Businesses use social media measurement and digital analytics to cultivate great customer service models. A sense of fairness in business applies to leaders and followers, as they use social media, break down organizational silos, and improve business and corporate social responsibility (CSR) objectives. A customer focus requires that businesses or nonprofits examine stakeholder relationships and seek a common good.

Small Business and Nonprofit Social Media Marketing Strategy

Small organizations often have a large problem. Social media have become more important for branding, awareness, engagement, and business goals, but one community manager can only do so much. Obviously, there is an importance of strategy in setting clear goals through research data. Large companies examine big data, but also qualitative relationships. The focus is on content matched to a particular social media channel that engages a targeted audience.

Brand strategist Michael Brito (@Britopian) says "you can't just interrupt the conversation" within social media. Instead, Brito urges bringing value to each interaction:

- **Utility:** help customers solve a problem or achieve a goal.
- **Entertainment:** people like enjoyable experiences.
- **Exclusivity:** your organization has expertise.
- **Promotion:** offer coupons or help spread the word.

By starting with communication value, a small business can then decide what to do about its Facebook page and Twitter account. This should include at least a small budget for paid media. "The social networks, while free to create an account and leave comments, and post updates, you're not always going to reach the people you want to reach," Brito says.

The Facebook filtering algorithm will slow page growth and reach without paid promoted posts. Brito adds that a small business can re-target on Facebook through an advertisement aimed at people visiting their website. These strategies also work for nonprofit organizations.

> *I would say the ultimate goal for a nonprofit organization is donation, and being able to acquire new donors, or people donating and giving based upon what they care about. You can certainly track that. It's not hard to do.*

—*Michael Brito*

Unique promotion codes allow nonprofits to track donations made through specific media channels. Events, including Facebook events, also are opportunities to track donor behavior. Targeting and data tracking may be particularly important, if your small business or nonprofit is located in a small, rural community with limited resources.

Entrepreneur and BCom Solutions CEO Brent Comstock knows time is precious. He owned an Auburn, Nebraska company while studying again this fall at the University of North Carolina. Beginning at age 12, Comstock found his knowledge of computer technology was valuable to businesses in his community. Comstock says his small business must sell older companies on the idea of new technology solutions—different from competing with other digital firms in a large city. That takes creativity and a focus on what they do very well. "There has to be a constant source of learning," Comstock adds.

Social media marketing efforts are quickly shifting to mobile devices. Facebook and Twitter may help close the gap between urban and rural companies in the next five years, Comstock says. "I'm learning that it takes a lot of work to balance 500 different things."

"The starting point is the analytics and what that tells you, and the insights from the analytics that will help you define your brand, your narrative, and what you want to say [and] where you want to say it," Brito says. "It all starts with looking at what customers are saying, either about your company, your topic or your industry." Remember, you may be the social media manager also doing other work within a small business or nonprofit organization, but strive to ignite management team interest and curiosity by sharing outcomes and success stories. Organizations also may be able to get some help from a social media lab at a nearby university. As you learn more about data analytics and social media technologies, your small business or nonprofit will develop stronger plans for producing positive results.

Sources: Lipschultz, J. H. (2018, May). Michael Brito on Participation Marketing. SoundCloud. https://soundcloud.com/jeremy-lipschultz/michael-brito-on-participation-marketing

Lipschultz, J. H. (2015, August 26). Small Business and Non-profit Social Media Marketing Strategy. *Huffington Post*. www.huffingtonpost.com/entry/small-business-and-non-profit-social-media-marketing-strategy_b_8034612.html

CUSTOMER RELATIONS MANAGEMENT (CRM), C-SUITES, AND CORPORATE SOCIAL RESPONSIBILITY (CSR)

CSR has become popular among those practicing management in large firms interested in trust and loyalty (Asatryan & Asamoah, 2014; McWilliams & Siegel, 2001). This has led to some critical academic study of the promotion of commerce and consumption (Pompper, 2015, 2018). Corporate interests sometimes use social media engagement for PR purposes that may not reflect actual values and behavior. Employees may participate in CSR social media (CSR/SoMe) campaigns promoting, for example, sustainable environmental policies. PR and HR offices could play a role is a social media internal or external campaign (Bhattacharya, 2016). Strategic management through PR (Broom & Sha, 2013) has a focus on stakeholders and "collaborative decision making" within an organization (Heath & Coombs, 2006, p. 396). Social networks imply interpersonal social interaction, popularity, and isolation through network structure and linkages (Hansen, et al., 2011), clustering or grouping of online communities, and connections of "ties" or "edges" with others (Hansen, et al., 2011, p. 33). SNA has its roots in the personal influence, diffusion, and social change (Rogers, 1995). Organizations may be seen as a collection of productive and non-productive employees—either working within a small group or isolated. Social connection, then, is a form of prestigious relationships within an organization (Gao, 2017; Guo, et al., 2016).

Leaders frequently seek to promote organizational cohesion based upon messaging that externally connects with consumers or other stakeholders. Online brand advocacy by employees can be achieved across social networks through trustworthy electronic word-of-mouth (eWOM) information (Lu & Keng, 2014; Miller, 2013; Sandes & Urdan, 2013). Employee credibility with family, friends, and others on social media is a matter of using social capital (Johnston, et al., 2013). Ethical community engagement, such as was discussed in the previous chapter, reflects not only loyalty, but also satisfaction and trust "to improve customer identification and customer support" (Asatryan & Asamoah, 2014, p. 8). Global, cross-cultural social networks may consist of consumers evaluating corporate-laced eWOM and potentially learning new ideas (Brandtzaeg, 2012; Chu & Choi, 2011; Doh & Hwang, 2009; Sandes & Urdan, 2013). The diffusion of new ideas and practices, including corporate promotion of pro-social information through social media posts, reflects a need to continuously innovate to survive within a competitive environment. Entrepreneurs frequently discuss such a paradigm in explaining their need to use social media within branding efforts.

Customer reviews may be positive, neutral, or negative and potentially may hurt a business. For example, a bad Yelp review of a Long Island bar visited during a bachelorette party night out was followed by cyberbullying and harassment on a woman's Facebook page and wedding site. *The Daily Beast* reported that it began with this negative review:

> I would give zero stars but google doesn't let you, . . . The owner is very rude and nasty. I came here with a bachelorette party with 16 girls. The bar was completely empty aside from 2 people so we definitely were the only ones providing any type of revenue on a Friday night.

As designated driver, I was the most sober person at the bar at this point and did nothing except ask [the bartender] not to yell at our group, . . . If you want to get yelled at, drink crap drinks (they don't have seltzer for vodka sodas) and be in an empty bar, then definitely come here! If not, look elsewhere.

(Briquelet, 2018, paras. 17–18)

Apparently, one-star reviews may lead to business retaliation in the form of trolling and even sexual harassment. These unethical responses run counter to the social media engagement idea of responding to customer complaints through transparent communication that promotes new business growth.

Peter Shankman on Entrepreneurship

Imagine hard failure: "Like, oh my god, Earth open up and swallow my ass, it's going to be terrible." Peter Shankman says that he will not hire

FIGURE 8.1 *Peter Shankman (@petershankman). Photograph by Jeremy Harris Lipschultz, courtesy Peter Shankman.*

someone who has not failed, but they must learn important lessons from it, and "brand everything." Shankman's early AOL newsroom experience taught him "a very valuable lesson to get shit right because you only have one chance to not screw that up."

His *Faster than Normal* leading podcast focuses on the ADD/ADHD brain, and how to use it as "a gift, not a curse" in life: "Own that shit, that means you have a faster brain," Shankman says, "and that means your brain is better than normal." Shankman offers four simple rules: 1. transparency; 2. relevance; 3. brevity; 4 top of mind.

As a PR media relations expert, Shankman applauds the demise of the online publication Gawker, which had a file on him and published articles about his online career. "It didn't bother me," Shankman says, except that his mother read the gossip, which called him "an asshole." His career is a series of chances, and he encourages students to try their ideas.

> *If you're thinking about doing something, and you're worried about doing it, . . . ask yourself a simple question: Is what I'm about to do going to land me in jail? Is it going to cause an international incident? Or, am I going to be homeless? . . . The worst that happens is you fail, and you try again, and as long as you learn something from the failure, I don't consider it a failure. I will never hire anyone who has not failed. I want you guys to fail. I want you to fail so god damn hard that it blows your mind. You can't imagine. Trust me when I say this, if you continue down the entrepreneurial path, you have no clue right now, how hard you're going to fail . . . It's going to be awesome . . . because every time I've failed, and I've failed a ton, I learn so much.*

—Peter Shankman

Shankman's early business success involved selling t-shirts in Times Square. "I'm learning if I try to do that shit today, . . . some idiot with a camera on Instagram would take a picture and post it online in five seconds, and within 20 minutes 15 sites would be selling my idea."

"When you have an idea," Shankman adds, "you will work really, really hard at, you will get . . . the customer's advice to help you grow it, and you will brand the shit out of everything you do because if you can't get what you're building to come back to you—people need to associate the cool idea you have with the fact that you have it." Shankman also sold a public relations agency, as well as the **Help A Reporter Out (HARO)** media relations email list to Cision, apparently for about $10 million—or about ten times what he thought it was worth, he says. The value came from its 97 percent open rates, which were very attractive to advertisers. That start-up began as a 1,500 member Facebook group grown in four days, and then transferred to a site built in about one hour. HARO continues to publish daily media email queries from reporters looking for experts to interview and quote in news stories.

Part of Shankman's success is that he quickly responds to all email. In fact, his response time to my recent "thank you" note was about two minutes. "You are entering the entrepreneurial world," Shankman told students, "at a time where the bar for the customer experience has never been lower." At the same time, entrepreneurs fail in a "screw-up" or hire someone who does, Shankman says, "because someone who has a big following, you pissed them off. It's gonna happen. This is life." It might lead to a tweet storm on Twitter. "What do you do?" Shankman asks and then answers by saying, "Get in front of it."

"Transparency simply means owning your mistakes," Shankman says. On Twitter, people "don't need a fix . . . they need . . . a response—they need to feel heard," he adds. "When you own your mistake, you turn a hater into a lover, and . . . that lover is going to take the next bullet that's coming for your heart."

Entrepreneurs must take risks, but they also need to take care of themselves. Shankman rises early each day to exercise, eat healthily, avoid drinking, and offer his brand of advice. There is a value proposition in the art of listening, responding, and using communication to grow a business one branded moment at a time.

Source: Lipschultz, J. H. (2018, April 9). Peter Shankman on Entrepreneurship. *LinkedIn* article. www.linkedin.com/pulse/peter-shankman-entrepreneurship-jeremy-harris-lipschultz/

MEDIA STORYTELLING, CONTENT SHARING BLOGS, AND MICROBLOGS

The basics of media storytelling are fundamental to the sharing of social media content within a specific campaign. Branded content creation and promotion typically precede a social media managers' evaluation of data, but analytics also may inform future posts and PR. While traditional media relations involve pitching story ideas to journalists, social media storytelling often begins with organization thought leaders posting content on blogs or microblogs. In other words, entrepreneurial social media communication may be direct-to-audience engagement.

 Thought Leader Dana Dyksterhuis

Influencer Marketing and the Future of Social Media Entrepreneurs

There are many sides to influencer marketing, and it has been so exciting to watch it evolve. When it comes to using influencers to market your product or create buzz for your start-up, I am a huge believer in influencer marketing and began using it about ten years ago before it became massively popular. At that time, I was living in Seattle and just beginning my marketing and communications consulting business, BoastHouse.

FIGURE 8.2 *Dana Dyksterhuis (@DanaDyksterhuis). Photograph courtesy Dana Dyksterhuis.*

A friend of mine, who was an architectural designer, had a side business creating eco-chic, sustainable jewelry from recyclable materials they used in the architectural world. Not only was this cool, but the jewelry was beautiful! I found a fashion-focused social media influencer in Twitter, and we gave her free product, photo, and video shoots in exchange for promoting ThinkNOW jewelry on Twitter and Facebook. At that time, this was all it took for my friend and her eco-friendly jewelry to take off in Seattle, including nice sales and media coverage.

Since then, I also developed a successful influencer marketing program for my first start-up, Fanzo, in order to drive app downloads. It took some iterations; however, I ultimately scored big with Manchester United influencers who promoted our app like crazy, resulting in a CPI of sometimes 2 cents to 12 cents. During this time, entrepreneurs figured out that it was lucrative to build influencer marketing platforms, many of which have been hugely successful, such as Opendorse in Lincoln, Nebraska. As we move forward, a friend and peer of mine, Jessica Gioglio, also here in London on the Tech Nation Exceptional Talent Visa, pointed out that influencer marketing has evolved to the point that influencers are now creating and marketing their own products with great success. From fitness and beauty products, to cookbooks and even food brands, influencers are now generating money not just by being an influencer, but by becoming a much bigger brand.

As an entrepreneur, I would think about ways to tap into this truth and build something in the e-commerce space. Artificial intelligence (AI) also presents a big opportunity in influencer marketing. In the past when I've done campaigns, it's all been incredibly manual and tedious. However, AI can help marketers out now, by pinpointing the right incentives to offer, predict performance, find the most influential influencers, etc. Keep your eye out here!

AI start-ups are getting funded like crazy in all global markets. AI can help in social media by finding new clients, promoting the right brands, and identifying demographics (via SmartData Collective, April 2018). Just one example is Dataminr out of New York. "Datamin's clients are the first to know about high-impact events and critical breaking information, enabling them to act faster and stay one step ahead." Dataminr uses AI and has raised $577 million to date in a Series E according to Crunchbase.

Virtual reality is such a fun space and in the grand scheme of things, brands are still trying to figure out. However, there is a lot of buzz and a lot of potential for this tech. Emily Sappington, who is another UK Tech Nation Exceptional Talent Visa friend of mine here in London, talked about one of the latest social VR ideas creating some buzz, which is the idea of paying to attend lectures, conferences, and concerts in VR. "What does a networking event or conference booth look like in VR and how people use it?" There is not a lot in this space, but it is a space that entrepreneurs should explore.

Niche and Authenticity

In the early days of social media, it was quite normal to get as many followers as possible no matter who they were, and even use platforms to generate likes and followers in order to increase these numbers. These days, however, this is totally inauthentic, and many consumers are averse to it. When it comes to brand value, high-quality niche markets are an incredible opportunity. Look at Twitch and gamers as a huge success story for example. Here in London, there is also Peanut for mamas to meet and connect, funded by Felix Capital. MEIYOU (MEETYOU) in China, funded by Cathay Innovation, has a user base of more than 100 million Chinese women and helps them manage their health, cycles, and maternity. ChefSteps in Seattle (recipes and classes) is another niche success story, as is RealSelf (community of cosmetic surgery and beauty treatment reviews). I can't leave out WhatsApp. WhatsApp has become a tool not only for one-on-one communication, but also a place to create special interest groups for messaging and marketing. I believe niche, social communities will only continue to grow and evolve.

Social Good, "Tech for Good"

"Tech for Good" is really big here in London as organizations and institutions actively work to fund start-ups and implement initiatives that work to enhance wellbeing in the lives of community members. The Royal Foundation, for example, has two major initiatives in Mental Health and Early Years for families, where they are actively seeking to partner with organizations and start-ups to make a difference. Bethnal Green Ventures is a VC firm that exists to fund tech for good start-ups. Their portfolio includes start-ups such as Chatterbox, which is an online language learning service that trains and employs refugees as language tutors, GoodGym, which is a community of runners who combine regular exercise with helping our communities, and Pillar, which is a support network for happier healthier mums.

I have mentioned the UK Tech Nation Exceptional Talent Visa here for a reason. Tech Nation, along with the UK government, created this Visa a few years ago, in order to attract global tech talent, nurture start-up teams, and be a leader in innovation. I am a proud recipient of this Visa and it has changed my life in unbelievable ways. With that, the UK is not the only country actively working to recruit tech talent. Other hubs (cities and countries) include Berlin, Paris, Amsterdam, Singapore, Canada, Chile, Italy, Israel, Australia, and New Zealand, to name a few, all of which have efforts to recruit tech talent and start-ups. A 2018 report by Tech Nation also stated that jobs in digital tech are on the rise here in the UK, and workers in digital tech command higher salaries. If you are considering going down the path of social media entrepreneurship, I would encourage you to research opportunities on a global scale, as well as the Visas that could be available. It's a huge, incredible world out here with vast experiences and opportunities to make a difference.

Dana Dyksterhuis is co-founder of Here for You for Them, Founder of Boasthouse and Fanzo (www.linkedin.com/in/danadyksterhuis). She was creator and executive producer at Foodie Empire and has worked in media and media relations. She welcomes email at: dana@boasthouse.com.

Social media measurement and management entrepreneurship may involve leveraging the social networks of employees within an organization. This raises important questions about the tricky boundaries between public work and private life.

AS SEEN ON YOUTUBE

Assignment

Watch Edelman Digital President Jay Porter talk about the importance of employee engagement: www.youtube.com/watch?v=ofasyCTDwr8

Questions

1. How many employees and customers on a purchasing journey effectively collaborate in an ethical way? Why is satisfaction related to company and community culture?

2. What opportunities exist to innovate in the employee engagement space?

USEFUL TOOLS

Explore the Dynamic Signal employee engagement platform site (https://dynamic-signal.com/product/). This is an app designed for organizations with 5,000 or more employees. It is focused on internal and external communication opportunities for HR and PR offices.

PROJECT IDEAS

Visit a local store. Interview the store owner or manager, How is the physical location being impacted by social media engagement? What could the store owners and managers do to improve face-to-face and online customer experiences?

DISCUSSION QUESTIONS

1. What is an example of your best and worst online experience as a customer? How, if at all, were social media used as a tool in the interaction? How could social media measurement and management improve these experiences?

2. Are there times when you would prefer a bot responded to your question as a customer? Why or why not? How do you believe AI is changing your experience as a customer?

UNIT FOUR

Social Media Planning and Campaigns

Employee Engagement

> *This idea of the power of giving credit to others—as opposed to your own individual accomplishment—has shaped my entire career. Most people don't really think about that. They mostly think, "Look at me." But really if you say, "Look at what others are accomplishing," it's so much more powerful in terms of your ability to attract the best people, to get things done.*

—PayPal CEO Dan Schulman (@Dan_Schulman, via David Gelles, 2018, para. 9)

Employee engagement refers to the growing need to see all people within an organization as social media influencers who may help amplify important branded messages. Leaders must help set positive examples and support systematic social media management. From culture wars to office politics, social media can be an effective corporate tool for internal and external communication or a disaster in the making. Particularly for large and diverse organizations, CEOs and other top executives need new leadership tools to reach employees that may not behave in traditional ways yet bring value to business teams.

A starting point is to consider the degree of organizational acceptance of data literacy. Sterne (2018a) outlined a spectrum of organizational marketing data literacy—from "data denier" to "data forward" (para. 1):

- *Data Denier* reflect "stubborn" and "antagonistic" views about use of data.

- *Data Agnostic* people tend to be "disinterested."

- *Data Aware* may be "curious."

- *Data Literate* may aspire, but they also can be "careless" or "imprecise."

- *Data Capable* show evidence of proficiency.

- *Data Gifted* are "thoughtful" about uses.

- *Data Savvy* reflects thought leadership status.

- *Data Forward* employees may be on the "bleeding edge" of data science.

A true understanding about data science and error estimation is that research requires ongoing evaluation and revision of models based upon experimentation:

> This requires a willingness to fail in order to learn. The person who tries something and fails, but has no resulting data about the effort, has no opportunity to learn. The one who fails and learns from it is on the path of continuous improvement.
>
> (para. 6)

Much as we see with Rogers' (1995) diffusion of innovation during an adoption of change cycle, the goal is to move employees along with innovators and other early adopters. If a new practice catches on, then we see early and later majorities under the model. The process relies upon personal influence and social networks of persuasion. One example can be found in newspaper and radio news reporters who learned the value of Twitter and podcasting and adopted these methods in promoting their traditional journalism.

Unlike Long and Cameron, other veteran journalists across the U.S. rejecting change tended to be the first facing layoffs and unemployment. This is why all employees would be wise to embrace innovation and entrepreneurship. In the end, the diffusion model predicts there will be a group of laggards who will resist change. These are Sterne's data deniers—employees who want to rely upon old knowledge and methods.

If we dive deeper into organizational learning about data science and data-driven decisions, then we also can see that innovation and entrepreneurial thinking and action rely upon metrics, tools, and statistical knowledge with a complex set of practices.

FIGURE 9.1 *Chicago Tribune reporter Ray Long (@RayLong) on Connected to Chicago with Bill Cameron (@billjcameron) podcast. Photograph by Jeremy Harris Lipschultz, courtesy Ray Long, Chicago Tribune, and Bill Cameron, WLS-AM.*

These may begin with understanding and developing agreement within an organization on KPIs and measurement norms (Sterne, 2018b).

A campaign mindset helps organizations to be strategic. The historic planning models include: research, action, communication and evaluation (RACE); research, objectives, strategies and planning, implementation, and evaluation (ROSIE); and research, objectives, strategies, tactics, implementation, and reporting (ROSTIR), to name a few (Luttrell & Capizzo, 2019, pp. 10–11). Each model emphasizes the need for managers to adopt a research orientation, develop explicit goals and objectives, build measurable strategies and tactics, and follow continuous evaluation and improvement. It is recommended that social media managers develop a spreadsheet to track KPIs over time. Public relations, advertising, and marketing social media managers build strategy around the various content forms—paid, earned, shared, and owned (PESO) media (pp. 18–19. Paid advertising and owned websites tend to be seen as "controlled" media, while earned and shared social media are more aligned with "uncontrolled," yet sometimes "credible" content (p. 41). However, within employee social networks there are social media spaces to encourage credible and approved company content. One particularly effective area is corporate social responsibility (CSR) programs and practices. The key is to follow ethical management guidelines. "In this transparent age, any hypocrisy or perception of hypocrisy can seriously damage your CSR efforts" (Page & Parnell. 2019, p. 119). Social media branding efforts, for example, may be most effective when aligned with broader "community relations" programs (p. 231). Management through "organizational clarity" of goals should strengthen employee buy-in to these efforts (pp. 254–255). Much of what has been learned from modern PR models is centered upon identification of stakeholders and organizational values. Social media measurement and management plans must be consistent with leadership desires to guide priorities and outcomes.

The alignment of goals and objectives begins with hiring employees who share organizational values. For example, one GlassDoor.com search of "Senior Social Media Manager" produced a regional bank advertisement that began with a simple question: "Are you passionate about helping create amazing customer experiences?" The bank sought to welcome and retain its customers through the use of social media communication. This was defined as "customer strategies to onboard and increase engagement." The social media manager needed an interest in testing customer loyalty programs, creative engagement, collaboration in business goals, media storytelling skills, as well as building "a community of brand advocates." The company articulated important values—passion, nurturing relationships, project management, and "analytical skills to determine marketing effectiveness and ROI of customer efforts." Strategic thinking extended to the value of the internal team in order to "create a stronger brand." Organizational thought leadership happens within an organization through subject expertise, cross-functional working relationships (CFWR), and industry regulation compliance. Social media managers must have the general knowledge described in this book, as well as industry-specific knowledge and experience. For example, the banking and financial industry seek social media managers with the MBA degree, Salesforce software experience, and a complete set of marketing and communication skills.

ENGAGEMENT AND EMPLOYEE ADVOCACY

Smart social media managers understand that employees may be influencers and brand advocates. After all, for large numbers of employees, the workplace is most important outside the home. As *Advertising Age* noted, the industry wants content to make its way into consumer social media streams. The Dynamic Signal app has been a leader in guiding companies to leverage employee social networks. The goal is to track how social media communication value can be observed through specific results from employee content posts. The data suggest that company employees are trusted more than leaders as sources for information that customers want. At the same time, however, criticism has been expressed about harnessing employee social networks for reach. The argument is that when an employee shares approved social media content, she or he essentially transforms into a paid influencer and loses a degree of authentic and trusted social capital (Lin & Lu, 2011). It is important to limit the use of employees within a brand engagement strategy to sharing a limited amount of high-value content—emphasizing to employees that they should put their own spin on social media messages. This requires an obvious loss of control, but it also recognizes social media norms that favor individual opinions.

While the size of reach for social media content remains important, an emerging marketing perspective is that strategy should focus upon network structure and key influencers. A *Harvard Business Review* analysis suggests that a "handful of influencers" may "give the impression that everyone is talking about your brand." The so-called "majority illusion" may make "some ideas, behaviors, or attributes appear widespread." Not unlike what public opinion researchers have called "pluralistic ignorance," people may fall into a group because they incorrectly perceive it to be the majority. At the same time, we may become aware of key influencers within specific topics and contexts.

Social network analysis on platforms, such as Twitter, allow us to visualize the structural nature of influence. It is not always the case that the accounts with the most followers seem to wield the greatest influence. Likewise, the influencers may not be those who traditionally were atop an organizational chart.

Marketing strategist Jennifer Neely is right when she focuses on the context of big data, or "contextual intelligence," in the study of influencers and content. We can study local television newsrooms, as one example of organizations leveraging large numbers of employees on social media sites. Some TV news anchors are among the most influential, but this is not always the case. Even an entry-level employee may sometimes be among the most influential on a specific, salient community topic. The social network analysis methodology allows us to also track employee performance compared to competitors. Accounts also may appear on top lists of replied to and mentioned Twitter handles. These measures are likely much more important than which accounts are the top tweets—those tweeting often to the large numbers of followers. In short, noise does not equal social influence.

Consider a specific strategic goal of a TV station, such as driving traffic from social media to a website that is monetizing through advertisements. Tagging an official station Twitter account in a tweet would be much less important than including web story links to news, sports or weather pages. Likewise, hashtags may be used strategically or not. An official branded hashtag may be more central to social media strategy than use of a currently popular one. Twubs.com is a tool that allows for registration and promotion of branded hashtags.

If the goal is to expand the community, then engagement with a trending hashtag could produce a positive result. While it is tempting to focus on the size of message reach, the lesson of electronic word-of-mouth (eWOM) research is that meaningful engagement is more important. Each one of your employees has her or his personal network of trusted friends, peers, colleagues, and associates. When an employee is positive about your brand, those within the social network take notice. This raises some legal and ethical concerns. Organic employee social media conversation may be positive, but there are issues about forcing employees to post, offering incentives for leveraging their networks, and using sophisticated monitoring of social channels to evaluate performance. While a social media community manager is paid based upon job description, other employees have rights when not on the job. There is not much case law in this area, but we would expect future conflict between social media branding and employee autonomy and privacy within a personal social network. Influence is best thought of as earned, authentic, and transparent social media communication, and not yet another form of obscured paid messaging and marketing.

Effective Employee Mobile Communication

Employers at large organizations face internal communication challenges. Employees are frequent social media users, and they expect timely and accurate information at work: "All of them want to know what's going on," Dynamic Signal Chief Marketing Office (CMO) Joelle Kaufman says, "and employers want everybody to understand organizational priorities." Frequently a pressing challenge is "the cacophony of messages that come at people all day from so many sources," Kaufman says. More than two decades after email transformed the workplace with computer-mediated communication (CMC) employees often spend too much time sifting through the inbox. Mobile phone apps offer a more efficient path by targeting messages to the right people at the right time.

Dynamic Signal sells "the ability to measure who got it: Did they engage with it? Did it have the desired impact?" While external social media reach and impressions may be a company goal, "80 to 90 percent of what you need to communicate with your employees is not actually what you need or want them to share," she adds. Instead, leaders need effective ways to move a team in a strategic direction.

> *Those metrics really are about impact. It's not just that they saw it, but did they by segment—we're very big on segmentation—so, by segment, did they click on it? Read it? Did they engage with it?*

—Joelle Kaufman

Health, wellness and safety compliance are among key use cases. Some companies share short videos as, "snackable, so that the other person doesn't have to interrupt their day to do it," Kaufman says. "I'm hard pressed to find a circumstance where being able to communicate effectively with your employees isn't needed." This form of internal communication may work best when the goal is to clearly define employee roles within a set of organizational priorities. Ideally, clear vision allows teams to identify opportunities to collaborate. "That just catalyzes energy and can truly break down silos," Kaufman says. Dynamic Signal, though, is not a chat-room environment found within Slack, Facebook, Yammer, Microsoft Teams, or other collaboration tools. Rather, it can be used as a strategic internal communication option. Its model is based upon "authentic relationships," and "credible communication," Kaufman says. "It's just my instinct that people like to communicate with real people."

While AI chatbots and augmented reality (AR) continue to grow in popularity (Pavlik & Bridges, 2013), human communication knowledge and skills will continue to be important. Marketing AI, though, may help improve efficiency for people in search of simple information within noisy internal and external social media spaces. Data help identify target audiences for creative media storytelling within appropriate communication channels. The loss of effectiveness for email and company newsletters helped attract interest in the Dynamic Signal app, which offers an alternative for large organizations (500 to 400,000 employees) to track effectiveness of internal messages. "They're getting the data and measuring," Kaufman says. "They can actually show the value of what they're doing, and that is how they can unlock and are unlocking more resources for communicating."

As is the case with external media monitoring tools, data analytics help communication professionals make the argument to the C-suite for justifying staffing and budget. Active users, post views, reactions, comments, and other engagement data offer important insights into the value of content through employee engagement in 2018 and beyond.

Source: Lipschultz, J. H. (2017, December 30), Key 2018 Goal: Effective Employee Mobile Communication. *Huffington Post*. www.huffingtonpost.com/entry/key-2018-goal-effective-employee-mobile-communication_us_5a480037e4b0df0de8b06aae

Use of mobile apps for employee social media engagement is built upon the strategic need to push back against loss of trust. Business leaders are among authority figures suffering from a lack of public trust.

Employee Social Media Engagement May Help with Business Trust

In an age of declining public trust of authority, businesses are turning to their employees for sharing influence across social networks. Public relations effectiveness may be measured, but big data quickly produce complex results. "Everybody is in some way chasing that same holy grail of being able to attribute everything back to its source," Edelman Chicago President Jay Porter says. "So, certainly, brands are trying to do that, understanding all of the impacts along the customer journey."

The results from Edelman's global Trust Barometer may be related research about social media and news sources lacking credibility. Brand voice and customer loyalty are important in building social media trust. "It's theoretically easier to do with employees who are sort of a captive audience, but you're still faced with that same question," Porter says. The sources for trustworthy shared content, for example, may be:

- Employee "loyalty and advocacy"
- The chief executive officer (CEO)
- Transparent internal communication
- Company culture and a "bond with managers"
- Team collaboration

These "multiple inputs," Porter says, make it challenging to isolate factors driving behavior. Employee satisfaction can be studied through surveys or observed behavior in search of deeper relationships within the data. Millennial employees appear to be particularly interested in brand voice and impact when it comes to solving large social problems. The loss of trust in government offers businesses an opportunity to step up through authentic engagement. "There's a huge desire for action and advocacy around issues that consumers care about," Porter says. "So, I don't think it's optional, I mean the first, second and third requirements are just transparency."

> *I think it's all going to relate to culture, and those have to feel sort of on-brand of the internal brand to your employees. A Cisco shouldn't try to do something that's right for Starbucks and expect the same result.*

—Jay Porter

Porter says it is critical to gather employee engagement and satisfaction data and be as analytical with internal communication as with external PR: "I think we're going to see a lot of really exciting creativity around employee engagement and internal conversations, and some of the same firepower." The Edelman data showed some companies are better than competitors at building trust, but the largest predictor remains an industry sector. It appears that the public tends to make sweeping judgments about types of businesses.

"I think the good news is that beyond that transparency, consumers—and again, particularly Millennials and I would suspect Gen Z—come with this tremendous built-in filter for authenticity," Porter says. "If a brand is engaging on something in-authentically, they've sort of been trained to decode that kind of natively." If companies are guided by transparency, authenticity and stakeholder expectations, then Porter says, "it's going to be hard to be really off-base."

Trust may be considered the "meta construct" used to build successful internal and external communication programs. Porter adds that trust informs Edelman research and insights, the PR work done, and evaluation of effectiveness. In a sense, this is like an academic research program in which social science data feed new research questions.

Social marketers have developed *specific strategic planning frameworks* that begin with a scan of social media spaces, measure key performance indicators (KPIs), and generate results based upon long-term relationships. Communicators must be able to use critical thinking and the liberal arts as a foundation for responding to what Porter calls "this incredibly complex multi-stakeholder world" that includes social media. "Just because the campaign is about emojis, somewhere in there you're going to have to think strategically about what that's supposed to do."

Source: Lipschultz, J. H. (2017, October 8). Employee Social Media Engagement May Help Business Trust. *Huffington Post*. www.huffingtonpost.com/entry/employee-social-media-engagement-may-help-business_us_59da7f59 e4b0cf2548b3384e

PARTICIPATION MARKETING

While some companies are encouraging social media participation by employees, others have removed access. One of the arguments against leveraging employee social networks is that clients may be concerned about data privacy from an industry compliance perspective. Regulated industries, such as finance and health, tend to be the most concerned. Despite the potential increase in social media content reach, what one industry professional called a "force multiplier" employee effect, this frequently must be balanced against other organizational concerns. Consider what happens when a college campus confronts a crisis that plays out on social media sites. One option is to let the chips fall where they may. However, a smarter course of action is to use crisis PR and manage, as well as measure, social media conversation.

 Thought Leaders Donna Presnell, Betty Farmer, and Rylee Roquemore

Managing Social Media during the Death of a Leader—A Crisis Communications Case Study in Higher Education
The proliferation of social media has had a profound impact on how organizations manage communications during crises. Utilizing social media during a crisis is no longer a choice but an expectation; the only choice is how to

FIGURE 9.2 *Donna Presnell, Betty Farmer, and Rylee Roquemore (@WCU).*
Photograph by Ashley Evans, courtesy Western Carolina University.

do so (Jin, et al. 2011). Moreover, social media managers must be an integral part of the crisis communications team. Fink (2013) argues that the social media department or manager is one of the "most valuable assets in the heat of an acute crisis" (p. 91).

Patashnick (2016) surmised that managing social media on college campuses during crises is particularly challenging because of its generational divide, its speed, its viral nature, and the lack of human and technological resources to support this function. Campus communicators must be prepared to reach a wide range of publics, including faculty, staff, students, alumni, parents, boards/trustees, government and legislative officials, donors and media, among others, and to match the platform to the targeted audience. For example, students will more likely turn to Twitter or Instagram for information, whereas older adults (alumni, community members, etc.) will more likely engage on Facebook. Some audiences, such as students, expect the university to be communicating via social media, and will search for and use hashtags related to the crisis (Patashnick 2016). While communicating via social media during crises is essential, communicating through other channels is also necessary. After reviewing 200 empirical research studies on risk, crisis, and social media over a seven-year period, and spanning 40 countries, Rasmussen and Ihlen (2015) concluded that social media should be "used in tandem with traditional media" and that social media should not be regarded as a "panacea for problems of risk and crisis" (p. 12).

Indeed, the integration of social media with traditional channels and the ability of communicators representing public relations, public affairs, marketing, internal communications, and digital (and other units) to coordinate and collaborate messages during crises is one of the biggest stumbling blocks to effective crisis communications today. Consistency in messaging has long been one of the guiding principles of effective crisis communications. The new media landscape makes achieving this ideal even more challenging.

The following case study provides highlights of the collaborative and integrated communications plan the Western Carolina University public relations, marketing, and social media team implemented in June 2018 to announce the death of and honor its chancellor David O. Belcher. How the social media manager coordinated with the other departments, how the social media strategy was developed, how the implementation of the plan was evaluated, and key takeaways will be shared.

About Chancellor David O. Belcher

Belcher served as Western Carolina University's chancellor from July 2011 until he took medical leave in December 2017 to battle a glioblastoma brain tumor. Belcher indicated he did not expect to return as chancellor, and an interim chancellor was named. In June 2018, WCU faculty, staff and students, and citizens and leaders from across the Western North Carolina region and state of North Carolina said goodbye to and celebrated the life of this charismatic and transformational leader.

From the students with whom he posed for selfies, to the faculty and staff members whose work he enthusiastically celebrated, to the legislators he enjoined to support his bold, student-focused vision, Belcher was, as Margaret Spellings, president of the University of North Carolina System, described it, "beloved."

Belcher's impact on WCU and the Western North Carolina region was enormous. During his tenure, WCU achieved all-time highs in student achievement, enrollment, retention, and graduation rates, in student and alumni engagement, and in philanthropic giving. His belief in the power and potential of higher education was encapsulated in his repeated refrain: "We are in the business of changing lives."

Bill Studenc, WCU's chief communications officer, added that, "Belcher's legacy at WCU includes support and implementation of two pivotal statewide initiatives . . . the NC Promise tuition program that dramatically lowers student college costs, and his efforts toward the successful passage of the Connect NC bond, which included $110 million in funding for WCU's Apodaca Science Building." Given the extent of Belcher's reach and reputation, WCU's public relations, marketing and social media departments knew that a comprehensive communications plan, which would both celebrate and honor Belcher's life and work, as well as provide a forum for the expected outpouring of grief and condolences from a wide variety of constituents, was needed. The foundation for such a communications plan was already in place, as WCU had developed a series of "Chancellor's Health Updates" after Belcher was diagnosed with the brain tumor in late April 2016. The updates kept the campus community and other constituencies informed about the treatment process and the chancellor's condition. The plan involved the use of website updates, email communications to the campus and to key external audiences, and a social media effort through which members of the university community could express support and best wishes. In February 2017 the Council for Advancement and Support presented an Award of Excellence to WCU in the category of crisis/issues management plan for the Chancellor's Health Updates series.

Building on the foundation laid with the health updates, the WCU team created and implemented a communications plan to announce Belcher's death and memorial celebration. The expectation in any crisis situation is that the communication flow will be multi-directional. That is, audiences will comment, like, share, etc. The expectation that Belcher's memorial posts on social media would be heavily shared and would drive up engagement numbers across all demographics motivated the WCU team to create the best possible content for users to share.

Following are highlights of that plan, with emphasis on social media.

Overall goal: To honor Belcher's work and his legacy of extraordinary leadership.

Objectives

- To inform both internal and external audiences of Belcher's death
- To remind the WCU community and community at large of Belcher's #1 priority: increased philanthropic support for student scholarships
- To enable all constituents to grieve his passing through communal forums
- To enable all constituents to express their appreciation for his service to WCU, the region, and to institutions where he previously held a leadership role through WCU-managed forums

Timeline and Summary

Because Belcher was terminally ill, the WCU team was able to work from a probable timeline in order to develop and deliver assets, gain all the necessary approvals from administration and family, and determine a deployment sequence.

WCU's chief of staff worked closely with Belcher's family, especially his wife, Susan, during the planning stage to ensure that the Belchers' wishes were respected. Representatives from marketing and communications teams met to discuss an overall approach, and the social media strategist developed a communications plan.

WCU's usual social media strategy is very targeted, as managers rarely post anything to all of its platforms. However, content such as Belcher's memorial is the rarest of all content—it is relevant to every demographic. With this in mind, WCU's social strategy for this case was to get the information out everywhere by pushing it widely, across all platforms. By mid-April, the WCU team had everything planned, and was ready to launch the social posts, emails, and dark website when the time came to do so.

On Sunday, June 17, WCU's "beloved" chancellor died. Within hours of his passing, the web manager activated the memorial website, http://belcher. wcu.edu; the social media manager sent the announcement of his death (which arrived in inboxes as having come from Susan Belcher's email account) to WCU faculty, staff, students, alumni, and boards; the chief communications officer issued a news release and posted the news to the WCU news site; and the initial round of social media posts went up across platforms.

All of this was done from the team members' respective homes.

The following Monday, the social media manager's office became command central and members of PR, Design, Web, and the entire social staff were all in the same space so they could communicate instantly with one another. This allowed them to react to and manage the multitude of engagement emails, website comments, and social media posts to ensure every voice was heard. The majority of the work was in monitoring the incoming messaging for appropriateness and then pushing it to social channels and the website.

Belcher's memorial was planned for Saturday, June 23, six days after his death, in the Bardo Fine and Performing Arts Center, a 1,000-seat facility where Belcher, an accomplished pianist, and Susan, an accomplished vocalist, had performed many times. Overflow seating was arranged in rooms nearby the stage, and a live stream of the service was provided. During the week leading up to the memorial, the WCU communications and social media team worked with personnel from Video, Information Technology, Bardo Fine and Performing Arts, Facilities Management and Parking to ensure the service was fitting and easy to access/attend.

During the week between his death and memorial service, the WCU social media team monitored, reacted, reposted, and engaged with the grieving constituents directly on its social media channels.

Specifics of the Communications Plan

Tactics/Assets

Microsite
- Develop a microsite as a memorial to Belcher and his legacy (belcher.wcu.edu)
- Microsite designed as a place for the community to celebrate his life and provide opportunities for action, focusing on share, support and serve

- Microsite pages include Home, Obituary, Memorial Service, Condolences, and In Lieu of Flowers. Some information intentionally duplicated between pages, in case visitors did not visit every page

Home
- Photo of Belcher with b/d dates
- Celebration of life video
- Memorial location and details
- (Share) Opportunities to share condolences, photos, memories
- (Support) In lieu of flowers opportunity to give to WCU or other Belcher philanthropic priorities
- Roll up shared memories (submitted on Condolences page)
- Photographs of Dr. Belcher's highlights at WCU

Obituary
- Photo
- Obituary

Memorial Service
- Celebration of life video
- Memorial service details
- Parking information and map
- (Share) Opportunities to share condolences, photos, memories
- (Support) In lieu of flowers opportunity to give to WCU or other Belcher philanthropic priorities

Condolences
- Online form to share written Belcher memories, express condolences to family, etc.
- Approved stories appear on Condolences page and selected messages appear on Home page
- Sharable graphics with same design elements as microsite available for anyone that wants to share these on their own social media platforms

- Post viewer displaying any tweets or Instagram posts using #beloved-belcher as well as selected messages shared via email and submitted through the online form

In Lieu of Flowers
- David and Susan Belcher requested that memorials be directed to the foundation endowments of Western Carolina University, Furman University, the University of Arkansas at Little Rock, and Missouri State University (institutions where he previously served)
- Posted photos, descriptions, and links to each of the organizations requested by the Belchers

Celebration of Life Video
- Developed from archived photos and videos from Belcher's young life, including his personal and professional passions and his work at institutions prior to WCU, but with major focus on his motto in higher education, "we are in the business of changing lives"
- Produced in-house with approval from administration and family

Email Campaigns
- Announcement of Death: Recipients—all students, faculty/staff, alumni and WCU boards
- Email leads with autoplay of Celebration of Life video
- Information at belcher.wcu.edu
- Funeral arrangements: Recipients—entire WCU community
- Post memorial wrap up: Recipients—entire WCU community
- Link to Dr. Belcher's final statement and notice of social channels going dark to reflect a 'moment of silence' for the remainder of the weekend

Media Kit
- Materials prepared for announcing Dr. Belcher's death to the greater community

- Media kit dispersed to local media as well as applicable media for other communities Belcher was a part of (his hometown, his alumni community, etc.)

Press Release
- Celebration of life video
- B-roll of Belcher
- Photos of Belcher
- Link to microsite
- Obituary

Memorial Service Program
- Passed out day of memorial service

Memorial Visuals
- Once service arrangements are made, predetermine what visuals are desired for this
- Belcher photos
- Looped footage (no audio)
- Previously created 16-minute mini-doc was excerpted to 5 minutes and played at the beginning of the memorial service

Social Media Takeover
All official WCU accounts were dedicated solely to honoring Belcher for one week after his passing.

Instagram:
- Push out #belovedbelcher sharing Belcher stories
- Re-post photos that are shared with this hashtag
- Graphics with Belcher signature phrases
- Share celebration of life video
- Share any other shorter videos that are relevant (use hashtag)

Facebook:
- Push to microsite—Share, Support messaging
- Push out #belovedbelcher for sharing Belcher stories

- Graphics with Belcher signature phrases
- Share celebration of life video
- Share any other shorter videos that are relevant (use hashtag)
- Links to any stories about him

Twitter:
- Push to microsite—Share, Support messaging
- Push out #belovedbelcher for sharing Belcher stories
- Graphics with Belcher signature phrases
- Share celebration of life video
- Share any other shorter videos that are relevant (use hashtag)
- Links to any stories about him
- Retweet what people are saying

LinkedIn:
- Share announcement article and/or video
- Focus on Share, Serve, Support content

Monitoring and Evaluation

WCU uses Hootsuite Enterprise, TintUp, and on platform monitoring. While it is difficult to accurately measure the full reach and scope of Belcher's memorial on social media channels because not everyone sharing thoughts and comments used #belovedbelcher, and because some uses of the hashtag are difficult to record due to Facebook's API and use of the hashtag in private accounts, the analytics compiled paint a picture of a beloved leader who will be deeply missed and remembered for all time.

#belovedbelcher Data

Twitter: 1,530 posts—2.4M impressions

   Instagram: 138 posts—759K impressions

   Of particular note on Instagram: WCU's School of Stage & Screen alums, along with the *Rent* 20th Anniversary cast, shared a message of love from the road. #BelovedBelcher, which garnered 3,182 views. www.instagram.com/p/BkRAc3mF9x-/

Facebook

A video of Belcher playing the piano at Spellings' home went "viral" with 23,000 views.

www.facebook.com/WesternCarolinaUniversity/videos/10155321900670689/

WCU Administration and Communications & Marketing offices received emails, phone calls, and personal compliments regarding the way Belcher's passing had been managed publicly. 100 percent positive responses.

Key Takeaways

Takeaway #1

Communicate the plan to all individuals who manage social media across the organization. During the post-memorial week, while the official WCU accounts were posting *only* to honor Belcher's memory, many other very visible social media accounts, including those for Athletics and Campus Dining, continued to post upbeat and audience-building posts that were not in keeping with the Belcher posts going out on the main accounts and were jarring to users following multiple WCU accounts.

In hindsight, a simple distribution of the communications plan around Belcher's passing to social media, marketing, and communications managers across campus ahead of his memorial service would have given other divisions not involved in the development and implementation of the university's communication plan time and direction to plan for appropriate posts.

Given that social media is often decentralized across large organizations, we believe this is an especially important takeaway.

Takeaway #2: Provide Opportunities for Engagement for Those Who Are Not Social Savvy

Although there was some heavy lifting on the backend to create an online form that anyone, regardless of social media expertise, could use to send condolences, WCU was very conscious about ensuring everyone could contribute to the public discussion. When someone submitted the form, it came through as an email to an account the social media manager managed. The social media team reviewed these messages, and those that were especially poignant were added to the bottom of the home page as a slider and/or were pushed up as social media posts through TintUp. The rest were collected here: www.wcu.edu/davidobelcher/condolences.html

Takeaway #3: Capitalize on Unexpected Content

We knew we were memorializing a popular, "beloved," and revered individual, but what we did not expect was that upon meeting in Raleigh shortly after his passing, the NC House of Representatives would call for a proclamation honoring Belcher. The WCU video team captured the Legislature's live video stream, and the social media team included this in their outreach the week following the memorial service. Also, at that same session, before the proclamation was voted on, the microphone was passed to member after member who all took the time to share memories of and admiration for Belcher. This all became social media content and the footage has been archived for potential future use. https://news-prod.wcu.edu/2018/06/nc-house-approves-resolution-honoring-life-and-memory-of-wcus-chancellor-belcher/

Takeaway #4: Don't Be Opportunistic

Belcher's death came in the midst of a fundraising campaign, "Lead the Way," which was developed essentially in his honor. WCU leaders made the decision early on *not* to use his death as an opportunity to solicit donations for the campaign, and the PR team helped ensure media would share that we were celebrating a life well lived—and nothing else. Without ever once connecting his passing to the currently running capital campaign in his name, WCU focused the language of his memorial to reflect his number one philanthropic priority, student scholarships. Additionally, WCU messaged the opportunity for individuals to contribute to the Foundations of several institutions Belcher had previously served, not just WCU. The result: WCU's Office of Advancement saw a marked increase in contributions in the week ahead of and the week after Dr. Belcher's memorial.

Conclusion

The death of a leader is a difficult crisis to manage. Given that stakeholders will look to social media both for information, as well as a forum for sharing grief and condolences, it is critical that social media managers are prepared to facilitate this exchange while simultaneously coordinating consistent messaging with other organizational communicators. The goal to honor a respected leader—and his/her family's wishes—requires nothing less.

References

Fink, S. (2013). *Crisis Communications: The Definitive Guide to Managing the Message*. New York: McGraw-Hill.

Jin, Y., Liu, B. F., & Austin, L.L. (2011). Examining the Role of Social Media in Effective Crisis Management: The Effects of Crisis Origin, Information Form, and Source on Publics' Crisis Responses. *Communication Research*, 41(1), 74–94.

Patashnick, M. J. (2016). Social Media and Crisis Communication: Supporting Best Practice on University Campuses. Doctoral Dissertation. Retrieved from: https://search.proquest.com/docview/1839273726

Rasmussen, J., & Ihlen, Ø. (2017). Risk, Crisis, and Social Media: A Systematic Review of Seven Years' Research. *Nordicom Review*, 38(2), 1–17.

Betty Farmer is Professor of Communication and Public Relations, Donna Presnell is Social Media and Digital Marketing Manager, and Rylee Roquemore is Social Media Strategist at Western Carolina University. Located in Cullowhee, North Carolina, WCU is one of the 16 universities in the University of North Carolina System.

Employees play an important role within social media communication (SMC), but it is not all about work. The origins of SMC come from people playing with Internet technologies in the 1990s and early 2000s. What began as social play evolved into Silicon Valley entrepreneurial start-ups and eventually global social media corporations—some with billions of users.

﹖ Thought Leader Jennifer Grygiel

Why You Should Stop Trying to Justify the Cost of Social Media and Play More

Chief marketing officers (CMOs), directors of communications, and countless PR professionals' jobs became more complicated after the 2016 U.S. election, but it became easier, too. Presidential crisis communications are something that PR teams at publicly traded companies must manage now. However, communications professionals also do not have to spend countless hours trying to convince senior leadership that this new medium is important and worth investing in. Communication professionals have to manage for social media impact on areas, such as stock price. If President Donald Trump mentions a company in a tweet, a decision about whether or not to respond must be made very quickly. Few would dispute the power of social media and its influence now; it's "self-evident" (*Business View*, 2016, para. 15).

FIGURE 9.3 *Jennifer Grygiel (@grygiel). Photograph by Andrea Basteris, courtesy Jennifer Grygiel.*

The Importance of Play

Previously, social media were seen as "child's play," something that young people and interns were doing. It was easy to think this given that early social media use was immature, filled with people sharing song lyrics, animated GIFs (so many cats), and spending countless hours doing things like maintaining virtual farms.

But there is value in play, which I learned early in my career from Rodney Brook's work. Brooks is the former Director of MIT's Computer Science and Artificial Intelligence Lab (CSAIL) where I worked as an administrator during the early days of social media. He is known as an expert in the field of robotics and artificial intelligence (AI) and helped to create companies such as iRobot and more recently Rethink Robots. One of the most important ethos I took away from him and my time at CSAIL was that learning could just be "fun" (Hafner, 2000, para. 13).

When I teach social media to my students at the S.I. Newhouse School of Public Communications at Syracuse University, I explain how I learned to use social media by promoting my band on Myspace. I talk about the importance of learning to like media and new technology before jumping in and trying to learn how to apply it professionally. How can we adopt what we do not like first? Adoption (Rogers, 1995) in the early years of professional social media was a challenge, and it can still be hard to get senior executives, and even students, to personally embrace it. One of our class exercises is focused on livestreaming as the ability to broadcast in real-time is still a new experience for many and is intimidating. The class exercise is called the "Periscope Heart Challenge," and students are encouraged to be "silly" on the livestreaming platform and earn as many "hearts" (likes) as possible to better understand how to create engaging content—the results yield some good laughs and potential. I have found that this challenge helps those without any broadcasting experience. Live broadcasting is a very rich form of media (Daft & Lengel, 1984) and it is intimidating to many. I teach another course in collaboration with BuzzFeed, which is focused on developing future media skills and one of the classes is called, "Embracing Your Weird Lab" where students are encouraged to "be weird together" to help inspire new creative content. Brainstorming and playful exercises such as these has helped #NHBuzzFeed students to achieve over 18 million views on class assignments posted via the BuzzFeed Community over the past two years—we work hard in the class, but we also play, and have fun, and I believe this has contributed to our success.

I have embraced language in my classroom such as "play" as it corresponds to learning, but you will be hard pressed to hear these types of words in corporate. They are sometimes disguised and represented in terms such as: thought leadership, innovation, brainstorming, whiteboarding, hackathons, competitions, and challenges, but all of these terms can be boiled down to play—which in many ways is the seed of creativity, but why do people not use this term more? Can you imagine a manager saying, "Go play for an hour." But I would argue that this clarity in language is exactly what we need more of otherwise people are going to sit around and try and impress management instead of having more fun—businesses need to embrace playfulness more as a professional trait.

I was lucky to have worked in a corporate marketing department that gave me time and space to develop a social listening program during a time when few committed the financial resources to essentially "play" in this area. There are still not many use cases for social listening in industry, and this type of program had not existed in the company, so it was all new development and my job to "figure it out." A few keys to my success were: (1) being playful, (2) being conscious of needing to measure success without working towards predefined success metrics, and (3) applying social listening to real-world, timely, problems and spontaneous opportunities. And, lastly, I used my human brain to maximize social business opportunities by analyzing a massive network of social media through strategic filtering and then taking action. But why is social media valuable?

Sensing Social Media Data

In order to better understand social media and its potential, it is helpful to look at Brooks' (1990) early work in AI on "physically grounded systems," which moved the development of robotics in the direction of reacting to sensors and machine controls (actuators) as opposed to other models which were dependent on typed inputs and outputs (p. 3). Brooks ties robotics to animal systems, which have muscles and are capable of fast motion, as opposed to plants which move much more slowly (Dawkins, 2016). Dawkins (2016), an evolutionary biologist known for insights on culture and communications and for coining the word "meme" in his book *The Selfish Gene* (p. 249), also discusses the evolution of animals and "behavior," which he defines as the "trick of rapid movement" (p. 60). He notes how natural selection has favored animals with sense organs and how they evolved to be "fast" because of muscles—animal cells also have neurons that are connected to a brain, which responds to senses (p. 61). Given the evolutionary benefits to sensory skills, *speed*, and action, it is no wonder that Twitter, recognized by industry as the fastest, most real-time social media platform, is at the center of social listening. One human, sitting behind a social listening station, is capable of real-time monitoring, and *sensing*, the collective feedback of millions of individuals—this is an evolutionary leap forward in communications. In this sense, social listening technology (e.g., Radian6) functions like a large sensory organ such as skin with nerves that bring new information (social media posts) into a human brain for processing. This new system is physically grounded as it uses cues and information from the real-world and is received by a human operator for use in "social business" (Oelrich, 2015, p. 14).

Brooks' work also notes how "the world is its own best model. It is always exactly up to date. It always contains every detail there is to be known. The trick is to sense it appropriately and often enough" (p. 3). In terms of real-time real-world modeling, I would argue again that Twitter is key as it is the best real-time model of the world and source for sensing what people are thinking, what changes are happening in the world, and for grounding to the physical world, which helps to explain why so many communications professionals have come to rely on this platform. There is work in automation and algorithms being developed so we can rely less on humans for processing, but as with the early days of computers, humans are still essential and our brains are still superior to the best computers in the world; that is if you do not agree with Brooks' belief that humans are nothing more than machines (Brooks, 2002).

Measuring Success

The founder of the MIT Media Lab, Nicholas Negroponte, has defined his success measurement as "self-evidence" and noted how "no one had to measure the effect of Uber. The impact of a big change is generally seen—self evidence is highly underrated" (*Business View*, 2016, para. 15). Negroponte also suggested at the 2014 MIT CFO Forum that if you have to measure the impact of what you are working on then it might not be worth doing (Hirst, 2014). I set out to find a corporate social listening program with Brooks' idea of play and Negroponte's success model in mind, but I also realized that I did indeed work for a corporation, so I would need to document some success use cases. By the time I left, the social listening program was described as the "crown jewel" of the marketing department; I took that as self-evidence.

Brooks (1990) also speaks to the challenge of proving success in physically grounded systems (things that are connected to the real-world via sensors, etc.) and the focus on generality (picking obscure use cases and demonstrating that your system can tackle it) that leads to a disease called "puzzlitis." When starting new and emerging programs such as social listening, it could be easy to try and make the program work for your needs instead of using social listening to try and solve for things that naturally arise. The old adage is "run before you walk," but I would argue we should tweak that mindset to "never stop playing," which can help to inspire innovation and entrepreneurship.

Key Skills and Hiring Tips

In founding a corporate social listening program, I learned and discovered ways to use social media data to help manage the company's reputation, aid global security, evaluate employee sentiment, listen for new business leads, measure the success of marketing campaigns, and, lastly, and what I found to be most interesting, listen for innovation. Leaders and entrepreneurs can attain a significant advantage if they are able to find social media insights before they hit the mainstream, and this includes monitoring disruptive technology and new market entrants.

The primary tools to social listening are access to data such as Twitter's firehose (full stream) or Instagram's garden house (a sample of the full stream), knowledge of Boolean search (the search queries that help you to filter the millions of posts that are created everyday), interpreting data (e.g., identifying communities and trends), and a strategic mind that asks useful questions and knows when they have identified something useful. The skills that are necessary to run a corporate social listening program extend beyond technical know-how to include things like empathy, emergency preparedness, and crisis response training, as well as ethics (given the potential for abuse) and business awareness. Yes, it may seem as though hiring managers are looking for a unicorn, but they are out there. Now, how do you find them?

Negroponte puts forward the idea of hiring "misfits" and even put this term in job descriptions at the MIT Media Lab (*Business View*, 2016, para. 14). In addition to recruiting self-identified misfits, managers could explore hiring for neurodiversity and disorders such as ADHD, which could be an asset in a fast-paced media environment where *speed* of action is needed (Wiklund, et al., 2017).

I have interviewed many managers and staff at BuzzFeed and one universal trait that keeps coming up—passion. Your passion could be music, sports, corgis, Lady Gaga—it does not matter what the subject is, but that you just are excited and engaged; energy and enthusiasm is not something that you can learn per se but it is something that you can learn to embrace and is also something that managers can cultivate and support. This might seem basic, but as new media and technology come to market, from blockchain to AI advances, we are all going to have to double-down on embracing change and developing an entrepreneurial, misfit spirit, mindset so that we can keep embracing innovation.

Conclusion

What each CMO should be making sure that they are asking beyond "What's the ROI?" is: "Am I investing in hiring smart, ethical, misfits?"; "Am I allowing employees enough space and encouraging 'play'?"; and "Am I excited to come to work?" If those three things are mixed right and in place, innovation will flourish and your success will be self-evident.

References

Brooks, R. A. (1990). Elephants Don't Play Chess. *Robotics and Autonomous Systems, 6*(1), 3–15. doi:10.1016/S0921–8890(05)80025–9

Brooks, R. A. (2002). *Flesh and Machines: How Robots Will Change Us* (1st ed.). New York: Pantheon Books.

Business View. (2016). Insights from Nicholas Negroponte at the World Business Forum. Retrieved from https://business.nab.com.au/insights-from-nicholas-negroponte-at-the-world-business-forum-16974/

Daft, R. L. & Lengel, R. H. (1984). Information Richness: A New Approach to Managerial Behavior and Organizational Design. In L. L. Cummings, & B. M. Staw (Eds.), *Research in Organizational Behavior 6* (191–233). Homewood, IL: JAI Press.

Dawkins, R. (1941/2016). *The Selfish Gene* (40th anniversary ed.). Oxford: Oxford University Press.

Hafner, K. (2000). A Robot That Coos, Cries and Knows When It Needs a New Diaper. *The New York Times*. Retrieved from www.nytimes.com/2000/11/16/technology/a-robot-that-coos-cries-and-knows-when-it-needs-a-new-diaper.html

Hirst, P. (2014, November 20). Nicholas Negroponte: If You Have to "Measure" the Impact Then it Might Not Have Been Worth Doing! #MITCFO #SELF-EVIDENT [TWEET]. Retrieved from https://twitter.com/PeterHirstMBE/status/535552147149324289

Oelrich, P. A. (2015). Role and Effect of Social Determinants on Moral Judgment: A Study of Employee Behavior when Communicating Using Social Technology (Doctoral Dissertation, Fielding Graduate University).

Rogers, E. M. (1995). *Diffusion of Innovations* (4th ed.). New York: Free Press.

Wiklund, J., Yu, W., Tucker, R., & Marino, L. D. (2017). ADHD, Impulsivity and Entrepreneurship. *Journal of Business Venturing, 32*(6), 627–656. doi:10.1016/j.jbusvent.2017.07.002

Jennifer Grygiel is an Assistant Professor of communications and magazine, news, and digital journalism at the S.I. Newhouse School of Public Communications at Syracuse University.

AS SEEN ON YOUTUBE

Assignment

Watch Chatterkick President and Founder Beth Trejo discuss the challenges and opportunities of growing one of the first social media agencies in the U.S.: www.youtube.com/watch?v=MMUpHCzKjXw

FIGURE 9.4 *Beth Trejo. Photograph courtesy Beth Trejo and Chatterkick.*

Questions

1. How does the integration of PR planning strengthen social media measurement and management processes? What are some of the opportunities and risks in starting your own social media firm?

2. What are some of the dramatic changes in the past few years, since Trejo spoke to students in the video? How do these shifts reflect a need to constantly innovate social media measurement and management methods?

USEFUL TOOLS

Use Union Metrics Twitter Assistant and Instagram Checkup (https://app.unionmet-rics.com/tools/) to evaluate your use of Twitter and Instagram. Answer the following questions:

1. What were your top performing tweets and why?

2. Why are image tweets important to follower engagement growth?

3. What are your top Twitter and Instagram hashtags? Do they reflect your personal and professional brands?

4. Is there a day and time when you are most effective in posting on Instagram? Why might this be important?

5. What insights can be learned from your top performing Instagram hashtag?

PROJECT IDEAS

Use LinkedIn or GlassDoor to search employee and former employee recommendations about a potential employer. How do these reviews impact your perception? Would the reviews lead you to change your mind about working for a company? Why or why not?

DISCUSSION QUESTIONS

1. How does personal branding and employer branding influence communication between prospective employers and employees? Why?

2. How does your immediate supervisor or former boss use social media? Why is this helpful or not? Does your employer or former employer make social media sharing suggestions? Do you welcome these? Why or why not?

The Future of Social Media Measurement and Management

> *I've always believed in taking risks and creating change in my life and work. Blowing up a business model that had been successful for more than 50 years was a little intimidating, but I learned a lot in the process.*

—Fred Cook (@Golin, via Jacobs, 2018, p. 7)

> *Organizations shouldn't just invest in voice capabilities because they can. The technology must take the end-user into account. As organizations continue to see voice as a key differentiator to the business . . . it's important for them to remember that voice-activated technology should always be relevant, desired and make an obvious improvement for the people directly impacted.*

—Juan José López Murphy (@Globant, via Alaimo, 2018a, para. 6)

The rapid diffusion of technological change is already impacting the future of social media measurement and management. Virtual and augmented reality, drones, robotics, and machine-learning require social media managers to be entrepreneurial in how they measure human behavior. Digital analytics are continuously refined and updated because chatbots and other new tools require organizations to keep pace with business competition. The demise of many U.S. retail giants, such as Toys 'R Us, seems to support VaynerMedia CEO Gary Vaynerchuk's view that, as he said in a LinkedIn video, "when you don't innovate, you die."

Similarly, Golin Chairman and University of Southern California Center for Public Relations Director Fred Cook applies an innovative and entrepreneurial mindset to seeing early trends and positioning strategies and tactics. "I realized that the speed of change is critical," he told *PRSA Strategies & Tactics*:

> If you go too fast, you leave the skeptics behind. If you go too slowly, the go-getters get frustrated. You have to find a pace somewhere in the middle . . . Change is a constant process and you have to keep pushing, while also celebrating your successes along the way. Otherwise, people naturally fall back into familiar patterns.
>
> (Jacobs, 2018, p. 7)

Golin's g4 reorganized business structure around four roles—explorers (researchers), creators (ideas, design and content), connectors (consumer and business engagement), and catalysts (champions of business growth). "Explorers deliver insight and measurement through research, analytics and planning (Golin, 2016). The emphasis in this framework on research data within paid, earned, social, and owned media is important in continuous improvement and change. The challenge and opportunity for social media managers is that the job frequently requires a single person or small team to work across all four Golin areas. Management of high-quality social media is driven by research and measurement in creating engaging content that connects organizations to stakeholders and champions growth. The upside of this is that social media managers should be positioned to rise to transformational leadership roles within an organization.

As we look ahead to the next phase of social media measurement and management innovation, voice commands to a wide variety of IoT devices also is expected to transform the nature of social media communication. Alaimo's (2018a) data suggest that diffusion of voice-activated devices use for personal life and professional work is in the early-majority stage with about half of U.S. consumers already on board. Voice commands are only part of the innovation context, as entrepreneurs also drive interest in AR, VR, facial recognition, and matching, and filters through new forms of social media influencer marketing (Digiday, 2017). Snapchat AR lenses, for example, may offer high levels of engagement and "brand lift" data to "quantify brand awareness" (para. 15), but adoption continued to be slow. At the same time, however, some express the fear that AI will further widen the economic inequality gap. Former Microsoft and Google executive Kai-Fu Lee was blunt about how new technologies further disadvantage the poor:

I think AI will exacerbate wealth and inequality . . . at the very bottom rank are the people, many of whose jobs will be replaced because they're routine and AI will do their jobs for them, so it's actually having a doubling effect on giving more wealth to the wealthiest, creating new AI tycoons at the same time taking away from the poorest of society.

(Sandoval, 2018, para. 6)

As has been the case with former Facebook managers, regret tends to be expressed after executives leave technology companies. Facebook and other social network sites received critical news media coverage, and data suggested that users had lost trust between 2017 and 2018 in these businesses. A majority of adults polled (N = 3,622) responded that social media do more to hurt than help democracy. While 43 percent in 2017 responded that social media hurt, this had grown to 57 percent a year later (Fischer & Snyder, 2018). Democrats and independents joined a Republican majority in their skepticism about social. Only 40 percent of adults surveyed viewed social media as a positive, while 65 percent responded that mobile smartphones improved the quality of their lives. As social media source and message credibility are questioned, social media are becoming more complex because of AI. Starting with Google and SEO, digital marketing was defined by optimization of search and impacted by active social media users. By one estimate, the rapidly diffusing voice search space of Google Home, Alexa, Apple Siri, and Facebook Portal was nearly one-fourth of searches in 2018. As appliances, cars, and other IoT devices become the norm, the blurring of human and machine-learning functions will have an enormous impact upon social media measurement and management. Algorithm changes at Google and Facebook are designed to serve consumers and advertisers, but it is not clear how AI will blend with human communication.

Computer-mediated communication (CMC) research extended knowledge about human interaction with artificially intelligent avatars, online content, and automated machine learning. In the case of social media measurement and management, a mindset of entrepreneurship is essential because technological change quickly comes to social media spaces. In this sense, management of social media assets does not assert the hardest of scientific methods in search of objective truths. It owes as much to qualitative interpretation as it does the massive amount of big data generated over time. One critical perspective is that "multimodal discourse analysis" (MDA) may be relevant as a path to explore complex social media messaging and how the content may be "exploited for commercial purposes" (Djonov & Zhao, 2014, p. 5). This approach, as well as critical discourse analysis (CDA), may be useful in deconstructing images present and shared across distinct social networks sites (SNSs) with followers and fans. SNS social capital may be measured through "bridging" or "bonding" (Steinfeld et al., 2013, pp. 121–122). Perhaps one of the most significant changes is that innovation is no longer limited to the magic of primarily men in Silicon Valley, as other parts of the country and world make important contributions to the next wave of technological and social change.

In New York, social media spaces are perfect for female entrepreneurs to use innovation in marketplace change. For example, Amra (@AmraBeganovich) and Elma Beganovich and their a & e digital marketing agency leveraged millions of followers in the beauty and travel social media area. Founder Elma Beganovich and her sister mastered Google, Instagram, and YouTube by identifying targeted Millennial audiences and offering quality content. Beganovich was on a securities and financial regulation career path at Georgetown Law when taking photos of herself and posting them changed everything. As an early adopter in 2012 of Instagram and then Facebook pages, she and Amra (trained as an economist) began with low-cost do-it-yourself (DIY) beauty recipes and tips. The idea was to disrupt traditional lifestyle publications, such as *Vogue* magazine.

"Most consumers don't have to spend tens of thousands of dollars in skin care, or millions of dollars in plastic surgery," Beganovich says. The sisters also took time to learn computer coding, as they built a website. Bloggers helped attract more than 100,000 unique visitors in the first three months. Topics such as "travel to Croatia on a budget" helped build a following and celebrity status by using video and remarkable photography. "Even those 'vanity metrics' . . . you can essentially monetize," Beganovich says. Brands also evaluate an influencer's "healthy engagement" through comments and likes.

Lifestyle influencers may target clothing as one way to attract brand interest. A "really clever" influencer develops an "online persona" to attract a target demographic, Beganovich says. The combination of mobile technologies and social media data has freed women entrepreneurs from the traditional boardroom and office, Beganovich says. The sisters completed a 2014 programming course, and they developed proprietary agency software.

> *The software allows you to do a very quick search based on filters in Instagram and YouTube—so, for example, location, following number, and keywords (our main filters)—and so brands are able to quickly find the influencers they want to see.*

—Elma Beganovich

Beganovich says the launch of an influencer analytics platform was their next step. One strategy for clients is to match influencers with upcoming brand events. "They can quickly . . . get to those influencers, find them (rather than doing it manually), and then . . . "click on the influencers' profile, and you're able to see the engagement rate."

A Millennial is likely to begin shopping on Instagram rather than at an upscale store. "We make them 'explode digitally' . . . your digital footprint has become everything," Beganovich says. "Basically, Instagram has become your store . . . So, yeah, we are sort of matchmakers" between brands and social media influencers, Beganovich agrees.

DATA SCIENCE

In Miami, Formulated.by Founder Anna Anisin's boutique marketing firm incorporated data science in her entrepreneurship focused on digital and face-to-face experiences. "We specialize on servicing B2B enterprise clients," Anisin says. There remain a host of data problems, "so there's a lot of opportunity still to be had in this market," Anisin says. "The biggest thing right now is marketing and social media texts and segments . . . basically, taking all of your data . . . scraping data." At the Data Science Salon in Los Angeles, media companies examined current issues. New algorithms and models help social marketers dive "into those conversations and . . . patterns (what people are saying about your products)" because negative sentiment may adversely impact sales for large and small brands alike, Anisin says. At the same time, Anisin warns against falling for marketing buzzwords. In the end, the key techniques remain text mining and sentiment analysis, and human coders continue to have an edge over artificial intelligence (AI). "Contextual marketing," Anisin says determines, "the right time to give you that ad, so it's relevant."

Brand relationships imply the need for a steady stream of great content, as defined by social media communities. Media such as Netflix are at the cutting edge of developing predictive analytics through granular data. It's no easy task. "I don't think everybody is meant to be an entrepreneur," Anisin says. "You have to figure out if that's really you . . . first, before you go out there and try to start a business."

Despite the risks in new business development, many traditional companies also will fail in the ongoing digital shift. They could, however, learn to be agile by listening to a new generation of women entrepreneurs.

Entrepreneurs can learn a lot from business innovator principles that have been tested over decades. Effective social media measurement and management begins and ends with strategies that keep a brand in focus. Goals, objectives, and media-specific tactics must be sensitive to a brand's value proposition, fans wants and needs, and the power of clear and persuasive content.

The attention wars are growing in fragmented social media spaces. Social media are here to stay, but how we use the tools is fluid. For businesses and non-profit organizations, it is essential to connect with the social media online community in your area and industry. Clear goals, strategies and tactics must connect best practices to broader marketing plans. A counter-argument to marketing each is that social media may be effectively managed through the cultivation of meaningful relationships. It is a quality over quantity perspective. It is tempting to want to expand social media reach, but mere exposure to larger numbers rarely offers a return on investment of marketing costs. In this fragmented media time, brands need to carefully plan for how social media tools strengthen broader business goals.

In the social media spaces, paid sponsored and promoted posts are increasingly invading otherwise carefully curated Twitter and Facebook feeds. Noisy blasts are purchased by brands in search of quasi-targeted reach that truthfully is not much better than the scattershot of TV advertising. This old marketing approach also seems to be reaching into newer social media channels. *Social Media Today* urged, "Snapchat for Business: How to Reach Millennials Through Storytelling." Yet, the hype of Snapchat turned out to be more of a bust. Strategist Carlos Gill was an early adopter of the youth-oriented site of more than 100 million Snapchat users and their billions of daily videos. Gil's argument was that Snaps result in increased YouTube channel subscription, website traffic, and email subscriptions—all within the soon-to-be leading 13- to 34-year-old demographic. Storytelling through 10-second native "micro-moments" seeks to activate influencers and sharing in the promotion of brand activities and events. The need for interactive content also speaks to the emerging desire of large companies to activate employees and their social networks.

Lenovo, for example, launched a company-wide social network to take advantage of the fact that about half of all employees post messages about their employers. Through internal and external public relations content, employees may become PR workforce in extending reach by sharing content with their friends, family, and colleagues. Cool stories can serve to boost employee morale, improve company image, and even raise awareness about new events, products, or services. If reach serves specific business goals, it may complement broader strategy. If not, storytelling may fail as introducing even more noise within the fragmented social sphere.

Long-term relationship building is the cornerstone of any business and brand. Here, I think more than ever, organic and authentic conversation wins out over forced social media sharing through strategic plans and content management systems. Engaging second screen content may reinforce brand loyalty and later behavior. None of this may be as influential as online conversation with other friends who are fans. Electronic word-of-mouth (eWOM) is an extension of what happens face-to-face with our proximate social networks. We share common interests and enthusiasm.

When it comes down to business, use social media when it makes sense to join obvious conversation about new or developing events. Most importantly, keep your eye on the ball (sales). Social media content may help raise awareness and increase engagement—it will take more to convert people into customers.

New technologies companies, such as Globant.com, have developed plans for use of voice within an organization's larger digital strategies. While adoption of voice technologies in personal daily life has become common, workplace adoption was happening at a slower pace. Most organizations see a business value in investing in the newest technologies, but company leaders felt their organizations were not prepared for the change in consumer preference. At least 39 million Americans were early adopters of voice-activated speakers, and the best estimate in 2018 was that about one-third of companies were beginning to respond to the trend. As bots become more common within social media communication, though, news issues emerge. For example, collaboration by people in social media boiler rooms sometimes look similar to bots, with frequent tweets and retweets on Twitter, and platforms may block them (Burnett, 2018). The future of social media measurement and management will be defined by increasing difficulty in categorizing human and non-human communication.

Beyond new technologies, social media measurement and management is becoming a diverse field of practice. The Digital Analytics Association (DAA) developed a Women in Analytics mentoring program to promote gender diversity in a historically male-dominated area. Female and male mentors may "empower fellow analysts" through shared experiences, perspectives, and volunteer work. New social media managers benefit from finding a mentor who can offer advice, guidance, and counsel in facing difficult situations. It is not necessary to join a formal mentoring program to take advantage of the benefits found in intergenerational professional communication.

What Microsoft's Bill Gates once called "the road ahead" continues to be impacted by rapid diffusion and adoption of social media technologies. Nielsen (2018a) found that U.S. adults spend more than *eleven* hours each day reading, listening, watching, and interacting with media—including social media. Mobile access has transformed social media into an "always on" habit, as about half of our day appears to be spent immersed in media.

> Digital usage also continues to play a growing role with the adult U.S. consumer. Digital platforms—think computers, smartphones and tablets—have become a major catalyst for this frequent content exposure. In first-quarter 2018, consumers spent three hours and 48 minutes a day on digital mediums. This is a 13-minute increase from the prior quarter, and 62% of that time is attributed to app/web usage on the ubiquitous smartphone.
>
> (para. 6)

Increasingly, social media managers must adopt a global perspective. It would be incorrect, for example, to use U.S. Facebook data to understand the rest of the world. In Japan, eMarketer discovered that nearly two-thirds of social media users are on Twitter—well ahead of Facebook and Instagram. The Japanese language, as well as a 2011 earthquake and tsunami, cemented Twitter as a leading cultural social media platform.

Clearly, ubiquitous mobile media use presents measurement and management opportunities and challenges. This is likely the tip of an iceberg, as parents turn mobile phones and tablets over to their youngest children. The newest generation knows no other world than the one that quickly responds to touch, voice and other interfaces. Each action generates a flow of new data.

Social media crowds are here to stay. So, strategic management of share of voice through personal and organization branding are essential. Events and campaigns drive social media interest across social network sites. In these spaces, we have the tools to measure and manage social media conversation. Specialists in this growing area have the opportunity to focus on metrics that reflect KPIs, observe data in real time using sophisticated dashboards and other tools, and focus on continuous improvement. Too often, there is a temptation to evaluate only at the end of a calendar or fiscal year. However, real-time social media measurement and management allows us to set hourly, daily, weekly, and quarterly goals. Data analysis offers insights into effectiveness of our events and campaigns. Through A/B testing and KPIs, social media managers have an opportunity to refine methods, improve measured outcomes, and develop successful work habits.

It is clear that industry best practices continue to shift toward the integration of media storytelling through PR, advertising, and marketing channels. Increasingly, social media managers will be impacted by law and regulation, such as GDPR privacy rules in the EU. Even where laws do not exist, strategists should be concerned about their professional reputation and the role that ethical communication plays in the long term. Transparency must be accompanied by reduction in conflicts of interest. This is not easy when representing proprietary business interests. The desire for transparency frequently clashes with the need for business secrets.

Customers or other stakeholders remain at the core of solid planning. Social media relationships grow through the sharing of engaging content that is audience centered. Successful social media measurement and management requires close attention to planning, strategy and tactics. Campaigns may be organized or not, so managers must strive to reduce chaos where possible. Employees, particularly within the largest organizations, offer amazing opportunities to expand reach and amplify messages through social networks. Communication, however, must be interactive with employees sharing in governance and responsibilities to promote explicitly stated goals.

Tech Entrepreneurship on the Silicon Prairie

Experienced entrepreneurs increasingly can be found outside of Silicon Valley in California and the East Coast corridor. In Chicago, for example, there is a hub of entrepreneurship happening that is relevant to social media measurement and management. John Macleod's team built a news app and went on to develop "news on-hold" technologies to compete with the more common music on-hold when waiting on a telephone line for customer service. MacLeod's experience includes Navteq, Sony, and Disney, and this breadth and depth may have been behind a shift from a consumer app to a B2B business model. After the initial flurry of interest in building mobile apps, entrepreneurs quickly discovered that getting people to download and use an app was not as easy as first thought. MacLeod's focus at Navtaq (a leader in digital car GPS navigation), as well as the larger media companies, "has always been to look for new opportunities to try to identify new businesses." The "iterative, agile process" begins with identifying needs and opportunities, and then offering solutions:

> *It's proposing, testing, proposing again, adjusting. So, it's a lot of iteration. A lot of times you are failing more than you're succeeding, and so I think a big part of being an entrepreneur or anybody who's trying to develop something new is you have to have a very healthy attitude about failure.*

—John Macleod

It is not easy to shift ideas or even stop altogether because entrepreneurship is an investment of time and money. "I think a lot of being an entrepreneur is really having a mindset around a willingness to put yourself out there, test things, be open-minded, not be biased in terms of what you think the outcome will be because then that will lead you down paths that are not as successful," MacLeod says. By shifting away from mobile phone apps and pivoting to be a "smart audio creation and distribution company," media storytelling content could be delivered to Amazon Alexa or Google Home devices. The smart part of Rivet audio is, "the way our stories are created . . . to sound great, but they also are indexed and tagged with data, so that they're easily searched and discovered," MacLeod says.

As an example of entrepreneurship, MacLeod's Rivet lives by a set of basic "good show" principles:

- Produce great content
- Be accurate
- Offer entertaining and engaging content
- Know the "guests" (a Disney term for audience members)

The smart audio concept is innovative by combining high-quality content with accurate and consistent new data technologies. MacLeod says, "voice . . . in a sense, it's a new operating system."

Artificial intelligence (AI) uses "natural language understanding your voice to basically interact with devices," MacLeod says. The work of "trying to infer the context and sort of who you are and why you're asking the question to help with the answer" is complex because "the ear is really far more sensitive than your eye in terms of being able to pick up emotion and thoughts."

The entrepreneurial challenge is that podcasting audiences remain relatively small; hence the opportunities are seen within the internet of things (IoT) and smart speakers. Time will tell if these devices become ubiquitous, but large companies are continuing to invest.

While iterative development at MacLeod's start-up represents one Chicago success story, across the river at the Merchandise Mart, there are more than 500 companies at various stages of entrepreneurial development. 1871 Chicago has become a new business incubator boasting resources from major universities in the city.

1871 Chicago is a growing complex that includes hundreds of members and mentors. The campus environment features a podcasting studio and many resources for teaching new entrepreneurs how to launch a business and keep it going. This includes understanding how to develop business models around great ideas and pivot when necessary. It remains to be seen whether or not entrepreneurs in B2C spaces can find success on the Silicon Prairie instead of going to one of the coasts to follow the more traditional path of new business technologies. Kansas City, Omaha, Des Moines, and

FIGURE 10.1 *Entrepreneur Carol Fowler (@carolfowler) developed her TV news consulting software business at 1871. Photograph by Jeremy Harris Lipschultz, courtesy Carol Fowler.*

St. Louis are among the smaller Midwestern cities in search of tech entrepreneurial success. Chicago took a place among the global leaders for high-tech jobs:

1. San Francisco
2. New York
3. London
4. Los Angeles
5. Taipei
6. Seoul

7. Boston
8. Singapore
9. Toronto
10. Chicago

Chicago was ranked ahead of Dallas (11) and Washington, D.C. (25), as well as many large cities in Asia and Europe.

New entrepreneurs need to learn from and be mentored by those with experience and expertise in how to start, build, and maintain a new business. Frequently, this means learning to repeatedly fail and pivot toward better ideas. John MacLeod likes to think about smaller chunks of failure: "the smaller you can break the pieces down, so that you can get 'fast to succeed' or 'fast to fail' with different phases of the program, the better informed you are, the sooner you can make an adjustment or pivot . . . in a different direction, or decide to stop doing it."

Source: Lipschultz, J. H. (2017, October 6). Chicago Startup Entrepreneurs Learn to Pivot. *Huffington Post*. www.huffingtonpost.com/entry/chicago-startup-entrepreneurs-learn-to-pivot_us_59d7d647e4b08ce873a8cda7

Social media changes are rapid and sometimes dramatic. Measurement and management is a field that begins its second decade with numerous challenges and opportunities: consumer trust may be weakened by disclosure of lack of data privacy; Twitter and other platforms have an uncomfortable relationship with social media management automation through the use of chatbots; strategists are challenged to find a balance between organic and paid Facebook; appropriate use on YouTube, Instagram, IGTV, and other sites continues to evolve; and popular use of Stories and groups is impacted by platform revision (Stelzner, 2019). It means that social media managers must remain current through continuous innovation. In this context, there is renewed interest in quality of content through narrative storytelling, as well as "hyper-targeted personalization" (Patel, 2018d, para. 25):

Customers have come to expect brands to tailor special offers and discounts to their wants and needs. To keep up with expectations, businesses need to step up their game when it comes to targeted advertising. Nearly every social media platform offers some level of audience filtering when you opt to pay for advertising. These options range from simple geographic targeting to advanced filters that refine audiences into highly specific segments.

(para. 25)

The growing field of social media entrepreneurship is grounded in the media technology sector that increasingly overlaps with IoT devices. The entrepreneurs behind the diffusion of innovation seem to defy traditional boundaries. Jeff Hoffman (@SpeakerJeff), for example, focuses on solving common problems in numerous successful startups, including Priceline.com.

Hoffman's first success was development of automated airline ticket kiosks to end long airport lines, but he has gone on to be a producer of Hollywood films, and an Emmy Award-winning TV show, as well as a Grammy-winning jazz album. He has spoken in more than 50 countries about entrepreneurship, innovation, and leadership. Hoffman urges students to focus on dreams and making them happen, such as when he produced a benefit concert with Elton John.

FIGURE 10.2 *MasterCard Conversation Suite data (@MasterCardBrian). Photograph by Jeremy Harris Lipschultz, courtesy AEJMC San Francisco, 2015.*

Social media managers have an opportunity to be entrepreneurial with start-up business ideas, as well as within organizations of all sizes. At MasterCard's New York headquarters, for example, a few years ago collaborated with software developers in Germany to create its proprietary Conversation Suite.

The company positioned social media monitor screens near a public lunch area to engage employees across departments in its external efforts. Gendron has since moved onto innovation in digital wallets and payments, and mobile eCommerce, peer-to-peer (p2p) through MasterCard's incubator developing, testing, and scaling ideas. Some of the most exciting social media innovation is happening within the media monitoring area. Traditionally, PR professionals pitch stories to news reporters and later need evidence of publication and broadcast. Social media, though, disrupted the model for demonstrating ROI.

((•)) Thought Leader Todd Murphy

#SameRulesNewTools

Media monitoring is rapidly evolving from a way to measure earned media exposure, to a discipline that allows organizations to understand their efforts and outcomes, similar to other departmental functions such as marketing and sales. Universal Information Services subscribes to the tenants promoted through the work of the International Association for Measurement and Evaluation of Communication (AMEC), a global organization whose mission focuses on "education and innovation in PR and communications measurement and evaluation." Truly accurate and insightful media measurement comes through a defined framework that is not only transparent in methods, but also holistic in content and centered upon accuracy.

FIGURE 10.3 *Todd Murphy (@Todder4News). Photograph courtesy Universal Information Services.*

Volume of results, audience, circulation, and other quantitative measures have a relevant place in media measurement, but services must include *qualitative* measurements—strength of message points, degrees of impact, and prominence of sentiment. Many automated measurement services attempt to simulate qualitative measures, but overall the accuracy of those algorithms is too low.

AI, machine learning, and other computer programming efforts could only automate the more fundamental areas of media measurement, at least with any degree of statistical accuracy. Universal continues to view machine learning and AI as tools to automate the routine tasks, serving up valid information and data so it can be further analyzed by trained analysis professionals. Our research shows that analyst-assisted media measurement continues to be the most accurate approach for gauging the success and impact of public relations and communication outreach efforts.

One breakthrough area for analysis has been in Universal's development of the Alpha Clips tool. Alpha Clips uses AI to better focus the summarization and clustering of media mentions, delivering the key article points indexed with similar stories, so users can more quickly determine content and impact. Alpha Clips is both a client user tool for consuming media results and an enhancement for trained analysts that need to efficiently evaluate media mentions. The summarization Alpha Clips provides allows PR professionals to consume their media mentions in 75 percent less time than normal media monitoring reports, as well as identify the first occurrence of a story, so it can be indexed along with the other outlets that ran the materially same story.

Universal's analysis process has moved beyond basic earned media measurement and into measuring across the entire Paid, Earned, Shared, Owned (PESO) model. Taking a measure of your media presence is the first step in the communications measurement process. While Alpha Clips is helping us work more efficiently, we have found that nothing fully replaces a trained analyst when qualitative insight must be interpreted, especially when you are measuring across many different media channels. By counseling our clients to consider a blend of complementary communications metrics, it allows us to open the door to more meaningful reporting and measuring down the line. Finding relationships between fundamental *business* metrics is always the place we recommend our clients start their measurement journey. Baseline measurement of fundamental metrics allows us to move our clients into deeper insights.

To get an idea of how valuable earned media is in relation to our clients' business efforts, we made a change several years back to focus more on helping communications professionals prove that their earned media is making an impact. At that time, Universal started to track if consumers were buying their goods when they engaged with a media story or if they wanted to engage in other actions beyond just seeing their media story. Basically, would communication actions lead to behavioral changes in a direction desired by our client? Using analytics platforms, such as Google Analytics, and tying that data to earned media campaigns, helped us to find parallels, or the absence of, between revenue impact and organizational change. The truth is there is no one way to track the impact of your earned media unless you are able to blend owned metrics into the mix, such as referral traffic, sales, clicks, opens, and many more.

Tracking metrics, such as conversions (or conversion rate), and spikes in coverage to a key landing page are some simple ways to introduce yourself into the world of integrated communications measurement. For Universal, simply being attentive to how much new website traffic a specific earned media story brings to your organization can help jumpstart more integrated measurement projects. Are those viewing your website, those that saw your earned media story, within your target audience? What else do they do on your website? What actions are they taking? When you see the answers to these questions, you reveal how valuable that media story was for the overall health of your earned media strategy. Do the desired outcome result from your communications effort, or not.

The AI automation that we have implanted for the routine processes, such as searching for content, clustering articles, etc., cannot complete the measurement process for our clients. It is the job of our professional analysts to take in all measures and make sense of the data according to a defined, proven methodology. Universal subscribes to the theory that tracking can be done mostly by automation, but nothing can replace the analytical insight of people.

Todd Murphy is CEO at Universal Information Services. He has developed innovative public relations and news monitoring client tools for more than 27 years. Austin Gaule (@austininomaha), PR measurement director for five years, contributed to this analysis.

Throughout this book, readers have been pointed to YouTube video. The social media content platform offers tremendous opportunities to innovate direct-to-audience experiences. In fact, entertainment television content has been disrupted, and entrepreneurs are migrating shows away from TV and to YouTube, where audience measurement is more direct than traditional TV ratings.

ᵗ🗼 Thought Leader Matt Tompkins

From TV to the Web—*Omaha Live!*
Local entertainment and humor have long been part of how I spend my days (and nights) in Omaha, Nebraska. With a nearly 15-year career spanning AM, FM, and satellite radio, it seemed only fitting that my next stop would be the Internet. With the great sprawl that occurred when Twitter, Facebook, and YouTube took hold, communication professionals and novices alike have found audiences online both large and small.

FIGURE 10.4 *Matt Tompkins (@MattTonTV and @livefromOmaha). Photograph by Chris Holtmeier, courtesy Matt Tompkins.*

I built solid followings on social media for various stops in radio, including 1110 KFAB-AM, 96.1 KISO-FM, 93.3-KTWI/KFFF FM, and 1290 KOIL-AM. I had only dipped my creative toe into the waters of YouTube when NBC's Omaha affiliate, WOWT-6, came calling in 2014. The station's general manager was a fan of the work I'd done with my brother, Ben. Our brotherly duo was known for emceeing local events, concerts, and fundraisers. Our unique blend of humor differed from anything else on the airwaves utilizing our production skills, musical talent, and quirky style that was proven to entertain fans of all ages.

At WOWT-6, the Saturday night midnight time slot, immediately following entertainment Goliath *Saturday Night Live*, had potential. Late-night infomercials were the easy choice, but WOWT-6 management wanted to try something new. This is how a meeting lead to the creation of Omaha's first, locally produced sketch comedy show.

With just a single camera and tripod, a used pair of headphones, zero production staff, and a church basement where our father served as pastor, we took years of comedic writing, entertaining, and producing to create a sketch comedy show not just for the Internet, mind you, but for local television. A presence on YouTube, Facebook, Twitter, and even Instagram would soon follow, but the first priority for *Omaha Live!* was to build an audience—an audience on a platform that many may say is slowly being replaced by subscription television and the Internet.

Each week I would edit the 30-minute episode in my home production studio. Sketch comedy segments skewering Nebraska tourism, the football Cornhuskers, and even local politicians were filmed throughout the week in and around the Omaha area. We recruited a few family members, friends, and even former coworkers to appear in scripted parodies.

And every Saturday night, when a new episode of *Omaha Live!* debuted at midnight, I would take to Twitter on my iPhone, live-tweeting each episode from @livefromomaha and including the hashtag #omahalive. At first the chatter was quiet. But as buzz built locally online and, on the streets, we saw Facebook and Twitter traffic increase. And not just at midnight; throughout the week fans of all ages—men and women alike—shared feedback on a particular sketch, segment, joke, or parody song that they loved. I was selective, however, in what episodes and segments we uploaded and *how* they were shared with fans on YouTube and Facebook. In the first season the goal was to not do any standard promotion on radio, print, or traditional commercials. This was intentional because the workload for the show was so heavy that my time was limited, and our small team did not have any production or promotional staff to assist.

"Superfans," as I like to call them, were the vital key to generating online buzz and more followers, likes and views. My brother Ben and I catered directly to just a handful of superfans in the beginning by always responding to them, interacting with them, even sharing their tweets on television and letting fans online decide what sketches would air in our "Fan-Favorites" episodes. These "superfans" were vital because once they felt like they were part of the *Omaha Live!* community, they quickly spread the word throughout the week and during the Saturday-night hours leading up to the show. The online influencers consistently shared *Omaha Live!* full episodes and shorter videos via Facebook and YouTube.

It didn't hurt that we also recruited local celebrities to appear on *Omaha Live!*, including former Huskers Eric Crouch and Johnny Rodgers, former U.S. Senator Ben Nelson, Omaha Mayor Jean Stothert, Congressman Don Bacon, and many more. Most of these well-known faces are also active on social media, and in turn promoted their segments on *Omaha Live!* and online.

Cross-promotion was another key element to building the audience for *Omaha Live!* Celebrities generated a lot of buzz online, but we also have had guests on the show who simply had huge social media fans and followers. MMA/UFC fighter Houston Alexander joined the cast and brought with him his 50,000 Facebook fans. As the show grew to 23 cast members and writers, everyone connected to the show added more and more cross-promotion.

With seven seasons of *Omaha Live!* and a rare television milestone of 100 episodes, consisting of 234 weeks of episodes, what started as a local DIY television show grew into a success story that far surpassed the expectations of their creators.

Omaha Live! is not only the no. 1 late-night television program in the Omaha market, but the ratings for the show are higher than the daytime programming on WOWT-6 (11a-2p), as well as beating out national programs such as *Late Night with Seth Meyers*, *Last Call with Carson Daly*, *Meet the Press*, and nearly tied *The Tonight Show with Jimmy Fallon*. In the first season commercial blocks were filled with station promos, but it wasn't long until national advertising agencies were buying into the show along with local sponsorships.

We accomplished what most people would say is impossible, but proved that with hard work, creativity, passion, and a multitude of skill sets anything can be accomplished. With strong leadership we convinced more than 30 people over the years to volunteer their time for what would be the equivalent of a part-time job every week.

The key to our success has been one simple strategy: "Actually do it." Everyone has a great idea, but it's those people who put in the work and take the risks that find success. We also worked very hard to build relationships with people in the industry by being dependable and reliable with the work we did for them. That approach to building relationships with people is also how we approached social media engagement. People don't want advertisements, they want to connect with you whether it's in person or on the Internet. The bottom line is to work hard, be yourself, help others, and actually do it.

Matt Tompkins *is a cross-platform media producer and entertainer.* **Wendy Townley** *(@wtownley), executive producer and author of* Nerdy Thirty, *contributed to this analysis.*

MESSENGER BOT SEQUENCES

The front line of social media entrepreneurship is chatbots. A useful tool to enhance a Facebook Live or other live event is a Messenger bot sequence that interacts with audience members. Dana Tran writes about a step-by-step process that may be a valuable introduction to the use of artificial intelligence tools within social media measurement and management. The real-time nature of live-streaming video has long been understood on the Internet. But measurement and management of live events has trailed the innovation. "Messenger bots allow you to create a personalized 'choose your own adventure' experience" (Tran, 2018a, para. 5). "You can also leverage bots to provide people with relevant and helpful information on a platform where open rates are extremely high, often resulting in greater reach." Messenger bots are seen as a way to:

- Increase event registrations and attendance—it is easy to get people to register for an event on Facebook then it is to have follow through. Reminders may increase event attendance. Facebook message open rates (80–90%) are believed to be as much as three times higher than email reminders (17–28%) (paras. 6–9).

- Bots may be used "as a listening and research tool" to "learn about your audience," as well as "customize" the presentation—perhaps to increase conversion rates (para. #).

- A chatbot may spark user action by increasing engagement through the use of a form, free PDF download, or video replay link—early stems within a marketing journey funnel that may generate leads and eventually sales or other action (para. 10).

Typically, a "reminder sequence" begins with a registration thank you message, and event reminder, and finally follow-up messages. In terms of engagement, these are opportunities to call a Facebook Live viewer to further, perhaps deeper, action. Tran (2018) suggests use of the tools Chatfuel or ManyChat to automate the sequence. It begins with what is known as a scheduled "broadcast message" to live video subscribers (para. 17).

The idea is to create engaging messages that lead a subscriber to reply that they are interested in the live event or not. The filtering through message interaction and follow-up essentially qualifies leads for further engagement. The use of positive AI interaction saves time and assists in target marketing efforts. Confirming registration for a live event is an act that represents a higher level of interest and engagement. At a minimum, these further brands a live event. The most sophisticated bot communication mimics human interaction. It is possible that you have interacted with a bot without even knowing it. This raises important ethical issues. First, Facebook and other social media platforms place constraints on what is appropriate to not to communicate through a chatbot. Second, it can be argued that all bot interaction should be transparent and also reflect financial and other interests. Users should know they are communicating with AI technology and why. For example, a Facebook Live host could say, "I am unable to individually chat with all of my webinar viewers, but this chatbot will allow you to send us important information for follow-up." Or, "Our AI communication with you here helps with a request for free resources." However, chatbots are used to manage a Facebook Live or other video event, Tran (2018) suggests that the need to "build trust" is a key goal (para. 82). It is clear that is brand trust is lost in the use of AI, then this runs counter to marketing goals and objectives. We know that it is common for users to subscribe, but then be unable to attend an event. So, reminders and replays can be helpful. This is true, so long as the marketer does not cross a line and annoy by seeking engagement when it is no longer desired.

Google offers many excellent resources to assist search engine marketers. The inclusion of video content has become a game-changer in terms of data measurement and prediction. There remains a lot of debate about use of video in digital marketing campaigns, but the technologies used to view it continue to grow—watches, glasses, home devices, and a wide range of projection screens. For marketers, a key traditional issue is whether or not video helps move a potential customer through the marketing funnel. As digital advances, though, there is more interest in the customer journey. It may involve online and physical sites. Rapid technological change, at the same time, is opening new and creative opportunities for entrepreneurship. Exploration of AI ethics, at the same time, is expected to grow in importance, as entrepreneurs seek cover from the threat of regulation (Kahn, 2019).

The future of social media measurement and management also can be found in media storytelling platforms—including immersive game environments. Multi-player online games, in this sense, return social media to Internet chatroom roots. Immersive virtual reality, however, is a sophisticated way to transport individuals to a common space for specific purposes, such as a fundraising event that reaches a younger target demographic group. One example is a global social entrepreneurship event.

ʈ(ʀ) Thought Leader Jurge Cruz-Alvarez

Case Study—Extra Life Fundraising Campaign

Video game players and their online gaming communities may not always be known for their charitable giving, but each autumn more than one hundred thousand players join together for a greater cause. A subsidiary of the Children's Miracle Network, a nonprofit that fundraises for hospitals across North America, Extra Life was established in 2008 with the goal of setting up an infrastructure to empower game players to raise money for children's hospitals by doing what they do best—playing video games. By creating a fundraiser page and a way to transfer

FIGURE 10.5 *Jurge Cruz-Alvarez (@jcruzalvarez26). Photograph courtesy Jurge Cruz-Alvarez.*

money to a hospital campaign, similar to sponsoring a marathon contestant, players then broadcast themselves playing video games with the goal of raising money for their designated charity.

In the Fall of 2017, myself and a couple dozen others descended upon Maryland to put on our own 24-hour Extra Life charity broadcast. The broadcast represented video games editorial website Irrational Passions and the entertainment company known as Kinda Funny. My goal was to use social media, primarily Twitter, to communicate with our community and the public at large about our fundraiser. I promoted our Extra Life broadcast as an event. However, in reality, we were a large group of people packed into a private home. I wanted to use social media, combined with our broadcast, to tell an engaging multi-social story that would draw audiences to our fundraiser. Quesenberry (2019) says that the best social media does not just tell a story, but it also has an understanding of what the story is and where is the story. We approached the event as a social marketing campaign.

Twitter, unlike platforms Facebook and Instagram, is designed for real-time, moment-to-moment live tweeting. Twitter's quick, micro-blogging format is great when you have an event because you can create quick and meaningful content to regularly update your audience. The Irrational Passions brand account already had a Twitter following of about 600, and most of our members participating and performing on the broadcast were internet content creators with some sort of following on the platform—with between 200 and, in one case, one million followers. Most of our team was tweeting about the event. I used the #IPExtraLife hashtag to funnel all of the separate conversations to spread the event across their social networks.

Ma, et al. (2013) mention that making a successful and popular hashtag is difficult because it is dependent on a number of users using the hashtag in a certain time frame and with a certain frequency. Because of this, it can be difficult to predict the success of a hashtag. The combined social power of our group, the quality of our stream, and the hashtag grabbed the attention of our social networks. The Union Metrics data analysis tool suggested, that our hashtag had a potential reach of 1,103,732 with almost nine million impressions. Additionally, we were able to increase by about 100 our number of account followers, as well as grow impressions over 3,000 percent based upon Twitter Analytics data.

These are great social media results, but having popular posts was not the end game of our group. As Quesenberry said, it is important to have a deeper understanding of the story. Every post I put out from the Irrational Passions Twitter account also was designed to stand alone as a piece of quality content for our followers, as well as including a link back to our broadcast and fundraiser page. Ultimately, the goal of this social media campaign was to draw attention to our broadcast and raise funds. We found that linking to

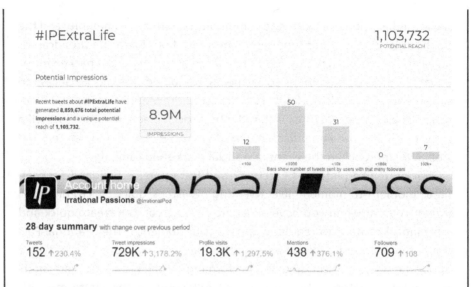

FIGURE 10.6 *Extra Life data. Image courtesy Jurge Cruz-Alvarez.*

destinations was successful because the percentage of our link click through rates (CTRs) were substantially higher than usual.

During this campaign, I was also able to witness the effectiveness of the changes Twitter implemented in 2017 to raise their post character limit from 140 characters to 280 characters. By doubling tweet length limits, I was able to write quality posts that included images, the hashtag, member tags, and links for our broadcast and fundraiser pages.

At the end of our campaign, we raised over $2,300 dollars for Johns Hopkins Hospital of Baltimore, surpassing our goal of $1,500. The #IPExtraLife campaign was the first time I implemented and managed a social media campaign. It was a very powerful learning experience and a first-hand look at the effectiveness of social media for event management when you have the right people, resources, and a strategic plan of attack.

References

Ma, Z., Sun, A., & Cong, G. (2013). On Predicting the Popularity of Newly Emerging Hashtags in Twitter. *Journal of The American Society for Information Science & Technology*, 64(7), 1399–1410, 1399.

Quesenberry, K. A. (2019). *Social Media Strategy: Marketing and Advertising in the Consumer Revolution*, second edition. Lanham, MD: Rowman & Littlefield.

Rosen, A. (2017, November 7). Tweeting Made Easier. Twitter Blog. Retrieved from https://blog.twitter.com/official/en_us/topics/product/2017/tweeting madeeasier.html

Jurge Cruz-Alvarez graduated in Journalism and Media Communication (JMC) at the University of Nebraska at Omaha in 2019. He was named by JMC faculty as the outstanding undergraduate. He served as UNO Social Media Lab technician in 2018–19.

Social measurement and management are colliding with an accelerating stage of technological diffusion of new products, services, and processes. Nielsen (2019), for example, is selling a product called Visual IQ that focuses on holistic and strategic media measurement of consumer journey touchpoint attribution, advertising audiences, and activation. "Time spent with the television set is shifting, with consumers spending more time using TV-connected devices to stream content in addition to traditional TV" (Nielsen, 2018b, para. 1). Consumers can be thought of as taking a journey through specific digital media, and they tend to avoid pain points that block them from immediately meeting needs and wants. The ability to observe online clicks is a form of "surveillance capitalism" (Singer, 2019, para. 3). Visit a local television newsroom, and you are likely to see data for real-time Google Analytics website hits, as well as competitive market data presenting social media platform performance measures.

Social media managers also activate awareness and interest of employees at all levels. Behind the computer code driving social change is a frequently hidden world of data and algorithms. From search marketing to social media campaigns, professionals must manage and continuously measure business effectiveness. Data from Altimiter suggest that engagement (clicks, shares, comments, and mentions) reflect nearly one-third (30%) of performance, followed by efficiency (cost savings, customer support) (23%), conversion (downloads, direct sales) (23%), reach (likes, views) (12%), and inbound (website time, other owned media (12%) (Baer, 2018b, para. 9). Beyond measuring content impact, Baer (2018b) suggests that brands should focus on customer interaction, product attributes over thought leadership, short video, and data expertise (data analysis, project management, and marketing automation) over traditional content editing and design skills.

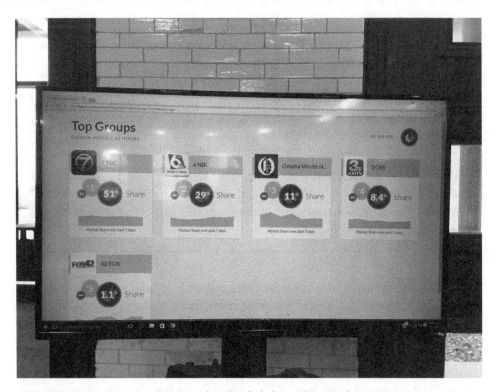

FIGURE 10.7 *KETV newsroom social media desk data. Photograph by Jeremy Harris Lipschultz.*

A variety of tools, such as Union Metrics' Twitter Assistant and Instagram Checkup, aggregate data and present a contextual picture of social media effectiveness within a relatively simple presentation for busy social media managers. Basic data dashboards are offered free to users, and advanced analytics are premium paid services.

Social media measurement and management begins with amplifying branded messages through increased reach and awareness—a precursor to sparking engagement, building relationships, and moving toward measurable conversion to behavioral action and change. Tools such as TweetReach present data on use of event or campaign hashtags. A prudent social media manager should triangulate all data from available tools to visualize patterns. As yet, no single tool captures every piece of data that may be useful. Paid dashboards, such as Nuvi, come closest. However, these tend to be expensive and require that social media manager make an extensive ROI case for the expense.

We have entered an era in which Instagram celebrities seek to monetize posts as paid influencers. Some seek fame for its own sake. Others are artists wanting to be

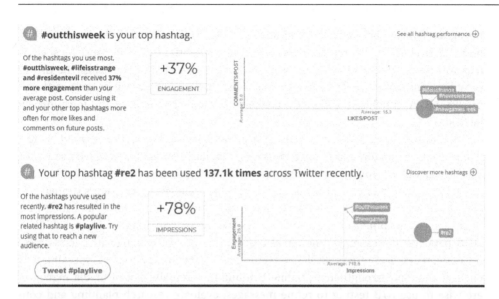

FIGURE 10.8 *Union Metrics data. Images courtesy the UNO Socia Media Lab.*

discovered or small business people desiring growth. At times, events lead to instant fame—brief or for the longer term. It is fair to say that successful social media managers play to brand strengths, build upon positive outcomes, address issues, and use continuous improvement techniques. Increasingly, we can visualize social networks as clustered communities focused around topics and interests. Large brands, such as Target in Minneapolis, use a command center for real-time monitoring and response. Social media managers must move beyond growing followers and reach, as mentions happen within a conversational context and set of business goals. This involves identifying and tracking KPIs. Social media posts may burst in a viral explosion, or they may quickly decay, as happens to most content. Frequently, social media users want valuable and personalized information the answers common questions. Within a marketing funnel, awareness should lead to some level of consideration about a product or service. Clearly, social media may help amplify messages. That said, the sheer size of social media platforms means that we are awash in noise and clutter. In 2018, for example, there were an estimated four million YouTube video views, two million snaps, one million Facebook logins, and half a million tweets every minute. The best that a social media manager can do is focus on branded page management of engaging posts. At the individual level, LinkedIn by 2019 was the dominant social media site for executives and one of the most popular for their employees. LinkedIn articles, as well as other blogging, vlogging, and podcasting offered structured ways to share and grow as thought leaders. The popular

Instagram Stories content model emphasizes importance of views and swipes. If social media managers are to inform, educate, or persuade, then content must be seen as trustworthy to billions of monthly users. However, when Kylie Jenner lost the title of most liked Instagram photo to an egg, it signaled that social media users are not always predictable. As much as social media managers try to be strategic, communication can be fickle.

The future of social media marketing rests on using data analytics to audit performance, refining media storytelling messages, emphasis on video, effective use of key social media platforms, and networking with other marketing professionals (Stelzner, 2018b). A grounding in social science method helps social media managers strategically align goals with larger business priorities. Paid social media celebrity and micro-influencers—what some call "nano-influencers" with less than 10,000 followers (Talbot, 2018, para. 5)—increasingly function as brand spokespersons, along with friends, family, co-workers, and others. Still, the larger goals of raising awareness, sparking new engagement, and strengthening online communities remain. Social media managers are wise to use A/B testing to refine messages, evaluate research planning and content execution, and develop best practices that work in a current context. In this sense, social media managers must stay current with new tools and methods for measurement and management.

Help can be found by reading current academic and industry research, integrating PR, advertising and marketing plans, cultivating stakeholder relationships through collaboration, engaging with relevant conversation, and bravely immersing in the newest technologies that virtually make possible social media communication from any time and place. Social media entrepreneurs will survive by being lifelong learners, embracing change, passionately meeting the needs of others, and recognizing the opportunities available, as well as those not yet imagined.

USEFUL TOOLS

Social media automation has become more common practice among social media managers. *Social Media Today* (Sarma, 2018) published five tools designed to save time and create more efficient operation of plans and tactics.

1. *DrumUp* is a content curation and scheduling tool that helps social media managers use keywords and RSS feeds for auto-scheduling.

2. *IFTTT* is a popular tool that uses "recipes" to automate social media posts, save social media photographs, and avoid repetitive and time-consuming work.

3. *Survey Anyplace* creates survey to learn more about a target audience.

4. *Brand24* tracks keywords and help manage brand reputation.

5. *CoScheduler* is a flexible content calendar.

Many popular tools such as IFTTT help social media managers automate a repetitive work function. Pettijohn (2018) mentions Hootsuite and Sprout Social for scheduling posts: "If used correctly, automation can be liberating" (paras. 1–2). IFTTT, for example, allows users to automatically save social media photographs to a Dropbox folder, or send an email alert. Some apps have been developed to assist content managers with following and unfollowing decisions for Twitter and Instagram. Social media measurement and management should grow over time—requiring additional freelance or permanent staff positions. Use of Google Docs is common for team collaboration, as are Skype, Zoom, and other video conferencing tools. "Google Sheets is great for tracking outreach and creating content calendars" (para. 11). Pettijohn (2018) suggests the following format:

TIME   TYPE   TOPIC   POST   LINK

A content calendar allows a social media management team to approve and schedule content each month. This project management mindset should help with organizing hashtags across platforms, using scheduling tools, and developing ongoing goals, objectives, and tactics. Ultimately, social media managers must focus on ROI of time spent with social media engagement compared to other work activities. It is reasonable to consider efficiency tools and processes because social media measurement and management can be an extremely time-consuming effort. Social media platforms, similar to the earlier larger Web, began with few restrictions. However, as Google, Facebook and other corporate giants face large fines over data privacy, social media managers may have less access to useful data. Strategic thinking should be increasingly important in order to use data science skills and practices in discerning meaningful metrics and valuable insights. Social media management works when it happens within the context of online community and relationship-building, authoritative influence and authentic, conversational media storytelling.

AS SEEN ON YOUTUBE

Assignment

Watch Thyng CEO Ed LaHood explain augmented reality (AR) technologies and look for connections that could be made to social media strategy and tactics: www.youtube.com/watch?v=nCqzvC4dx0Y

Questions

1. Think about one of your favorite brands: How could it use AR to spark new social media engagement?

2. What concerns should there be in protecting user data within AR? What other issues may there be in the future?

PROJECT IDEAS

Social media listening is key to the ability of social media managers to collect and analyze data in the future. "Social media monitoring is an excellent technique to reach your potential customers where they are, and build a genuine, authentic, customer–brand relationship" (Barysevich, 2018, para. 2). Use Boolean search operators, such as "and" and "or," to find current social media activity on Twitter. For example, select the brand mentions for your college or local sports team. See if you can determine any AI or bot activity on Twitter. How is this likely to be impacted by voice and other new technologies in the future?

DISCUSSION QUESTIONS

1. Given the speed of technological disruption, what are the greatest SWOT strengths, weaknesses, opportunities, and threats when it comes to your campus social media branding efforts?

2. Develop a set of three SMART goal that a social media manager for your campus could develop and implement. How should she respond to technological change represented by AI and bots?

Appendix A
Social Media Planning Template Options

STEP ONE: IDENTIFY INFLUENCERS
Instagram   Facebook   Twitter   LinkedIn

- Organic and/or paid influence opportunities
- Key hashtags
- Related topics or issues

STEP TWO: CREATE EVENTS
IGTV   FB Live   Periscope   YouTube

- Face-to-face opportunities
- SWOT (strengths, weaknesses, opportunities, and threats) analysis
- SMART (specific, measurable, achievable, realistic, timed) goals, objectives, tactics

STEP THREE: OPERATIONALIZE ONLINE

- Twitter live chat
- Live video
- Webinar
- Podcast

STEP FOUR: WEBSITE AND OTHER OWNED MEDIA MEASUREMENT

- Benchmarked data
- Google Analytics KPIs
- Facebook and Instagram Insights, Twitter Analytics, etc.

STEP FIVE: TESTING AND REFINEMENT

- A/B testing
- Paid post boost testing
- Use of dashboard widgets
- Refinement of influence model

Appendix B
Social Media Marketing Evaluation

To: *Supervisor*

From: *Author, Title*

Subject: *Social Media Marketing Evaluation Report*

The following social media marketing evaluation summary outlines key insights for the current reporting period. Key performance indicators (KPIs) are used to compare current to previous goals. Each SMART goal is evaluated based upon available data and any research limitation that is identified for future efforts in our ongoing process.

A. Key Insights

    1. Project Results?

    2. Project Challenges?

    3. Project Opportunities?

    4. Future Planning

    Comments:

B. KPIs Observed   Current Goal   Previous Goal

    1. Data

    2. Data

    3. Data

    Comments:

   C. <u>Current SMART Goals (Y/N)</u> **Specific Measurable Achievable Realistic Timely**

      1. <u>Goal 1</u>

      2. <u>Goal 2</u>

      3. <u>Goal 3</u>

    Comments:

       Adapted from K. Kosaka (2018, November 20). Alexa.com, *Free Marketing Report Template: Make Client Reporting Fast and Easy*. https://blog.alexa.com/marketing-report-template

Glossary

Administrative law—U.S. regulation by agencies, such as the Federal Trade Commission, focused on complex and specific areas.

Adoption—in the diffusion model refers to people who use a new product, service, process, or idea.

Advertising—paid and commercial messages purchased by an advertiser or agency representative to appear within mainstream traditional or hybrid digital media.

Advertising Value Equivalency (AVE)—a largely discredited model of placing a dollar figure on the value of earned media, such as a news story, and relating it to advertising rates. It was used as a way for PR people to claim ROI for their media relations work.

Algorithm—computer code that filters and organizes social media content based upon a set of goals and objectives.

Analytics—measurement of social media behavior through a variety of metrics. A stream of new tools has been developed to present real-time and near real-time data on social media dashboards, such as Google Analytics.

Application Programming Interface (API)—the computer code granting access to data, such as the Twitter search window code.

Apps—short for *applications*, an app is software, for use on a desktop, laptop, tablet, or smartphone, that allows the user to apply the power of system software for a particular purpose.

Artificial Intelligence (AI)—computer-based chatbots and other machine learning.

Attribution—a credited source of an online click. **Last-click attribution** gives credit for a conversion.

Augmented reality (AR)—use of geographic data and mobile smartphone data and images to augment physical spaces with vast amounts of computer data.

Authority—the presence of links and backlinks builds SEO authority and tends to improve page rank.

Benchmark—use of foundational data within a social media campaign. By benchmarking, a social media entity may set and track longer-term goals and objectives, as well as effectiveness of tactics.

Best practices—standard practices of an industry, developed gradually, that are the processes and social media content that have worked well over time.

Big data—huge and complex data collection over time that typically requires cloud computing and sophisticated algorithms designed to interpret it.

Blockchain—connection of big data computing, part of the Internet of Things (IoT).

Blog—these are online sites, often owned media, in which somewhat formal and regular posts (information and commentary) are published. Early blogs were characterized by authenticity, which is the idea that the author presents a more "real" and unfiltered identity.

Board—Pinterest uses the term "board' to reflect the online space where users "pin" content to a virtual message board.

Bounce rate—percentage of sessions with a single user interaction on a website.

Brand ambassadors—support brands by sharing their stories and broadening reach.

Brand evangelists—tend to be fans of products or services with a desire to spread enthusiasm.

Brand storytellers—narrative influencers promoting a specific brand.

Branding—the marketing technique of emphasizing a brand for a product, service, organization, or individual. A logo, face, or even a song may reinforce the brand for consumers.

Business-to business (B2B)—business between two businesses rather than between a business and consumer.

Buzz—the aggregate social network activity from a word, term, phrase, or other content. On Twitter, for example, we can track #BreakingNews buzz on a graph of time (X) and total number of tweets (Y).

Call to action (CTA)—social media content with a clear message through explicit words, such as retweet, follow, share, like, and download that increase engagement rates. The emphasis is on direct communication with an audience.

C-suite—top-level corporate executives making key decisions that may include social media policies.

Chatbot—artificial intelligence that generates an automatic response to a social media user each time she or he responds.

Chief executive officer (CEO)—a top decision-maker within a corporation.

Chief marketing officer (CMO)—the person in charge of marketing and reporting to the CEO within a C-suite of organizational leaders.

Clickbait—content primarily designed to drive clicks and traffic that may have little storytelling value.

Clickstream—data follow customers' online journeys from click to click.

Click-through rates (CTR)—a measure of user clicks on sponsored results.

Cloud computing—Internet storage and management of data in remote computer servers, such as at Amazon.

Community—a core CMC concept that describes how individuals create groups, including interest groups, by sharing information within social networks.

Computer-mediated communication (CMC)—a social and research construct that begins to explain the nature of social network and social media behavior and culture.

Conversation monitoring—the process of monitoring online activity, emphasizing engagement through responding to comments, reactions, and posts by others.

Conversion—marketers convert social media activity to sales or other outcomes.

Corporate Social Responsibility (CSR)—is a progressive business movement designed to include social concerns in decision-making that go beyond public relations value to, for example, environmental impact and sustainability.

Cost per click (CPC)—a social media alternative advertising measure to the traditional cost per thousand mainstream method for pricing commercial messages. CPC charges advertisers for every audience user click.

Cost per thousand (CPM)—a traditional advertising price method estimating how much to charge for each 1,000 audience members who will see the ad. For example, one online national video service charges about $25 CPM. The Super Bowl, which has the largest national audience, has increased over the years from $5 to $27 CPM, while a popular primetime show may cost $35 CPM.

Credibility—is related to trust and believability. In media research, we talk about source and message credibility. The more content has both, the more likely audience members will be to trust it.

Crowdsourcing—collective influence within a social network.

Customer relationship management (CRM)—organizes engagement around customer satisfaction, loyalty and retention.

Dark social—click data that cannot be attributed to a source.

Demographic—data describing individual attributes, such as age, education, income, and gender.

Dependent—effects variables that may be impacted by variation of independent variables.

Digital rights management (DRM)—systems of control over content access to seek user payments.

Diffusion—the spread of new ideas, new practices, new processes, and new products. Diffusion research identifies the earliest innovators (2.5%), early adopters (13.5%), early majority (34%), late majority (34%), and laggards (16%). The percentage of adopters (Y) is graphed using an S-shaped curve over time (X).

Early adopters—in a diffusion cycle, the first to adopt new technologies and/or ideas.

Earned exposure—customer reviewer expressions of positive feelings about products or services.

Earned media—public relations professionals work to receive positive attention for their clients through content that is not paid advertising. Earned media may be the product of media relations, a campaign, real-time engagement, or other activities.

eCommerce—online sales and business.

Electronic word-of-mouth (eWOM)—an extension of face-to-face communication applied to social media marketing.

Empirical—research based upon the human behavior that we may observe.

Engagement—the term that describes strengthening social network interaction from passive to more active. It goes beyond passive viewing to clicking on a link, liking content, sharing content, and responding to content in some way that can be seen by social media users.

Enterprise—large corporate use cases, typically of 5,000 or more employees, for specialized software applications and processes.

Entrepreneurs—social media sites have been created and developed by the technology sector, which values an innovative culture. Personal computer hardware and software were first developed by young entrepreneurs, such as Bill Gates and Steve Jobs, and the current industry features inventors and their start-ups.

Facebook Insights—a dashboard showing social media managers' performance over time of fan page posts.

Facebook Live—a real-time streaming video app within Facebook that allows for viewing, commenting, and use of like, love, sad, and angry emoji.

Fan—a Facebook user may like a page and become a fan. By doing this, the posts on this page appear on the user's news feed.

Fremium—sites may offer a free trial to advance the diffusion process in the marketing funnel toward purchase.

General Data Protection Regulation (GDPR)—a European Union (EU) legal privacy framework applied to personal data that U.S. sites adopted in 2018.

Geographic—data based upon location, such as found through mobile smartphone towers, WiFi, and Bluetooth positioning.

Geotags—link geographic location to social media content, sometimes within a geofenced area. Social media conversation, business, and entertainment may be related to location.

Governance—policy documents, such as a company's social media policy.

Hardware—the physical computing equipment, such as a desktop, laptop, tablet, or smartphone. We also speak of components—keyboard, mouse, monitor, router, modem, etc.—as hardware.

Hashflag—a paid emoji that automatically appears when a promoted hashtag is used.

Hashjacking—hijacking a hashtag already in use on Twitter for an event.

Hashtag (#)—the number sign used on Twitter and, more recently, Facebook as a filtering device. By searching for and using hashtags, subsets of the larger feed can be seen and used.

Help A Reporter Out (HARO)—Cision-owned daily emails pitching story ideas to potential media news sources.

Human–computer interaction (HCI)—early research into how humans engaged with computer hardware and software.

Hybrid media—new media that incorporate some older media rules, such as news editorial practices.

Hyperlinks—Web links to other content via an Internet URL address.

Hypotheses—formal prediction based upon theory, concepts, and previous research.

Identity—what we present online through the use of words, photographs, sounds, videos, emoticons, avatar, or other means. Each time we decide to communicate (and even when we do not) we suggest an identity to social network site users.

Impact measurement—analysis of impact, including nonprofit value of news stories.

Impressions—awareness of information, such as from seeing it during a search.

Independent—variables may be seen as statistically contributing causes to measured effects or outcomes.

Influence—users with a lot of fans, followers or connections tend to be considered influencers. Celebrities' large reach affords them monetized influence, but micro-influencers with 1,000 to 100,000 followers also may be influential due to higher engagement with fans.

Innovation—a business culture favoring change over stability. Entrepreneurs may be motivated to create new products and services.

Integrated marketing communication (IMC)—planning and strategies that integrate traditional advertising, marketing, and PR approaches.

Interaction—each engagement with another SNS account reflects a decision to interact. Interaction and engagement are a key foundation for social media use.

Internet of things (IoT)—increasing use of online commands to control home and business devices.

Intervening—variables may contribute between change measured for independent and dependent variables.

Key performance indicators (KPIs)—continuous monitoring of important business variables.

Keywords—words used within SEO to move page placement higher in a search by relating to common user language.

LinkedIn—professional business network site purchased by Microsoft.

Listicle—popular social media content may be structured as a numbered list in which longer articles can be divided into smaller chunks.

Literature review—academics review previous research to develop a project.

Location-based services (LBS)—designed to allow users to check in at locations.

Marketing—promoting and selling products and services targeted at a specific market. Research is usually utilized to focus marketing, which may involve use of advertising and social media marketing.

Marketing funnel—a traditional marketing model of awareness, consideration, and purchase.

Measurement error—all measurement has error, and researchers estimate amounts.

Media cloverleaf—Edelman PR divides the media environment into four overlapping parts: traditional media, owned media, hybrid media, and social media.

Media communication—a theoretical perspective that moves away from mass communication and mass audiences toward fragmentation.

Meme—social media content that features cultural imitation. Production typically uses easily identifiable characters, iterations, and humor. For example, there is a persistent use of an image from the 1971 *Willy Wonka and the Chocolate Factory* movie because of an early meme generator site.

Metrics—the measurement of behavior within social media. A variety of social media "dashboards," such as Google Analytics, Sprout, Chartbeat, Hootsuite, Cision, Tweetdeck, Argyle Social, Sprout Social, and Radian6 are in use.

Micro-influencers—on Instagram and other popular social media sites tend to have about 1,000 followers. Brands offer free products or payments to reach individual social networks.

Mobile communication—smartphones and tablets connected through WiFi or cell-phone data. Mobile Internet connections allow for the use of a wide variety of social media apps.

Monetization—generating revenue from views, such as through YouTube pre-roll advertising.

Multimedia storytelling—use of photos, video, or other rich media.

Narrative—use of storytelling techniques, such as a story arc.

Native advertising—paid content designed to look like unpaid editorial articles.

Network visualization—social networks generate large amounts of data that may be viewed as a series of network maps of communication hubs and spokes. Visualization depicts through graphs the social space between SNS accounts.

Open rates—in an email campaign, these are percentages of those sent a newsletter who opened the message.

Operational definitions—in academic research specify procedures.

Opportunity costs—the cost of using money on one expense and not having it available for other possibilities.

Optimizing—content and page performance measurement leads to improvement that corrects errors and grows audience over time.

Organic—a way to describe naturally evolving social media content. Facebook contrasts content that organically circulates on the social network with paid content that is then boosted to the top of feeds, or given more prominent placement.

Owned media—typically company-owned media, such as a website.

Pageviews—Google Analytics uses page clicks as a raw exposure measure.

Paid—social media includes advertising, boosting, and promoting newsfeed content, as opposed to naturally occurring organic content spread.

Paid search—search engines charge advertisers for top placement within search results.

Pay-per-click (PPC)—an advertising model that monetizes website clicks.

Paywall—a system requiring registration and payment by users.

Personal brand—use of social media to cultivate branding of individual identity.

Pins—Pinterest describes any posting on a user board as a pin, which is the online metaphor for placing a scrap of paper on a bulletin board.

Platforms—online sites that offer various social media services.

Population—data include all members of a group under study. In survey research, we randomly sample to estimate population data.

Posting—is the act of uploading media content to a social media site. Beyond organic content, the text, photographs, or video distributed through a posting may receive wider distribution by paying for a promoted post or sponsored content on a site.

Privacy—a concept first suggested in the late nineteenth century that calls for legal protection of intimate details of life, especially when a person seeks to protect these from public view.

Promoted posts—social media sites charge advertisers to appear in prominent positions that are likely to be seen.

Psychographic—data focused on lifestyle variables.

Public relations (PR)—seeks through professional best practices to present, maintain, and manage public images and reputations. Ongoing campaigns use media relations tactics to present perceived positives. Reputation management efforts may be in response to a crisis from perceived negative information.

Random—collection of data gives everyone in a population an equal opportunity of being selected, such as for participation in a survey. Many Internet surveys are not random, and data may not be representative of the population.

Ranking—Google page rank data measure a page's search result presence, high or low, compared to other pages.

Reach—a traditional mass media measure of distribution, social media are also interested in measuring the broad distribution of content.

Real-time social media listening engagement—current PR best practices include nearly immediate response to conversation monitoring of social media. Within a relatively short time, sometimes a matter of minutes, a brand engages on a social network about a trending topic, issue, or person.

Reliability—social scientific measures of consistency or reproducibility of results.

Research, planning, implementation, and evaluation (RPIE)—a PRSA process of systematically measuring goal outcomes.

Return on investment (ROI)—calculation of a financial gain minus the cost of an investment. ROI is expressed as a percentage or ratio and is sometimes considered a measure of efficiency.

Retweet—re-distributing a previous tweet with the letters RT in front of it, this allows Twitter users to easily share content to their social network. Twitter users also post MT for modified tweets and PRT, if an item is a partial retweet.

Rich media—photographs, video, info-graphics, or other visual elements.

Right to be forgotten (RTBF)—European law empowering users to have personal information removed from the Internet and disconnected from search engines, such as Google.

Roles—individuals adopt roles, much as an actor might. A social media professional, for example, may perceive and express the role of an innovator or entrepreneur.

RPIE—the Public Relations Society of America PR process of research, planning, implementation, and evaluation.

Search engine optimization (SEO)—Google algorithms produce a system for pushing some Internet content to the top of any specific search.

Search engine marketing (SEM)—paid strategies of benefiting from SEO.

Search engine results pages (SERPs)—using SEO techniques to drive high placement during keyword searches.

Segmentation—Targeting specific demographic or other marketing groups.

Sentiment—computer analysis and human coding for positive, neutral, and negative comments.

Share of voice (SoV)—a percentage of conversation mentioning a brand compared to competitors.

Slideshare—a tool that is used to share PowerPoint or other slide presentations within social media. These appear on LinkedIn, which can help in personal branding efforts.

Smartphones—mobile telephones connected on cellular networks that provide an Internet connection through devices that have personal computer capabilities.

Snaps—Snapchat user postings to the site.

Social business—application of business strategy, goals, and tactics within social media marketing campaigns.

Social graph—on Facebook, this is a user's complete social network.

Social media dashboard—measurement tools that organize data for efficient analysis.

Social media emergency management (SMEM)—Coordinated emergency management social media planning and execution during natural and other disasters.

Social media policy—explicit organizational rules covering appropriate and inappropriate social media use.

Social network analysis (SNA)—a set of methods for studying social network structure.

Social networks—an array of online platforms used to connect with others.

Social network site (SNS)—any online platform that enables communication between site accounts.

Software—computer code that allows hardware to be used via an operating system, programs, and applications.

Sponsored content—paid media content that may appear near editorial media content and free social media content.

Start-ups—new business ventures, sometimes with the funding help of "angel investors," launch social media sites and apps. An innovation culture, annual events such as "South by Southwest" (#SXSW) and the tech journalism community drive interest and activity in the diffusion of new ideas and products.

Stories—mobile apps Instagram and Snapchat offer users Stories as a tool to string together a series of postings into a larger narrative.

Subject matter experts (SMEs)—people with expert knowledge in a specific area.

Tactics—strategic PR campaigns devise a set of tactics used to achieve communication goals. For example, if a campaign is designed to raise awareness about an issue, a tactic may be to create a YouTube video that can be shared by bloggers.

Tagging—On Facebook, a person can be tagged in a photograph. In doing so, a name is associated with a face and perhaps a place, and these data can be shared across the social network. More generally, geotagging is use of a computer software code that identifies location. A smartphone photograph may be geotagged with the location, and this data can be presented or used within the context of an application.

Terms of service (ToS)—contract law that users click and agree to use software, apps, or websites.

Thought leader—in each area of the social media communication industry, leaders emerge who can communicate as influencers of the field. These thought leaders may be very active in social media and are asked to speak at conferences and meetings. They frequently blog and publish articles and books.

Tracking calls—code that identifies the source of clicks.

Transparency—the social media approach of disclosing all relevant interests and not having a hidden agenda.

Trending—on Twitter, different words and hashtags trend at any given time. These are the most talked-about items. These can be organic or "promoted" as advertising.

Trust—is considered an important and fundamental characteristic for a lot of influential social media content. Trust is related to credibility and believability, which frequently is assessed by judging previous behavior, including communication.

Tweet—Twitter originally limited each individual message to no more than 140 characters, but this was relaxed. Twitter Limits also include: 1,000 Direct Messages and 2,400 tweets per day; 1,000 follows per day; and ratio limits after 5,000 follows.

Twitter Analytics—a dashboard for social media managers to track real-time account data.

Uniform resource locator (URL)—a location, as reflected through a https: or http: web address.

User-generated content (UGC)—created content by users, often not sponsored by traditional professional media organizations.

User profiles—online descriptions of user identities.

Uses and gratifications—a research perspective emphasizing active audience participation.

Validity—in social science, the determination that measurement is conceptually what it was planned to be.

Vanity metrics—measures that do not go beyond popularity, such as number of followers, when these data are not related to strategies and tactics.

Variables—measures of variation, such as age from 18 to 85, data may fall within a range.

Verification and verified accounts—authenticity of identity is an important online concern. Twitter created a blue checkmark to identify those accounts that have been verified through its internal process, and this also appears on some Facebook pages. Additionally, Facebook users may take advantage of a two-step verification for login that includes a text message code to a mobile phone for account security.

Viral—content that is shared quickly and widely because of high interest. Social media enables individuals to post viral videos on YouTube and rise to almost-instant fame.

Virtual communities—online spaces creating a community experience among users.

Vlog—video bloggers use video posts instead of text. Vlogs are regular commentary in a video medium.

Word clouds—a word visualization of frequently used social media language.

Word of mouth (WOM)—personal influence is spread through word-of-mouth communication. In the past, this was mostly done face-to-face. Now, CMC allows for mediated WOM through social media communication.

References

Abraham, J. (2018, July 26). How to Use LinkedIn Lead Gen Form Ads. *Social Media Examiner*. https://www.socialmediaexaminer.com/use-linkedin-lead-gen-form-ads/

Abrams, A. (2018, July 12). There Will Only Be 1 Blockbuster in America Soon. *Time*. http://time.com/5337725/last-blockbuster-america-oregon/

Alaimo, D. (2018a, July 20). Study: Voice Investment Plans Don't Align with Preparedness. *Retail Dive*. https://www.retaildive.com/news/study-voice-investment-plans-dont-align-with-preparedness/528259/

Alaimo, K. (2018b, October 16). Twitter's Misguided Barriers for Researchers. Bloomberg. https://www.bloomberg.com/view/articles/2018-10-16/twitter-s-barriers-for-academic-researchers-are-misguided

Allcott, H., & Gentzkow, M. (2017). Social Media and Fake News in the 2016 Election. *Journal of Economic Perspectives 31*(2), 211–236.

AMEC (2015, September 3; 2010). *Launch of Barcelona Principles 2.0, Barcelona Declaration of Measurement Principles*. https://amecorg.com/wp-content/uploads/2015/09/Barcelona-Principles-2.pdf.

Amichai-Hamburger, A., Wainapel, G., & Fox, S. (2002). On the Internet No One Knows I'm an Introvert: Extroversion, Neuroticism, and Internet Interaction. *CyberPsychology & Behavior 5*(2), 125–128.

Anderson, M. (2016, November 7). Social Media Causes Some Users to Rethink Their Views On an Issue. Pew Research Center. http://www.pewresearch.org/fact-tank/2016/11/07/social-media-causes-some-users-to-rethink-their-views-on-an-issue/

Anderson, M., & Hitlin, P. (2016, August 15). Social Media Conversations about Race. Pew Research Center. http://www.pewinternet.org/2016/08/15/social-media-conversations-about-race/.

Andersson, H. (2018, July 4). Social Media Apps are 'Deliberately' Addictive to Users. *BBC News*, Technology. https://www.bbc.com/news/technology-44640959

Appelman, A., & Sundar, S. S. (2016, Spring). Measuring Message Credibility: Construction and Validation of an Exclusive Scale. *Journalism & Mass Communication Quarterly 93*(1), 59–79.

Asatryan, R., &. Asamoah, E. (2014). Perceived Corporate Social Responsibility (CSR) Activities and the Antecedents of Customer Loyalty in the Airline Industry. *Scientific Papers of the University of Pardubice, Series D, Faculty of Economics And Administration 21*(32), 5–17.

Ashcroft v. ACLU, 535 U.S. 564 (2002).

Ashcroft v. Free Speech Coalition, 535 U.S. 234 (2002).

Baer, J. (2018a). 4 Ways to Increase Share of Voice. *Convince & Convert*. https://www.convinceandconvert.com/social-media-strategy/4-ways-to-increase-share-of-voice/

Baer, J. (2018b). Your 2019 Content Strategy: 5 Trends You Can't Ignore. https://www.convinceandconvert.com/content-marketing/content-trends-2019/

Baer, J. (2019, January 6). 5 Ways to Get More Customers and Improve Customer Experience with SMS. *Convince and Convert*. Email.

Bargh, J., & McKenna, K. (2004). The Internet and Social Life. *Annual Review of Psychology 55*(1), 573–590.

Barnes, S. B. (2003). *Computer-Mediated Communication, Human-to-Human Communication across the Internet*. Boston: Allyn & Bacon.

Barnhart, B. (2018, August 21). The Ultimate Guide on How to Use Instagram Stories. Sprout Social. https://sproutsocial.com/insights/how-to-use-instagram-stories/

Barysevich, A. (2018, July 17). 5 Ways You Can Use Social Media Listening to Your Advantage. *Social Media Today*. https://www.socialmediatoday.com/news/5-ways-you-can-use-social-media-listening-to-your-advantage/527897/

Bauer, R. A. (1964). The Obstinate Audience. *American Psychologist 19*, 319–328.

Baumer, E. P. S., Guha, S., Quan, E., Mimno, D., & Gay, G. K. (2015, July–December). Missing Photos, Suffering Withdrawal, or Finding Freedom? How Experiences of Social Media Non-Use Influence the Likelihood of Reversion. *Social Media + Society*, 1–14.

Bell, K. (2018, December 3). Apple reveals the Most Popular iPhone Apps of 2018. *Mashable*. https://mashable.com/article/apple-most-popular-iphone-apps-2018/#vq2zU9mhAGqR

Bene, M. (2018, Summer). Post Shared, Vote Shared: Investigating the Link between Facebook Performance and Electoral Success during the Hungarian General Election Campaign of 2014. *Journalism & Mass Communication Quarterly 95*(2), 363–380.

Berger, C. (2005). Interpersonal Communication: Theoretical Perspectives, Future Prospects. *Journal of Communication 55*(3), 415–447.

Bhattarcharya, C. B. (2016, November 17). How Companies Can Tap Sustainability to Motivate Staff. *The Edge of Risk*. http://www.brinknews.com/how-companies-can-tap-sustainability-to-motivate-staff

Bornstein, D., & Davis, S. (2010). *Social Entrepreneurship, What Everyone Needs to Know*. Oxford: Oxford University Press.

Bossetta, M. (2018, Summer). The Digital Architectures of Social Media: Comparing Political Campaigning on Facebook, Twitter, Instagram, and Snapchat in the 2016 U.S. Election. *Journalism and Mass Communication Quarterly 95*(2), 471–496.

boyd, d. m., & Ellison, N. B. (2008). Social Network Sites: Definition, History and Scholarship. *Journal of Computer-Mediated Communication 13*(1), 210–230.

Brandtzaeg, P. B. (2012). Social Networking Sites: Their Users and Social Implications – A Longitudinal Study. *Journal of Computer-Mediated Communication 17*(4), 467–488.

BrightVessel.com (2018, January 25). Customer Journey Map 2018. Bright Vessel. https://www. brightvessel.com/customer-journey-map-2018/

Briquelet, K. (2018, November 22). She Posted a Bad Yelp Review. Then Her Nightmare Began. *The Daily Beast*. https://www.thedailybeast.com/she-posted-a-bad-yelp-review-then-her-nightmare-began

Brito, M. (2018). *Participation Marketing*. London: Kogan Page.

Broom, G. M., & Sha, B.-.L (2013). *Cutlip and Center's Effective Public Relations*, eleventh edition. Boston: Pearson.

Bucknell, J. (2018, July 30). The Facebook Attribution Window: How Facebook Tracks Conversions. *Social Media Examiner*. https://www.socialmediaexaminer.com/facebook-attribution-window/

Bullock, L. (2017, December 6). 4 Recurring Hashtag Trends That Will Make Your Tweets More Impactful. Twitter Business. https://business.twitter.com/en/blog/4-recurring-hashtag-trends-that-will-make-Tweets-impactful.html

Bullock, L. (2018, July 5). 3 Influencer Marketplace Tools to Help Locate and Connect with Brand Relevant Voices. *Social Media Today*. www.socialmediatoday.com/news/3-influencer-marketplace-tools-to-help-locate-and-connect-with-brand-releva/527099/

Burnett, S. (2018, August 4). Crackdown on 'Bots' Sweep Up People Who Tweet Often. Associated Press. https://www.apnews.com/06efed5ede4d461fb2eac5b2c89e3c11

Butts, C. T. (2008). Social Network Analysis: A Methodological Introduction. *Asian Journal of Social Psychology 11*, 13–41.

California Consumer Privacy Act of 2018, AB-375. https://leginfo.legislature.ca.gov/faces/bill TextClient.xhtml?bill_id=201720180AB375

Caplan, S. (2003). Preference for Online Social Interaction: A Theory of Problematic Internet Use and Psychosocial Well-Being. *Communication Research 30*(6), 625–648. *Carpenter v. U.S.* 585 U.S. ___, 138 S.Ct. 2206 (2018)

Cashmore, E. (2014). *Celebrity Culture*, second edition. New York: Routledge.

Chaffee, S. H., & Metzger, M. J. (2001). The End of Mass Communication? *Mass Communication & Society 4*(4), 365–379.

Chan, M. (2017, Autumn). Media Use and Social Identity Model of Collective Action: Examining Roles of Online Alternative News and Social Media News. *Journalism & Mass Communication Quarterly 94*(3), 663–681.

Chan, M. (2018, Summer). Post Shared, Vote Shared: Investigating the Link between Partisan Strength and Social Media Use Among Voters During the 2016 Hong Kong Legislative Council Election: Examining the Roles of Ambivalence and Disagreement. *Journalism & Mass Communication Quarterly 95*(2), 343–362.

Chan-Olmsted, S., Rim, H., & Zerba, A. (2013). Mobile News Adoption among Young Adults: Examining the Roles of Perceptions, News Consumption, and Media Usage. *Journalism &Mass Communication Quarterly 90*(1), 126–147.

Chen, J. (2018, October 30). How to Get Started on Your Content Marketing Strategy. Sprout Social. https://sproutsocial.com/insights/content-marketing-strategy/

Chen, Y., & Persson, A. (2002). Internet Use among Young and Older Adults: Relation to Psychological Well-Being. *Educational Gerontology 28*(9), 731–744.

Cheong, P. H., Martin, J. N., & Macfadyen, L. P. (Eds.) (2012). *New Media and Intercultural Communication, Identity, Community and Politics.* New York: Peter Lang.

Cho, M., & Auger, G. A. (2013). Exploring Determinants of Relationship Quality Between Students and Their Academic Department. *Journalism & Mass Communication Educator 68*(3), 255–268.

Chu, S.-C., & Choi, S. M. (2011). Electronic Word-of-Mouth in Social Networking Sites: A Cross-Cultural Study of the United States and China. *Journal of Global Marketing 24*(1), 263–281.

Cision (2018). *Earned Media Management: The Evolution of PR and Comms.* Cision. https://www.cision.com/content/dam/cision/Resources/white-papers/Cision_earned_media_management.pdf

Coban, B. (2016). Social Media R/evolution, An Introduction. In B. Coban, *Social Media and Social Movements, The Transformation of Communication Patterns,* pp. vii–xix. Lanham, MD: Lexington Books.

Cohen, S. (2016, December 23). Kardashian–Chyna Reality Show Continues on Social Media. NBC Chicago. http://www.nbcchicago.com/entertainment/entertainment-news/Kardashian-Chyna-Reality-Show-Continues-on-Social-Media—408104915.html

Cole, J. I. (2003). *The UCLA Internet Report, Surveying the Digital Future, Year Three.* Los Angeles, CA: UCLA Center for Communication Policy. www.ccpa.ucla.edu

Confessore, N., & Kang, C. (2018, December 30). Facebook Data Scandals Stoke Criticism That a Privacy Watchdog Too Rarely Bites. *The New York Times.* https://www.nytimes.com/2018/12/30/technology/facebook-data-privacy-ftc.html

Conradt, S. (2013, December). 16 People Who Tweeted Themselves into Unemployment. Mental Floss. http://mentalfloss.com/article/54068/16-people-who-tweeted-themselves-unemployment

Coombs, W. T., & Holladay, S. J. (2007). *It's Not Just PR: Public Relations in Society.* Malden, MA: Blackwell.

Crestodina, A. (2018). *Content Chemistry: The Illustrated Handbook for Content Marketing,* fifth edition. Chicago: Orbit Media.

Curtis, L., Edwards, C., Fraser, K. L., Gudelsky, S., Holmquist, J., Thornton, K., & Sweetser, K. D. (2010). Adoption of Social Media for Public Relations by Nonprofit Organizations. *Public Relations Review 36,* 90–92.

Darling-Wolf, F. (2015). *Imagining the Global: Transnational Media and Popular Culture Beyond East and West.* Ann Arbor, MI: University of Michigan Press.

Dencik, L., & Leistert, O. (Eds.) (2015). *Critical Perspectives on Social Media and Protest: Between Control and Emancipation.* London: Rowman & Littlefield.

Denten, L. L., & Saghy, K. (2013, October 24). Bridging Social to Traditional PR. Cision. http://us.cision.com/events/on-demand-webinars/Bridging-the-Gap-to-Traditional-PR.asp

Digiday (2017, December 8). 'AR Is the Next Internet': Snapchat Gets $1 Mil. A Day for Branded Lenses. https://digiday.com/marketing/ar-next-internet-snapchat-gets-1-mil-day-branded-lenses/

Dimitrova, D. V., & Matthes, J. (2018, Summer). Social Media in Political Campaigning Round the World: Theoretical and Methodological Challenges. *Journalism & Mass Communication Quarterly 95*(2), 333–342.

Djonov, Emilia, & Zhao, S. (Eds.) (2014). *Critical Multimodal Studies of Popular Discourse*. New York: Routledge.

Doh, S.-J., & Hwang, J.-S. (2009). How Consumers Evaluate eWOM (Electronic Word-of-Mouth) Messages. *Cyberpsychology & Behavior 12*(2), 193–197.

Edelman (2019, January 20). Edelman Trust Barometer. www.edelman.com/trust-barometer

Edelman Singapore (2018, June 21). Edelman Singapore and EDB Launch Edelman Predictive Intelligence Centre. https://www.edelman.com/news-awards/edelman-singapore-and-edb-launch-edelman-predictive-intelligence-centre

Elonis v. United States, 575 U.S. ___, 135 S.Ct. 2001 (2015).

Ezrachi, A., & Stucke, M. E. (2016). *Virtual Competition: The Promise and Perils of the Algorithm Driven Economy*. Cambridge, MA: Harvard University Press.

Fertik, M., & Thompson, D. C. (2015). *The Reputation Economy*. New York: Crown Business.

Fischer, S., & Snyder, A. (2018, November 18). Exclusive Poll: America Sours On Social Media Giants. Axios. https://wwwww.axios.com/america-sours-on-social-media-giants-1542234046-c48fb55b-48d6-4c96-9ea9-a36e80ab5deb.html

Foley, R. J. (2018, July 22). Private Messaging Apps Undermine State Public Records Law. Associated Press. https://apnews.com/647b0f0328f942ceb63d54a03b5de265

Fontein, D. (2016, July 27). Top Demographics That Matter to Social Media Marketers. Hootsuite. https://blog.hootsuite.com/facebook-demographics/

Forrester (2018, December). The Total Economic Impact of Adobe Analytics & Adobe Audience Manager. Adobe. https://www.adobe.com/content/dam/acom/en/modal-offers/pdfs/54658.en.aec.report.total-economic-impact-analytics-audience-manager.pdf

Foster, Brian D., & Cadogan, John W. (2000). Relationship Selling and Customer Loyalty: An Empirical Investigation. *Marketing Intelligence & Planning 18*(4), 185–199.

Fournier, S., Breazeale, M., & Fetscherin, M. (Eds.) (2012). *Consumer–Brand Relationships: Theory and Practice*. London: Routledge.

Freberg, K. (2019). *Social Media for Strategic Communication: Creative Strategies and Research-Based Applications*. Los Angeles: Sage.

Freberg, K., & Kim, C. M. (2018). Social Media Education: Industry Leader Recommendations for Curriculum and Faculty Competencies. *Journalism & Mass Communication Educator 73*(4), 379–391.

Freeman, R. E. (1984/2010). *Strategic Management: A Stakeholder Approach*. Cambridge, UK: Cambridge University Press.

Frier, S. (2018, July 25). Facebook's Quarterly Ad revenue to Get Lift from Instagram. Bloomberg. https://www.bloomberg.com/news/articles/2018-07-25/facebook-s-quarterly-ad-revenue-to-get-lift-from-instagram

FTC (2012, August 10). FTC Approves Final Settlement with Facebook. https://www.ftc.gov/news-events/press-releases/2012/08/ftc-approves-final-settlement-facebook

FTC (2017, September 6). Signed Letters to Instagram Influences, 2017–01436. www.ftc.gov/system/files/documents/foia_requests/all_of_the_signed_letters.pdf

Fussell Sisco, H., Pressgrove, G., & Collins, E. L. (2013). Paralleling the Practice: An Analysis of the Scholarly Literature in Nonprofit Public Relations. *Journal of Public Relations Research 25*(4), 282–306.

Gallardo, R., Bell, R., & Jacknis, N. (2018, April 11). When It Comes to Broadband, Millennials Vote with Their Feet. *Daily Yonder*. https://www.dailyyonder.com/comes-broadband-millennials-vote-feet/2018/04/11/24960/

Gao, X. (2017, March 24). Networked Co-Production of 311 Services: Investigating the Use of Twitter in Five U.S. Cities. *International Journal of Public Administration*. www.tandfonline.com/doi/full/10.1080/01900692.2017.1298126

Garton, L., Haythornthwaite, C., & Wellman, B. (1997, June). Studying Online Social Networks. *Journal of Computer-Mediated Communication 3*, 1. http://reed.cs.depaul.edu/peterh/class/hci450/Papers/Garton.Haythornthwaite.Wellman.1997.pdf

Gelles, D. (2018, July 27). Dan Schulman of PayPal on Guns, Cash and Getting Punched. *The New York Times*. https://www.nytimes.com/2018/07/27/business/dan-schulman-paypal-corner-office.html

Gershon, R. A. (2017). *Digital Media Innovation: Management and Design Strategies in Communication*. Los Angeles: Sage.

Golin (2016). The g4. http://golin.com/about-us/g4/.

Google Opimize (2018). Help. https://support.google.com/optimize/answer/7012154

Greenhow, C., & Robelia, B. (2009, July). Old Communication, New Literacies: Social Network Sites as Social Learning Resources. *Journal of Computer-Mediated Communication 14*(4), 1130–1161.

Greer, C. F., & Ferguson, D. A. (2011). Using Twitter for Promotion and Branding: A Content Analysis of Local Television Twitter Sites. *Journal of Broadcasting & Electronic Media 55*(2), 198–214.

Gritters, J. (2018, December 3). The Psychological Toll of Becoming an Instagram Influencer. *Medium*. https://medium.com/s/love-hate/the-psychological-toll-of-becoming-an-instagram-influencer-5bbd1d9174c4

Grunig, J. E. (1989). Symmetrical Presuppositions as a Framework for Public Relations Theory. In C. H. Botan & V. Hazleton, Jr. (Eds.), *Public Relations Theory*, pp. 17–44. Hillsdale, NJ: Lawrence Erlbaum.

Guo, L., Vargo, C. J., Pan, Z., Ding, W., & Ishwar, P. (2016, Spring). Big Social Data Analytics in Journalism and Mass Communication: Comparing Dictionary-Based Text Analysis and Unsupervised Topic Modeling. *Journalism & Mass Communication Quarterly 93*(2), 332–359.

Haciyakupoglu, G., & Zhang, W. (2015). Social Media Trust during the Gezi Protests in Turkey. *Journal of Computer-Mediated Communication 20*, 450–466.

Hale, B. J., & Grabe, M. E. (2018, Summer). Visual War: A Content Analysis of Clinton and Trump Subreddits during the 2016 Campaign. *Journalism & Mass Communication Quarterly 95*(2), 449–470.

Hamilton, P. K. (1989). Application of a Generalized Persuasion Model to Public Relations Research. In C. H. Botan & V. Hazleton, Jr. (Eds.), *Public Relations Theory*, pp. 323–334. Hillsdale, NJ: Lawrence Erlbaum.

Hansen, D. L., Shneiderman, B., & Smith, M. A. (2011). *Analyzing Social Media Networks with NodeXL*. Burlington, MA: Elsevier.

Harper, T., & Norelli, B. P. (2007). The Business of Collaboration and Electronic Collection Development. *Collection Building 26*(1), 15–19.

Hassan, R., & Sutherland, T. (2017). *Philosophy of Media: A Short History of Ideas and Innovations from Socrates to Social Media.* London: Routledge.

Heath, R. L., & Coombs, W. T. (2006). *Today's Public Relation: An Introduction.* Thousand Oaks, CA: Sage.

Hesmondhalgh, D., and Toynbee, J. (Eds.) (2008). *The Media and Social Theory.* London: Routledge.

Himelboim, I., McCreery, S., & Smith, M. (2013). Birds of a Feather Tweet Together: Integrating Network and Content Analyses to Examine Cross-Ideology Exposure on Twitter. *Journal of Computer-Mediated Communication 18*, 154–174.

Hitz, L. (2018, July 26). How to Build an Audience-aligned Social Marketing Strategy. Sprout Social. https://sproutsocial.com/insights/build-audience-aligned-strategy/

Hootsuite (2018). The Social Customer Experience. How Enterprise Organizations Are Using Social Media to manage the Customer Experience. https://hootsuite.com/resources/social-customer-experience

Hopp, T., & Gallicano (2016). Development and Test of a Multidimensional Scale of Blog Engagement. *Journal of Public Relations Research 28*(3–4), 127–145.

Huff, D. (1954). *How to Lie with Statistics.* New York: W. W. Norton &. Company.

Huffaker, D. (2010, October). Dimensions of Leadership and Social Influence in Online Communities. *Human Communication Research 36*(4), 593–617.

Hunsinger, J., & Senft, T. (2014). Introduction. In J. Hunsinger and T. Senft (Eds.), *The Social Media Handbook*, pp. 1–4. New York: Routledge.

Hutchinson, A. (2016, July 14). Facebook Releases New Data on What Users Are Looking for on Facebook and Instagram. *Social Media Today.* http://www.socialmediatoday.com/social-business/facebook-releases-new-data-what-users-are-looking-facebook-and-instagram

Huynh, K. P., Lim, S. W., & Skoric, M. M. (2013). Stepping Out of the Magic Circle: Regulation of Play/Life Boundary in MMO-Mediated Romantic Relationship. *Journal of Computer-Mediated Communication 18*(3), 251–264.

Hwang, S. (2013). The Effect of Twitter Use on Politicians' Credibility and Attitudes toward Politicians. *Journal of Public Relations Research 25*(3), 246–258.

Jacobs, K. (2018, October). Fred Cook on Rebranding Golin and Gaining Trust. *Strategies & Tactics.* PRSA, p. 7. http://apps.prsa.org/StrategiesTactics/Articles/view/12355/1162/Fred_Cook_on_Rebranding_Golin_and_Gaining_Trust#.W887QBNKhyc

Jahng, M. R., & Littau, J. (2016, Spring). Interacting is Believing: Interactivity, Social Cue, and Perceptions of Journalistic Credibility on Twitter. *Journalism & Mass Communication Quarterly 93*(1), 38–58.

Jansen, J. (Ed.) (2011). *Understanding Sponsored Search, Core Elements of Keyword Advertising.* New York: Cambridge University Press.

Jarreau, P. B., & Porter, L. (2018, Spring). Science in the Social Media Age: Profiles of Science Blog Readers. *Journalism & Mass Communication Quarterly 95*(1), 142–168.

Jensen, K. B. (Ed.) (2012). *A Handbook of Media and Communication Research*, second edition. London: Routledge.

Johnston, K., Tanner, N., Lalla, N., & Kawalski, D. (2013). Social Capital: The Benefit of Facebook 'Friends.' *Behavior & Information Technology 32*(1), 24–36.

Jugenheimer, D. W., Kelley, L. D., Hudson, J., & Bradley, S. D. (2014). *Advertising and Public Relations Research*, second edition. Armonk, NY: M. E. Sharpe.

Kahn, J. (2019, February 2). Deep Learning 'Godfather' Bengio Worries About China's Use of AI. Bloomberg. www.bloomberg.com/news/articles/2019-02-02/deep-learning-godfather-bengio-worries-about-china-s-use-of-ai

Kaplan, A. (1964). *The Conduct of Inquiry: Methodology for Behavioral Science.* New York: Chandler.

Kapoor, N. (2018, August 12). 8 Fascinating Faces of Social Media Usage in 2018 [Infographic]. *Social Media Today.* https://www.socialmediatoday.com/news/8-fascinating-facts-of-social-media-usage-in-2018-infographic/529882/

Kassing, J. W., & Sanderson, J. (2015). Playing in the New Media Game or Riding the Virtual Bench: Confirming and Disconfirming Membership in the Community of Sport. *Journal of Sport & Social Issues 39*(1), 3–18.

Katz, E. (1957). The Two-Step Flow of Communication: An Up-To-Date Report on an Hypothesis. Departmental Papers (ASC). Annenberg School for Communication. http://repository.upenn.edu/cgi/viewcontent.cgi

Katz, E. (2006, November). Afterward: True Stories. *ANNALS, AAPSS, 608,* 301–314. https://journals.sagepub.com/doi/pdf/10.1177/0002716206293441

Kaushik, A. (2010). *Web Analytics 2.0: The Art and Science of Online Accountability & Science of Customer Centricity.* Indianapolis, IN: Wiley; also see, Occam's Razor. https://www.kaushik.net/avinash/best-web-analytics-tools-quantitative-qualitative/.

Khang, H., Ki, E.-J., & Ye, L. (2012). Social Media Research in Advertising, Communication, Marketing, and Public Relations. *Journalism & Mass Communication Quarterly 89*(2), 279–298.

Khatibloo, F., Pilecki, M., Shey, H., Liu, S., Flug, M., & Turley, C. (2018, May 14). How Dirty Is Your Data? *Strategic Plan: The Customer Trust and Privacy Playbook.* Forrester. https://reprints.forrester.com/#/assets/2/335/RES73121/reports

Kim, Jeong-Nam, & Ni, Lan (2013). Chapter 7: Conceptualizing Publics and Constructing Public Relations Theory of Problem Solving and its New Research, pp. 126–142. In Krishnamurthy Sriramesh, Ansgar Zerfass, & Jeong-Nam Kim (Eds.), *Public Relations and Communication Management: Current Trends and Emerging Topics.* New York: Routledge.

Kim, L. (2018, June 30). 9 Social Media Experts Share Their #1 Productivity Tip. *Inc.* https://www.inc.com/larry-kim/9-social-media-experts-share-their-1-productivity-tip.html

Koh, J., Kim, Y.-G., Butler, B., & Bock, G.-W. (2007, February). Encouraging Participation in Virtual Communities. *Communications of the ACM 50*(2), 69–73.

Konieczna, M (2018). *Journalism Without Profit: Making News When the Market Fails.* New York: Oxford University Press.

Kosaka, K. (2018). Customer Lifecycle Marketing: The Complete Guide. Alexa Blog. https://blog.alexa.com/customer-lifecycle-marketing/

Kurylo, A., & Dumova, T. (2016). Introduction: Social Networking Without Walls, pp. 1–8. In A. Kurylo and T. Dumova (Eds.), *Social Networking: Redefining Communication in a Digital Age*. Lanham, MD: Rowman & Littlefield.

Lake, L. (2018, August 30). Learn About Integrated Marketing Communications. *Small Business*. https://www.thebalancesmb.com/integrated-marketing-communication-imc-2295501

Lee, C.-J., & Sohn, D. (2016, Winter). Mapping the Social Capital Research in Communication: A Bibliometric Analysis. *Journalism & Mass Communication Quarterly 93*(4), 728–749.

Lee, Y. (2018, June 21). Predictive Analytics Is the Next Tectonic Shift. Edelman Singapore. https://www.edelman.com/post/predictive-analytics-is-the-next-tectonic-shift

Lerbinger, O. (2019). *Corporate Communication: An International and Management Perspective*. Hoboken, NJ: Wiley Blackwell.

Lieberman, M. D. (2013). *Social: Why Our Brains Are Wired to Connect*. New York: Crown Publishers.

Lim, S. S., & Soriano, C. R. R. (Eds.) (2016). *Asian Perspectives on Digital Culture: Emerging Phenomena, Enduring Concepts*. New York: Routledge.

Lin, K.-Y., & Lu, H.-P. (2011). Intention to Continue Using Facebook Fan Pages from the Perspective of Social Capital Theory. *Cyberpsychology, Behavior, and Social Networking 14*(10), 565–570.

Lindlof, T., & Taylor, B. (2002). *Qualitative Communication Research Methods*. Thousand Oaks, CA: Sage.

Ling, R., and Campbell, S. W. (Eds.) (2011). *Mobile Communication, Bringing Us Together and Tearing Us Apart*. New Brunswick, NJ: Transaction.

Lipschultz, J. H. (2017, December 6). Employee Social Media Advocacy Influence. *Huffington Post*. https://www.huffingtonpost.com/entry/employee-social-media-advocacy-influence_b_9400072.html.

Lipschultz, J. H. (2018). *Social Media Communication: Concepts, Practices, Data, Law and Ethics*, second edition. New York: Routledge.

Lipschultz, J. H. (2019). New Communications Technologies, in W. W. Hopkins (Ed.) *Communication and the Law*, pp. 223–256. Northport, AL: Vision Press.

Lorenz, T. (2018a, July 13). Unidentified Plane-Bae Woman's Statement Confirms the Worst: This is "Not a Romance" but a "Digital-age Cautionary Tale about Privacy, Identity, Ethics and Consent." *The Atlantic*. https://www.theatlantic.com/technology/archive/2018/07/unidentified-plane-bae-womans-statement-confirms-the-worst/565139/.

Lorenz, T. (2018b, December 18). Rising Instagram Stars are Posting Fake Sponsored Content. *The Atlantic*. https://www.theatlantic.com/technology/archive/2018/12/influencers-are-faking-brand-deals/578401/.

Lu, Y.-L., & Keng, C.-J. (2014). Cognitive Dissonance, Social Comparison, and Disseminating Untruthful or Negative Truthful eWOM Messages. *Social Behavior and Personality 42*(6), 979–994.

Luckie, M. S. (2011). *The Digital Journalist's Handbook*. Lexington, KY: Mark S. Luckie.

Lup, K., Trub, L., & Rosenthal, L. (2015). Instagram #Instasad? Exploring Associations Among Instagram Use, Depressive Symptoms, Negative Social Comparison, and Strangers Followed. *Cyberpsychology, Behavior and Social Networking 18*(5), 247–252.

Luttrell, R. (2016). *Social Media: How to Engage, Share, and Connect,* second edition. Lanham, MD: Rowman & Littlefield.

Luttrell, R. M., & Capizzo, L. W. (2019). *Public Relations Campaigns: An Integrated Approach.* Los Angeles: Sage.

Maheshwari, S. (2016, November 20). How Fake News Goes Viral. *The New York Times.* http://www.nytimes.com/2016/11/20/business/media/how-fake-news-spreads.html

MarketingCharts.com (2018, September 14). Marketers Clearly See Email as the Best Content Distribution Channel. https://www.marketingcharts.com/cross-media-and-traditional/content-marketing-105672

Martin, R. L., & Osberg, S. R. (2015). *Getting Beyond Better: How Social Entrepreneurship Works.* Boston: Harvard Business Review Press.

Massanari, A. L. (2015). *Participatory Culture, Community, and Play.* New York: Peter Lang.

Mathison, D. (2009). *Be the Media.* New York: natural E creative.

McIntosh, H. (2019). Social Media and Research Methods, in S. M. Croucher and D. Cronn-Mills (Eds.), *Understanding Communication Research Methods,* second edition, pp. 147–159. New York: Routledge.

McWilliams, A., & Siegel, D. (2001). Corporate Social Responsibility: A Theory of the Firm Perspective. *Academy of Management Review 26,* 117–127.

McWilliams, A., Siegel, D. S., & Wright, P. M. (2006). Corporate Social Responsibility: Strategic Implications. *Journal of Management Studies 43*(1), 1–18.

Mediakix (2017). Instagram Influencer Marketing is a 1 Billion Dollar Industry. *Mediakix.* http://mediakix.com/2017/03/instagram-influencer-marketing-industry-size-how-big/#gs.TgQqabg

Meredith, A. (2017, February 1). How to Use Psychographics in Your Marketing. Hubspot blog. https://blog.hubspot.com/insiders/marketing-psychographics

Mersey, R. D., Malthouse, E. C., & Calder, B. J. (2012). Focusing on the Reader: Engagement Trumps Satisfaction. *Journalism & Mass Communication Quarterly 89*(4), 695–709.

Miller, P. (2013). Social Media Marketing. In Alan B. Albarran (Ed.), *The Social Media Industries,* pp. 86–10. New York: Routledge.

Mills, J. L. (2015). *Privacy in the New Media Age.* Gainsville, FL: University Press of Florida.

Minnesota v. Tatro, 816 N.W. 2d 509 (Minn. 2012).

Mulrennan, D. (2018). Mobile Social Media and the News: Where Heutagogy Enables Journalism Education. *Journalism & Mass Communication Educator 73*(39), 322–333.

Nakashima, R. (2018, August 13). AP Exclusive: Google Tracks Your Movements Like It or Not. Associated Press. https://www.apnews.com/828aefab64d4411bac257a07c1af0ecb/AP-Exclusive:-Google-tracks-your-movements,-like-it-or-not

Nicholls, A., & Murdoch, A. (Eds.) (2012). *Social Innovation: Blurring Boundaries to Reconfigure Markets.* New York: Palgrave Macmillan.

Nielsen (2019). Visual IQ. https://www.visualiq.com/solutions

Nielsen (2018a, July 31). Time Flies: U.S. Adults Now Spend Nearly Half a Day Interacting with Media. Nielsen Media. http://www.nielsen.com/us/en/insights/news/2018/time-flies-us-adults-now-spend-nearly-half-a-day-interacting-with-media.html

Nielsen (2018b, December 12). The Nielsen Total Audience Report: Q2 2018. Nielsen. https://www.nielsen.com/us/en/insights/reports/2018/q2-2018-total-audience-report.html

Nielsen (2019). Visual IQ. www.visualiq.com/solutions

Noelle-Neumann, E. (1984). *The Spiral of Silence: Public Opinion—Our Social Skin.* Chicago: University of Chicago Press.

ObservePoint (2018). Top 21 Takeaways from Analytics Thought Leaders in 2018. *ObservePoint Analytics Summit eBook.* https://www.observepoint.com/wp-content/uploads/2018/11/Analytic-Summit-Ebook-2018-1.pdf

Ontario v. Quon, 560 U.S. 746 (2010).

Page, J. T., & Parnell, L. J. (2019). *Introduction to Strategic Public Relations: Digital, Global, and Socially Responsible Communication.* Los Angeles: Sage.

Patel, D. (2018, December 31). 10 Social Media Trends to Watch in 2019. *Entrepreneur.* www.entrepreneur.com/article/324901

Patel, N. (2018a, July 31). Why Content Marketing Works for Me and Not You. Neil Patel. https://neilpatel.com/blog/content-marketing-works/

Patel, N. (2018b, August 2). How to get Around Google's Latest Algorithm Change. Neil Patel. https://neilpatel.com/blog/google-algorithm-change/

Patel, N. (2018c, August 14). I Wish I Never Built a Personal Brand. Neil Patel. https://neilpatel.com/blog/build-personal-brand/

Pavlik, J. V., & Bridges, F. (2013, Spring). The Emergence of Augmented Reality (AR) as a Storytelling Medium in Journalism. *Journalism & Communication Monographs 15*(1), 1–59.

PBS (2018, 29 October). The Facebook Dilemma (Part One). *Frontline.* https://www.pbs.org/video/the-facebook-dilemma-part-one-voajnk/

Pettijohn, N. (2018, November, 18). Tools to Automate Your Social Media. *Forbes.* https://www.forbes.com/sites/nathanpettijohn/2018/11/19/why-you-should-automate-your-social-media-part-2-of-2/

Pompper, D. (2015). *Corporate Social Responsibility, Sustainability and Public Relations: Negotiating Multiple Complex Challenges.* London: Routledge.

Pompper, D. (Ed.) (2018). *Corporate Social Responsibility, Sustainability, and Ethical Public Relations: Strengthening Synergies with Human Resources.* Bingley: Emerald Publishing.

Porter, C. (2018, July 19). How to Audit Analytics Tracking Calls. Evolytics. https://www.evolytics.com/blog/how-to-audit-analytics-tracking-calls/

Pressgrove, G. N., & McKeever, B. W. (2016). Nonprofit Relationship Management: Extending the Organization-Public Relationship to Loyalty and Behaviors. *Journal of Public Relations Research 28*(3–4), 193–211.

Quesenberry, K. A. (2016/2019). *Social Media Strategy: Marketing, Advertising and Public Relations in the Consumer Revolution*, second edition. Lanham, MD: Rowman & Littlefield.

Quesenberry, K. (2017, August 4). Shedding light on dark social media. *Social Media Today.* www.socialmediatoday.com/social-networks/shedding-light-dark-social-media

Quesenberry, K. (2018, December 18). 337 Tools and Resources to Improve Your Social Media Strategy for 2019. http://www.postcontrolmarketing.com/337-tools-resources-improve-social-media-strategy-2019/

Raacke, J., & Bonds-Raacke, J. (2008). Myspace and Facebook: Applying the Uses and Gratifications Theory to Exploring Friend-Networking Sites. *CyberPsychology & Behavior 11*(2), 169–174.

Ramirez, A. (2007). The Effect of Anticipated Future Interaction and Initial Impression Valence on Relational Communication in Computer-Mediated Interaction. *Communication Studies 58*(1), 53–70.

Recode (2018, November 8). Twitter Co-founder Ev Williams Says in Retrospect That Showing How Many Followers You Have Wasn't 'Healthy.' *Recode*. https://www.recode.net/2018/11/8/18075998/ev-williams-twitter-follower-count-health-popularity

Reno v. ACLU, 521 U.S. 844 (1997).

Rheingold, H. (1993). *The Virtual Community*. Ontario: Addison-Wesley.

Rogers, E. M. (1995). *Diffusion of Innovations*, fourth edition. New York: Free Press.

Rogers, E. M. (2003). *Diffusion of Innovations*, fifth edition. New York: Free Press.

Roose, K. (2018a, December 3). TikTok, a Chinese Video App, Brings Fun Back to Social Media. *The New York Times*. https://www.nytimes.com/2018/12/03/technology/tiktok-a-chinese-video-app-brings-fun-back-to-social-media.html

Roose, K. (2018b, October 31). The Business of Internet Outrage. The Daily, podcast. *The New York Times*. https://www.nytimes.com/2018/10/31/podcasts/the-daily/mad-world-news-facebook-internet-anger.html

Rosenberg, J., & Egbert, N. (2011). Online Impression Management: Personality Traits and Concerns for Secondary Goals as Predictors of Self-Presentation Tactics on Facebook. *Journal of Computer-Mediated Communication 17*(1), 1–18.

Rubel, S. (2017, January 3). Why Brands Need Faces and Franchises in the Platform Age. *AdAge*. http://adage.com/article/steve-rubel/brands-invest-faces-franchises-platform-age/307272/

Russo, T. C., & Koesten, J. (2005, July). Prestige, Centrality, and Learning: A Social Network Analysis of an Online Class. *Communication Education 54*(3), 254–261.

Samuels, R. (2019, January 4). A Complete Calendar of Hashtag Holidays for 2019. Sprout Social. https://sproutsocial.com/insights/hashtag-holidays/

Sandes, F. S., & Urdan, A. T. (2013). Electronic Word-of-Mouth Impacts on Consumer Behavior: Exploratory and Experimental Studies. *Journal of International Consumer Marketing 25*(1), 181–197.

Sandoval, G. (2018, September, 8). Underneath all the AI Hype is the Likelihood It Threatens the Poor, Says This Former Microsoft and Google Exec. *Business Insider*. https://www.businessinsider.com/beneath-ai-hype-is-likelihood-it-threatens-the-poor-says-former-microsoft-exec-2018-9

Sarma, A. (2018, July 29). 5 Social Media Automation Tools to help You Manage Your Time More Efficiently. *Social Media Today*. https://www.socialmediatoday.com/news/5-social-media-automation-tools-to-help-you-manage-your-time-more-efficien/528828/

ShareRocket (2018, December 26). Dear Share Rocket Users. Email to author.

Shearer, E. (2018, December 10). Social Media Outpaces Print Newspapers in the U.S. as a News Source. *Pew Research Center*. http://www.pewresearch.org/fact-tank/2018/12/10/social-media-outpaces-print-newspapers-in-the-u-s-as-a-news-source/

Shen, H. (2017, Winter). Refining Organization–Public Relationship Quality Measurement in Student and Employee Samples. *Journalism & Mass Communication Quarterly 94*(4), 994–1010.

Shifman, L. (2013). Memes in a Digital World: Reconciling with a Conceptual Troublemaker. *Journal of Computer-Mediated Communication 18*(3), 362–377.

Simon, S. (2018, July 28). Opinion: When a Video Isn't the Whole Story. NPR. https://www.npr.org/2018/07/28/633199563/opinion-when-a-video-isnt-the-whole-story

Singer, N. (2018, December 22). Why the F.T.C. Is Taking a New Look at Facebook Privacy. *The New York Times*. https://www.nytimes.com/2018/12/22/technology/facebook-consent-decree-details.html

Slashdot (2018, November 12). Twitter CEO Jack Dorsey Says Follower Count Is Meaningless. Slashdot. https://slashdot.org/story/18/11/12/0818251/twitter-ceo-jack-dorsey-says-follower-count-is-meaningless

Smith, A., & Anderson, M. (2018, March 1). Social Media Use in 2018. *Pew Research Center*. http://www.pewinternet.org/2018/03/01/social-media-use-in-2018/

Smith, B. G., & Place, K. R. (2013). Integrating Power? Evaluating Public Relations Influence in an Integrated Communication Structure. *Public Relations Research 25*(2), 168–187.

Smith, B. G., & Gallicano, T. D. (2015, December). Terms of Engagement: Analyzing Public Engagement with Organizations through Social Media. *Computers in Human Behavior 53*, 82–90.

Smith, M. A., Ranie, L., Sneiderman, Ben, & Himelboim, I. (2014). Mapping Twitter Opic Networks: From Polarized Crowds to Community Clusters. PewResearch Center. http://www.pewinternet.org/2014/02/20/mapping-twitter-topic-networks-from-polarized-crowds-to-community-clusters/

SourceWatch (2008, August 10). Advertising Value Equivalenct (AVE). https://www.sourcewatch.org/index.php/Advertising_Value_Equivalency

Sprout Social (2018a, July 20). How Classic Culinary Brand America's test Kitchen Connects With New Consumers. Sprout Social. https://sproutsocial.com/insights/case-studies/americas-test-kitchen/

Sprout Social (2018b, August 14). Social Media & the Evolution of Transparency. http://downloads.sproutsocial.com/Sprout-Social-Brands-Get-Real-Evolution-of-Transparency.pdf

Steinfeld, C., Ellison, N. B., Lampe, C., & Vitak, J. (2013). Online Social Network Sites and the Concept of Social Capital, in Lee, F. L. F., Leung, L., Qiu, J. L., & Chu, D. S. C. (Eds.), *Frontiers in New Media Research*, pp. 115–131. New York: Routledge.

Stelzner, M. (2018a, July 20). Instagram Stories Strategy: How to Make Stories That Benefit Your Business. *Social Media Examiner*. https://www.socialmediaexaminer.com/instagram-stories-strategy-how-to-make-stories-benefit-your-business-tyler-j-mccall

Stelzner, M. (2018b, December 31). 5 Steps to Marketing Success in 2019. Email. *Social Media Examiner*.

Stelzner, M. (2019). Announcing More Change for 2019. Email. *Social Media Examiner*.

Sterne, J. (2010). *Social Media Metrics*. Hoboken, NJ: Wiley.

Sterne, J. (2018a, April 11). Where is Tour Organization on the Marketing Data Literacy Spectrum? LinkedIn. https://www.linkedin.com/pulse/where-your-organization-marketing-data-literacy-spectrum-jim-sterne/

Sterne, J. (2018b, June 29). Marketing Data Literacy Dimensions. LinkedIn. www.linkedin.com/pulse/marketing-data-literacy-dimensions-jim-sterne/

Stewart, D. R. (Ed.) (2017, 2013). *Social Media and the Law: A Guidebook for Communication Students and Professionals*, second edition. London: Routledge.

Stitt, G. (2018, November 12). 5 of the Biggest Influencer Marketing Trends for 2019 [Infographic]. *Social Media Today*. https://www.socialmediatoday.com/news/5-of-the-biggest-influencer-marketing-trends-for-2019-infographic/541911/

Sundar, S. S., & Limperos, A. M. (2013). Uses and Grats 2.0: New Gratifications for New Media. *Journal of Broadcasting & Electronic Media 57*(4), 504–525

Talbot, K. (2018, December 21). 5 Social Media Expert Predictions: What You'll Need to Know in 2019. *Forbes*. https://www.forbes.com/sites/katetalbot/2018/12/21/5-social-media-predictions-from-experts-what-to-know-in-2019/#4a983c992c62

Tanner, L., & O'Brien, M. (2018, August 8). Advocates Condemn Psych Techniques Used to Keep Kids Online/Associated Press. https://apnews.com/9b66a718567a459e9cb46c1f7a53b8d5

Tay, D. (2018, July 24). 10 Ways to Generate More Engagement with Your Social Media Posts. https://www.socialmediatoday.com/news/10-ways-to-generate-more-engagement-with-your-social-media-posts/528351/

Tran, D. (2018a, July 11). How to Create a Messenger Bot Sequence for Your Live Video or Webinar. Social Media Examiner. https://www.socialmediaexaminer.com/how-to-create-messenger-bot-sequence-for-live-video-or-webinar/

Tran, D. (2018b, June 21). ManyChat vs Chatfuel, An In-depth Review and Comparison. Think-Tuitive. https://www.thinktuitive.com/comparison-manychat-vs-chatfuel/

Treadwell, D. (2017). *Introducing Communication Research*, third edition. Los Angeles: Sage.

Trendkite (2018). Measuring PRs Impact: The Framework for Digital PR. Trendkite.com. https://www.trendkite.com/ebook-download/measuring-prs-impact-the-framework-for-digital-pr

Turkle, S. (1995). *Life on the Screen: Identity in the Age of the Internet*. New York: Simon & Schuster.

Valentino-DeVries, J., & Singer, N. (2019, January 3). Los Angeles Accuses Weather Channel App of Covertly Mining User Data. *The New York Times*. https://wwwwww.nytimes.com/2019/01/03/technology/weather-channel-app-lawsuit.html

Valmont (2018, November 8). Social & Digital Marketing Intern. Valmont.com. https://valmont.jobs.net/en-US/job/social-digital-marketing-intern/J3S5MH7584Y26K11759

Vasileva, T. (2018). 9 Things We Learned About Content Marketing By Analyzing 6,000 Blogs. Jeff Bullas. https://www.jeffbullas.com/content-marketing-best-practice/

Vaynerchuk, G. (2013). *Jab, Jab, Jab, Right Hook: How to Tell Your Story in a Noisy Social World*. New York: HarperCollins.

Vaynerchuk, G. (2018, July). What Makes You Happy? Instagram. https://www.instagram.com/p/Blf5VKxFxxn/?taken-by=garyvee

Verheyden, M., & Goeman, K. (2013, Winter). Does (Company) Size Matter? Differences in Social Media Usage for Business Purposes. *Journal of Applied Quantitative Methods 8*(4), 3–16.

Walker, R. (2015). *From Big Data to Big Profits: Success with Data and Analytics*. New York: Oxford University Press.

Ward, S. J. A. (2019). *Disrupting Journalism Ethics: Radical Change on the Frontier of Digital Media*. London: Routledge.

Webster, J. G. (2014). *The Marketplace of Attention: How Audiences Take Shape in a Digital Age*. Cambridge, MA: The MIT Press.

Weeks, B. E., & Holbert, R. L. (2013, Summer). Predicting Dissemination of News Content in Social Media: A Focus on Reception, Friending, and Partisanship. *Journalism & Mass Communication Quarterly 90*(2), 212–232.

Welsh, D., Kaciak, E., & Shahmah, R. (2018). Determinants of Woman Entrepreneurs' Firm performance in a Hostile Environment. *Journal of Business Research 88*, 481–491.

Yang, F., Zhong, B., Kumar, A., Chow, S.-M, & & Ouyang, A. (2018). Exchanging Social Support Online: A Longitudinal Social Network Analysis of Irritable Bowel Syndrome Patients' Interactions on a Health Forum. *Journalism & Mass Communication Quarterly 95*(4), 1033–1057.

Yesbeck, J. (2018, October 16). SEM vs. SEO: What's the Difference and Which is Right for My Brand? Alexa Blog. https://blog.alexa.com/sem-vs-seo/

Youm, K. H., & Park, A. (2016, Summer). The "Right to Be Forgotten" in European Union Law: Data Protection Balanced with Free Speech? *Journalism & Mass Communication Quarterly 93*(2), 273–295.

Yun, G. W., & Park, S.-Y. (2011). Selective Posting: Willingness to Post a Message Online. *Journal of Computer-Mediated Communication 16*(2), 201–227.

Zamith, R. (2018, Spring). A Computational Approach for Examining the Comparability of "Most-Viewed Lists" on Online News Sites. *Journalism & Mass Communication Quarterly 95*(1), 122–141.

Zuboff, S. (2019). *The Age of Surveillance Capitalism: The Fight for a Human Future at the New Frontier of Power*. New York: PublicAffairs.

Index

A/B testing 7, 11, 23, 43, 45, 53, 73, 98, 132, 141, 156–157, 164, 212, 248–249, 254, 268, 272

Abraham, Julbert 31–33, 289

Abrams, A. 7, 289

acquisition 32, 51, 53, 118, 150

AdAge 77, 300

ADD/ADHD 199

Adobe 12, 14, 31, 78, 113, 118, 121, 128, 150, 177, 210, 232, 242, 246–247, 275, 291–293; Analytics 12, 14, 121; Audience Manager 14

administrative law 174, 275

adoption 5–7, 15, 18, 61, 150; *see also* diffusion of innovation

advertising xix, xx, xxii, 4–5, 9, 12, 15–16, 20, 22, 24, 31, 33–34, 38–39–40, 44, 47–48, 51–52, 58–59, 61, 73, 87, 101, 111, 116, 120, 139, 149–170, 173, 175, 177, 180, 184, 194, 211–213, 246, 248, 252–253, 259, 265, 268, 275, 277–278, 280–282, 286, 295–296, 299, 301; sponsored endorsements 175; target xix, 59 *see also* Google; Facebook

advertising value equivalency (AVE) 39, 275, 301

advocacy 4, 23, 85, 92, 112, 119, 150, 185, 197, 212, 216, 297

Ahrefs 121

Alaimo, D. 241–242, 289

Alaimo, K. 153, 289

Alaska Airlines 172

Alexa.com 23, 43, 45–46, 121, 131, 165, 274, 296, 303

Allcott, H. 139, 289

algorithm xix, 4, 10, 14, 24, 26, 40, 45, 52, 84, 88, 113, 123–124, 132, 190, 195, 234, 243, 245, 255, 265, 275–276, 284, 293, 299

Amazon xix, 4, 8, 13, 74, 82, 123, 142, 145, 155, 185, 249, 277; Alexa 249; Mechanical Turk 142, 145

AMEC 38–40, 42, 254, 289; *see also* Barcelona Principles

American Psychological Association 130

Amichai-Hamburger, A. 6, 289

Anderson, M. 36, 62, 140, 289, 301

angel investors 285

Angel, Gary 54–57

Anison, Ann 245

Appelman, A. 133, 289

applications (apps) 7, 31, 36, 44, 61, 98, 130, 140, 172, 174, 177, 180, 184, 192, 214–216, 249, 269, 275, 281, 285, 289–290, 293, 295; *see also* mobile

Apple 82, 173

application programming interface (API) 11–12

Armano, David 115; *see also* Edelman

artificial intelligence (AI) I, 6, 8, 36–37, 42, 59, 73, 98, 102, 116, 130–131, 145, 158, 160, 202, 213, 232–233, 242–243, 245, 250, 255, 250, 275, 277, 293

Asamoah, E. 196–197, 290
Asatryan, R. 196–197, 290
Ashcroft v. ACLU 181, 290
Ashcroft v. Free Speech Coalition 181, 290
Associated Press (AP) 177, 291, 293,
    298, 302
Association for Education in Journalism and
    Mass Communication (AEJMC) 140
attribution 43–44, 87, 265, 275, 291; last–click
    attribution 43; *see also* SEO
audience-centered communication xix,
    14, 20–21, 24–26, 28–30, 33, 37, 40,
    44, 49, 58–62, 64–65, 68–71, 77, 82, 84,
    96–98, 110–113, 120–121, 124–125, 128,
    131–132, 127, 137–138, 149, 152–154,
    159–161, 163, 166, 168–170, 177–178,
    194, 201, 215–216, 219, 221–222, 228, 244,
    248, 250, 253, 254, 256–260, 263, 265, 268,
    277–278, 281–282, 286, 290, 293, 295, 299,
    303; audience disparity 166
augmented reality (AR) 215, 241, 269, 276,
    299
Auger, G. A. 129, 292
Austin, L. L. 230
authenticity 26, 42, 60, 101, 129, 187–188,
    203, 217, 276, 286; authentic 60, 81, 214; *see
    also* ethics
authority 5, 154, 183, 216, 276
awareness i, xx, 20–21, 23–24, 33, 36, 40–43,
    61, 63–64, 71, 73, 82, 84, 86, 88, 90–91,
    110, 113, 119–120, 129, 150–154, 162, 178,
    188, 194, 236, 242, 246, 265–268, 280–281,
    285

Baer, Jay xix, 37–38, 193, 265, 290
Bangladesh 83, 85
Barber, Peter 150
Barcelona Declaration of Measurement
    Principles 38–40, 289
Bargh, J. 6, 290
Barnes, S. B. 60, 290
Barnhart, B. 31, 290
Beganovich, Amra 244
Beganovich,Elma 244
Behind-the-scenes (BTS) 28
Belcher, David O. 220–230

Bell, K. 61
Bell, R. 92, 94, 294
benchmarking 6, 23, 36, 43, 90, 96, 98, 111,
    122, 153, 155, 157, 163, 272, 276
Bene, M. 131, 290
BePress Digital Commons 133
Berger, C. 130, 290
best practices i, xxii, 20, 25, 31, 38, 40, 45,
    54–57, 73, 75–76, 79, 119, 128, 147–171,
    172, 174, 176, 178–180, 182, 184,
    186–188, 194, 230, 245, 248, 268, 276,
    283, 302
Bhattacharya, C. B. 197
big data xix, 7–8, 35, 38, 59, 73, 83, 85, 119,
    132, 160, 172–173, 177, 184–185. 189, 192,
    194, 213, 216, 243, 276, 303; *see also* data
Bitly 121
Bitmoji 61
Blockbuster 7, 289
Blog I, 11, 13–14, 18–20, 22, 32–34, 45, 52,
    77–78, 91, 96, 120, 124, 128, 130, 139, 145,
    149, 151, 155–156, 159, 165, 170, 174, 180,
    192, 200–201, 244, 263, 265, 267, 274, 276,
    285–287, 291, 293, 295–296, 298–299,
    302–303; *see also* micro-influencers 151;
    paid bloggers 155
Bloomberg 6, 289, 293, 296
Boasthouse xv, 201–204
Bonds-Raacke, J. 21, 300
Boolean search 117, 235, 270
Bornstein, D. 17–18, 290
Bos, A E. R. 137–138
Bossetta, M. 132
bottom-line impact 153
boyd, d. m. 60, 290
brand and branding xvi, xx, xxii, 3–7, 10–11,
    13–34, 36, 42–43, 45, 58–60, 72–74,
    76–78, 87, 90–91, 95–96, 98, 105–106,
    110–112, 115–116, 119–125, 129–131,
    137 141, 144, 150, 153, 155, 160–161, 164,
    167, 170, 172, 174, 177, 180, 190, 193–197,
    199–203, 209, 212–214, 216–217,
    238–239, 242, 244–246, 248, 252, 261, 263,
    265–270, 276, 281–284, 290–295, 297,
    299–301, 303; brand advocate 212; brand
    ambassadors 20; brand awareness 120, 242;

branded content 160; brand engagement 72, 242; brand evangelist 20–21; brand impact 153; insights 177; lift 242; brand storytellers 4; brand voice 160; marketing communication 58, 72; *see also* marketing; personal branding 17; public relations
Brandtzaeg, P. B. 119, 197, 290
Brandwatch 122
breaking news 169, 276
Bright, Amanda xv, xxiii, 166–169
BrightVessel 150, 291
Briquelet, K. 198, 291
Brito, M. 4, 21–22, 42, 195–196, 291
broadband i, 7, 9, 61, 92, 294
Brooks, R. A. 233–236
Broom, G. M. 24, 197, 291
Brownmiller, S. 137–138
Buffer 101, 122
Bullock, Lilach 105,151, 170, 291
Bullock, P. 134, 138, 151, 170
Burrell 78
Business Review 231, 298
Business View **231**, 234, 236
Butts, C. T. 133, 291
buzz 58, 78, 106–107, 109, 201–203, 258–259, 276
Buzzell, Jason xv, 106–109
Buzzfeed xxi, 232, 236
Buzzsumo 122

Cadogan, J. W. 8, 293
California Consumer Privacy Act of 2018 173, 291
California v. TWC (2019) 173
call to action (CTA) 28, 33, 65, 107, 109, 194, 277
Cambridge Analytica xix, 130, 174, 184
Cameron, Bill 210–211
Canary & Coal xvii, xxiii, 62, 66–71; *see also* Randa Zalman
Capizzo, L. W. 211, 298
Carpenter v. United States 181, 291
Cashmore, E. 21, 36, 291
Chatterkick 237–238
CBS Interactive 82–83
Chaffee, S. H. 62, 291

Chan, M. 131, 133, 291
Chan-Olmsted, S. 6, 291
Chartbeat 122, 281
chatbot xx, 6–7, 37, 58, 74, 102, 158, 215, 242, 252, 260–261, 275, 277
Chaudoir, S. 137–138
Chen, J. 149–150, 153, 291
Chen, Y. 130, 291
Chicago xvi, xvii, xxii, xxiii, 17, 30, 49, 54, 114–115, 129, 150, 169, 211,216, 248, 250–252, 292, 299
Chicago Cubs 129
Chicago Tribune 211
Chief Executive Officer (CEO) 10, 16, 216, 277
Chief Marketing Officer (CMO) 15, 214, 231, 277
Chicago Public Square 169
Child Online Protection Act of 1998 (COPA) 181
Child Pornography Prevention Act 181
Children's Internet Protection Act of 2000 181
China xx, 21, 83, 203, 292, 296
Cho, M. 118, 129, 292
Choi, S. M. 118, 197, 292
Chow, S, M. 133, 303
Chu, S.-C. 118, 197, 292
Cisco 217
Cision 77–78, 120, 122, 200; earned media management (EMM) 120
civic engagement 92–93, 131
clickbait 4, 277
clickstream 43, 277
click-through rates (CTRs) 48, 98, 165, 264, 277
Clinton, Hillary 132, 136, 294
cloud computing 8, 45, 78, 95, 99, 101, 173, 276–277
coding 5, 78–80, 117, 158, 244, 284
collaboration xxiii, 17, 21, 23, 31, 36, 112–113, 130, 160, 164, 212, 215–216, 232, 247, 268–269, 295
communities i, 7, 23, 40, 42, 60–61, 72, 75, 79, 92–94, 97–98, 111, 119–120, 132–133, 157, 159, 167, 188, 190, 197, 203, 226, 235, 245, 262, 267–268, 287, 295–296
Collier, Marsha 81

Comcast NBC Universal 82–82
Communications Decency Act of 1996 181
communications plan 220–223, 228
communities of practice (CoP) 133
community relations 212; *see also* public
    relations
comScore 82, 122
computer-mediated communication (CMC)
    xx, 6, 62, 79, 120, 133, 214, 243, 277, 290,
    294–295, 300–301, 303; interpersonal
    communication research 130; online
    identities 120; organic 120; shared values
    120
Comstock, Brent 195–196
Confessore, N. 175, 292
Confide 172
Cong, G. 263–264
consent 29, 172, 176, 184, 297, 301
consumer xvii, xix, 4–6, 8, 12–13, 17, 22–24,
    30, 37–38, 42, 44, 48, 59, 69, 73, 78, 84, 90,
    99, 112, 118, 124, 128–131, 173, 177–180,
    184, 187, 197, 203, 212, 217, 242–244,
    246–247, 249, 252, 256, 265, 276, 291, 293,
    299–301; complaints 90; data 112; listening
    118; transparency 217; *see also* customer
conversion 11, 14, 16, 43–44, 53, 69, 72, 87,
    101, 106, 154, 160, 163, 179, 256, 260,
    265–266, 275, 277, 291; *see also* marketing
Cook, Fred 16–17, 241–242, 295
Cook, Kevin 114–116; *see also* Edelman
Coombs, W. T. 197, 292, 295
corporate social responsibility (CSR) 19, 194,
    196–200, 209, 211, 290, 298
cost per click (CPC) 14, 277
cost per engagement (CPE) 157
cost per thousand (CPM) 131, 277
Crawford, S. 93–94
CrazyEgg 107
creative class 18
Crestodina, A. 3–4, 18, 31, 292
Crimson Hexagon xix, 122
credibility 17, 26, 39–40, 58, 116, 118, 133,
    151, 175, 197, 216, 243, 278, 286, 289, 295;
    see also trust
crisis communication xvi, 84, 92, 134, 144,
    160, 218–231, 236, 283

critical discourse analysis (CDA) 243
cross-functional working relationships
    (CFWR) 212
crowds xxii, 33–33, 63, 117, 139–140, 145,
    189–191, 248, 278, 301
crowdsourcing 4, 145, 278
Cruz-Alvarez, Jurge xv, xxiii, 262–265
C-suite 15, 57, 125, 165, 196, 215, 277
culture xxi, 7, 21, 36–37, 47, 53, 61–62,
    73–74, 85, 108, 115, 136–137, 139, 205,
    209, 216–217, 233, 277, 279–280, 285,
    291–292, 297–298; meaning making 62; *see
    also* David Armano
Curtis, L. 15, 292
customers i, xx, ,xxii, 6–7, 13, 15–23, 36–38,
    40–43, 56, 58, 73, 99–102, 116, 120–124,
    131, 144, 149–150, 153, 155, 158, 161,
    165, 193–205, 212, 216, 246, 248–249,
    252, 261, 265, 270, 277–278, 290–291,
    293, 295–296; *see also* acquisition 150;
    consumer; experiences 212; loyalty 150,
    193; marketing, pain points 149–170;
    service 150
customer relationship management (CRM)
    xxii, 19, 40, 123–124, 194–205, 278
customer relationships 193–205

Daft, R. L. 232, 237
dark social 8, 44, 278, 299
Darling-Wolf, F. 9, 292
dashboard xix, 48–49, 76–79, 90, 96, 98–101,
    105–106, 109, 121–125, 152–153, 158, 165,
    170, 248, 266, 272, 275, 279, 281, 284, 286
data i, xvii, xix–xxiii, 3–24, 27–28, 33, 35–40,
    42–46, 48–50, 54, 57–62, 71–74, 76–79,
    82–88, 90, 92–97, 99, 101–102, 105–106,
    109–112, 114, 116–125, 127–133,
    135–137, 140, 142–143, 145, 149–167,
    170–175, 177–181, 183–185, 187–192,
    194–196, 201–202, 210, 212–213,
    215–218, 227, 233, 235, 242–245, 247–250,
    252–253, 255–256, 261, 263–270,
    272, 275–279, 281–286, 292, 294–297,
    302–303; analytics 43; benchmark data
    43; big data xix, 7–8, 35–36, 38, 59, 73, 83,
    85, 119, 132, 160, 172–173, 177, 184–185,

189, 192, 194, 213, 216, 243; cleaned 77; collection 78; conceptual 128; dashboards 78, 101, 266; dirty 77; geographics 11; population 11; premium 95; random 11; science 72, 245; segmentation 43; structured 86; unstructured 86; *see also* big data; reliability; validity

data science xix, 72, 74, 156, 210, 245, 269

Davis, S. 17–18, 290

Dawkins, Richard 233–234, 237

demographics xx, 11, 44, 48, 65, 73, 93, 96, 105, 121–123, 149–150, 154, 163, 166, 169–170, 202, 221–222, 244, 246, 262, 278, 284, 293

diffusion of innovation, 5, 61, 119, 197, 210, 237, 241; adoption 61; awareness 61; organizational 210; social change 197; S-shaped curve 61

Digiday 242, 292

digital i, xv–xxiii, 6–9, 12, 21–22, 30, 35, 42, 49, 51–52, 54, 57, 60, 70–71, 73, 76, 79, 82, 84, 86, 92–94, 109, 114, 121, 131–133, 139, 153–156, 159, 165, 169, 172, 176–178, 180–181, 183, 188, 194, 196, 204, 220, 230, 237 242, 244–247, 249, 254, 261, 265, 275, 278, 290, 292, 294, 297, 299, 301–303; analytics 194; behavior 188; impact 153; marketing 243–244, 261; wallets 254

Digital Analytics Association (DAA) 42, 54–57, 79, 82, 247

Digital Millennium Copyright Act of 1998 183

digital rights management (DRM) 183

Dimitrova, D. V. 131, 292

direct message (DM) 26, 141–143, 286

DiscoverText 117, 135–137, 139; *see also* Stu Shulman

Disney 82, 249–250

Djonov, E. 243, 293

Doh, S.-J. 118, 197, 293

Do-It-Yourself (DIY) 159, 244

Domonoske, C. 134, 138

Dorsey, Jack 10, 301

drones 241

Dropbox 123, 173, 269

Dumova, T. 159, 297

Dyksterhuis, Dana xv, 201–204

Dynamic Signal 21, 112, 115, 122, 205, 212, 214–215

earned media 77, 120, 122, 154, 162, 254–256, 275, 278, 292; *see also* public relations

echo chamber 93, 114–116, 139

Edelman xxiii, 9, 17, 112, 114–116, 130, 204, 216–217, 281, 293, 297; Edelman Digital 114; Edelman Predictive Intelligence Centre (EPIC) 130; public relations 115; traditional, owned and hybrid media x, x–x; Singapore 130; Trust Barometer 9, 114, 216

Electronic Privacy Information Center 184

electronic word-of-mouth (eWOM) xxii, 22, 58, 118–119, 197, 213, 246, 278, 292–293, 300

Ellison, N. B. 60, 243, 290, 301

Elonis v. United States 182, 293

email 4, 9, 12–13, 16, 23, 29, 37–38, 47, 51–52, 74, 76, 99, 108, 112, 122–123, 132, 149, 151–152, 154, 156, 165, 169–170, 172, 200, 204, 214–215, 221–223, 225, 228, 246, 260, 269, 279, 282, 290, 298, 300–301

eMarketer 247, 279

emoji 218

employees i, xxii, 4, 21–22, 32–33, 36, 47, 99, 102, 110–112, 115, 122, 124, 155, 172, 197, 204–205, 209–239, 246, 248, 254, 265, 267, 279, 297, 301

end-user agreements 173, 182, 192, 285; *see also* terms of service 192, 285

engagement i, xx–xxiii, 6, 10, 13–14, 17, 19–24, 31, 33–34, 36–37, 40, 42–43, 56–58, 60–61, 67–70, 72, 74, 76–78, 82, 87–88, 90–93, 96–97, 101, 105, 108, 110–111, 113, 115–116, 118–120, 123, 125, 127–128, 131, 133, 151, 154, 156–162, 164–165, 168–169, 178–179, 188–189, 193–194, 197–198, 201, 204–205, 209–239, 242, 244, 246, 260–261, 265–266, 268–270. 277–278, 280, 283, 295, 298, 301–302; brand 72; cost–per 157; effective 127; employee 115; ethical 188; data 36; measurement of 56; *see also* real-time

Enterprise 36, 78, 99, 115, 122–124, 128, 180, 227, 245, 279, 295

entertainment 32, 129, 131–132, 142–143, 195, 257, 262, 279, 292

entrepreneurship i, xvii–xxiii, 7–8, 10, 14, 17–19, 22, 24–25, 29–30, 32, 35, 41, 72–73, 75, 92, 99–102, 117, 128, 130, 132–133, 139, 145, 162, 165, 170–177, 187, 191–192, 195, 197–204, 210, 230, 235–237, 241–245, 248–254, 257, 260, 262, 268, 279–280, 284, 290, 298–299; influencer marketing 201; innovation 19 ; media 128; social 17; *see also* innovation, mobile

ethics i, 22, 42, 171, 185–192, 197, 214, 236, 262, 297, 303; accuracy 186; authenticity 188; character 188; community engagement 197; dignity 188; employee communication 214; extremism 188; fairness 186; holistic 188; honesty 185; ideals 188; impartiality 188; independence 186; justice 188; neutrality 188; PRSA Code of Ethics 187–187; public interest 186; public relations 185; respect; responsibility 186; truth 185; values 185 ; *see also* transparency; trust

European Union (EU) xx, 4, 130, 279, 303

events 26, 31, 36, 45, 48, 57–60, 87, 107–108, 138, 156–158, 169, 182, 184, 195, 202, 244, 246, 248, 257, 260, 267, 271, 285, 292–293

Evolytics 12, 57, 299; AUDIT 12

Excel spreadsheet 24, 60, 124, 158, 164, 189

Ezrachi, A. 8, 293

Facebook i, xix–xxi, 3–9, 12–15, 20–21, 23–25, 31, 33–33, 36, 38, 40, 45–46, 48, 54, 58, 61, 63, 66–74, 76, 78, 82–83, 87–88, 93, 95, 98, 102, 108–112, 115, 122, 124, 128–129, 131, 140, 142, 152–153, 155–159, 163–164, 166, 168, 174–175, 178–180, 182–185, 187, 190–191, 195–197, 200–210, 215, 219, 226–228, 243–244, 246–247, 252, 257–261, 263, 267, 269, 271–272, 279, 282, 284–287, 290–293, 295–301; Ads Manager 67, 87; algorithm 195; budget 157; clicks 67; comments 8; community boost xx; engagement 67; Insights 12, 87, 122; Instagram 61, 68; likes 3, 40; Live 33 ; Messenger 61, 175; post, 66; reach 67; reactions 8, 12; shares 8; stories xx ; users 182

Face-to-face (f2f) communication 42, 61–62, 129, 138, 170, 205, 245–246, 271, 278, 287

Farmer, Betty xv, 218–230

Fear of Missing Out (FOMO) 129–130

Federal Communications Commission (FCC) 111, 183

Federal Trade Commission (FTC) xx, 106, 174–181, 184, 275

filter bubble 95, 116

Fink, S. 219, 230

First Amendment law 172, 175, 178, 181–184

Fischer, J. 138, 243,293

Foley, R. J. 172, 293

Fontein, D. 150, 293

Ford, S. 139

Forrester 12, 14, 73, 293, 296

Foster, B. D. 8, 293

Fowler, Carol 251

Freberg, K. 134, 155, 293

freedom of expression 3, 22, 116, 137, 172, 184, 186

freemium 16

Frier, S. 6–7, 293

Gallardo, R. xvi, xxiii, 7, 92–95, 98, 294

Gallicano, T. 4, 127–128, 295, 301

Ganapathy, Deepti xvi, 83–86

Gao, X. 197, 294

Garton, L. 119, 294

Gates, Bill 247, 279

Gawker 199

General Data Protection Regulation (GDPR) 4, 130, 173, 184–185, 279

Gen Z 217

geolocation 11, 173; geo-graphics 11; *see also* data, mobile

Gentzkow, M. 139, 289

Germany 254

Gershon, R. A. xxii, 7, 294

Ginor, Omer 9

GlassDoor 33, 79, 212, 239
Global xx, 4, 6–9, 14, 17, 21–22, 46, 61–62, 64, 109, 113–115, 121, 124, 133, 155, 173, 175, 178, 180, 183–184, 188, 197, 202, 204, 216, 230, 235, 247, 251, 254, 262, 292, 299
Globant 241, 246
Goldsmith, S. 93–94
Goeman, K. 128, 302
Golin (Harris) xxiii, 17, 241–242, 294–295; The Bridge 17; *see also* real-time
Google xix–xxii, 4–5, 12–14, 20, 27, 32, 42–50, 52, 61, 63 76–77, 82–83, 87, 97–98, 107, 119, 121–124, 131, 151, 153–154, 156, 158, 163, 165, 173, 175, 177–178, 180, 183–185, 187, 192, 197, 242–244, 249, 256, 261, 265, 269, 272, 275, 281–284, 294, 298–300; Advanced Search 123; Adwords 14, Alerts 76, 153; Analytics 12–13; bounce rate 45–46, 48, 50, 53, 163; click–through rates (CTR) 48, 98, 165; Gmail 61; location data 177; Maps 61; Trends 76, 122; *see also* search engine optimization (SEO); YouTube 13
Google Analytics xxii, 12, 27, 42–46, 48–54, 107, 119, 122, 156, 256, 272, 275, 281–282; acquisition 51; bounce rate 50; call to action button 107; campaign traffic 52; direct traffic 51; landing pages 119; referral traffic 51; search traffic 52; sessions 50; top content 52;
Google Drive 151, 173
Google Sites 82
Goradia, Kuntal 56–57
Grabe M. J. 132, 294
Grady Newsource 167–168
Green, J. 139
Greenhow, C. 76, 294
Gritters, J. 159, 294
Grunig, J. E. 128, 294
Grygiel, Jennifer xvi, 231–237
Guo, I. 119, 132, 197, 294

Hacker xxi, 7
Hafner, K. 232, 237
Hale, B. J. 132, 294
Hansen, D. L. 113, 119, 197, 294
HARO (Help A Reporter Out) 77, 122, 200, 279; *see also* Cision

Harvard Business Journal 213
hashtag 11, 26, 30, 58, 60–61, 77–78, 84–85, 87–88, 91, 105, 123–125, 134–137, 152, 158, 172, 174, 190, 213, 219, 226–227, 238–239, 258 263–264, 266, 269, 271, 279, 286, 291, 300; branded 60; #PlaneBae 172
Hassan, R. 36, 295
hate speech 183
Haythornthwaite, C. 119, 294
Heath, R. L. 197, 295
Heffernan, E. 176
Hill, Chad 178–179
Himelboim, I. 113, 139, 295, 301
Hirst, P. 235, 237
Hitlin, P. 62, 289
Hitz, Lucy 149–150, 295
Hoffman, Jeff 253
Holbert, R. L. 140, 303
Home Instead Senior Care 62–71
Hong Kong 133, 291
Hootsuite 36, 60, 78, 91, 96, 101–102, 123, 158, 227, 269, 281, 293, 295
Hopp, T. 4, 128, 295
HowSociable 123
Hubshout 178; *see also* Chad Hill
Hubspot 123
Huff, D. 42, 295
Human-computer interaction (HCI) xx, 60, 280; *see also* computer-mediated communication
human dignity 173
Hutchinson, A. 32, 295
Huynh, K. P. 62, 295
Hwang, S. 118, 197, 293, 295
hypotheses 11, 280

IBM 173, 180
identity 19, 30, 75, 85–86, 133–134, 137–138, 182, 188, 276, 280, 282, 286, 291–292, 297, 302; *see also* computer-mediated communication (CMC)
IFTTT 123, 269
IGTV xx, 18, 20–21, 25, 33, 123, 169, 252, 271
Ihlen, Ø. 220, 230
Illinois Journalism Education Association xv, 166, 168–169

impact measurement 17, 280
impression 8, 12, 18, 40, 42, 67–68, 70, 76–78,
   88, 90, 98, 105, 119, 122, 125, 155, 157, 169,
   213–214, 227, 263, 280, 300
India xvi, xx, 21, 46, 83, 85–86
influence 16, 19–20, 109, 119–120, 201, 213,
   271; blog sites and 19–20; content 120;
   marketing 201; majority illusion 213
information 4, 8, 12, 15, 20, 29, 33, 43, 45–46,
   53–54, 59–60, 62, 74, 78, 85, 87, 93,
   99–100, 106–108, 112–115, 118–119, 121,
   123, 129–132, 134, 142–144, 150, 152, 158,
   160–161, 172–174, 179, 183–184, 186, 190,
   192, 197, 202, 212, 214–215, 219, 222–225,
   229–230, 234, 237, 255, 260–261, 264, 267,
   276–277, 280, 283–284, 296
innovation xxi–xxiii, 4–5, 8, 11, 18–19,
   22, 24, 36, 61–62, 73, 92, 113, 116, 132,
   139, 162, 165, 177, 203–204, 210, 233,
   235–236, 242, 243–244, 252–254, 260, 280,
   285, 294–295, 298, 300; boundaries 113;
   innovative–decision process 113
Instagram xix–xx, 7, 18, 20–21, 24–29,
   31–33, 54, 61, 67–70, 74, 77, 82, 87–89,
   95, 106, 109–110, 112, 123, 125, 131, 140,
   150–153, 155, 158–159, 162–163, 166,
   168–169, 174, 199, 219, 225–227, 235,
   238–239, 244, 247, 252, 258, 263, 266,
   268–269, 271–272, 281, 285, 290, 293,
   295–298, 301–302; IGTV 169; influencers
   158; Insights 24, 87, 123; Stories 31
integrated marketing communication (IMC)
   160–161, 280, 297
intellectual property (IP) 171, 183
intelligent communities xvi, 7, 77, 92–95, 130,
   188
Internet of things (IoT) 8, 20, 130, 178, 250,
   280
Internet Service Providers (ISPs) 183
intimacy 38, 62

Jacobs, K. 241–242, 295
Jahng, M. R. 133, 295
Jarreau, P. B. 132, 295
Jenkins, H. 135, 139
Jenner, Kylie 268, 296

Jensen, K. B. 4, 37
Jin, Y. 219, 230
Johnston, K. 197, 296
Jugenheimer, D. W. 9, 296
Jung, J. 94

Kaciak, E. 128, 303
Kamerer, David xvi, 8, 48–54
Kang, C. 175, 292
Kansas City xxiii, 250
Kaplan, A. 37, 296
Kassing, J. W. 21, 296
Katz, E. 5, 296; see also influencers
Katzman, Alan 179
Kaufman, Joelle 214–215
Kaushik, A. 43, 50–52, 54, 87, 296
Keng, C–J. 118–119, 197, 297
KETV xxii, 266
key performance indictors (KPIs) 15, 56, 64,
   87, 90, 93–95, 101, 105, 122, 133, 154–155,
   211, 217, 273, 280
keywords 5. 13, 19–20, 43, 45–46, 52, 73,
   76–78, 121, 123, 131, 153, 155, 244,
   268–269, 280, 284, 295; see also Moz; Neil
   Patel; SEO
Keywords Everywhere 123
Keyword Tool 43, 123
Khaled, DJ 95
Khang, H. 139, 296
Khatibloo, K. 12, 296
Kim, J.-N. 4, 293, 296
KidVid 175
Klipfolio 99–102, 123; see also Klipfolio
Knitowski, Alan 177–180
Koesten, J. 119, 300
Kosaka, Kim 23. 165, 274, 296
Kraft, Chris 110–111; see also ShareRocket
Kumar, A. 133, 303
Kunz, Jennifer 3
Kurylo, A. 159, 297
Kutcher, Ashton 10

LaHood, Ed. 269
Lake, L. 161, 297
Lampe, C. 243, 301
Latinos 46–48

Lee, C. J. 130, 133, 297
Lengel, R. H. 232, 237
Lerbinger, O. 185, 297
lifestyle influencers 244; *see also* influence
Likealyzer 76; *see also* Meltwater
Lim, S. S. 21, 297
Limperos, A. M. 133, 302
Lin, K.-Y. 212, 297
LinkedIn i, xv–xvi, 13–14, 19, 30–34, 54,
    60, 79, 96–98, 109, 112, 123, 128, 152,
    155, 158–159, 162, 166, 168, 179, 200,
    204, 227, 239, 242, 267, 271, 281, 284, 289,
    302; personal brand 19; profile 123, 158;
    SlideShare 19
Lipman Hearne 150, *see also* Peter Barber
Lipschultz, J. H. i, xxi–xxiii, 16–17, 48,
    55–57, 60, 74, 83, 102, 112, 114, 116, 150,
    174, 180, 196, 198, 200, 211, 214, 218,
    251–253, 266, 297
literature review 15, 281
Littau, J. 133, 295
Liu, B. F. 230, 296
London 202–203, 251, 291–293, 295–296,
    299, 302–303
Lorenz, T. 17, 172, 297
Los Angeles xx, 245, 251, 292–294, 298, 299,
    302
Lu, H.-P. 212
Lu, Y.-L. 118, 197, 297
Lufthansa 99
Lup, K. 159, 297
Luttrell, Regina M. 81–82, 211, 298
Lyft 175–176

Ma, Z. 263–263
MacLeod, John 249–250, 252
MailChimp 37, 151–152, 154, 165
Malthouse, E. C. 298
management xix–xxiii, 4, 6, 8–10, 12, 19, 197;
    strategic 197
Marino, L. D. 237
marketing xix–xxii, 4–6, 11, 13–16, 20–24,
    31, 33–38, 40, 42–43, 46–48, 51–52, 54,
    57–60, 71–72, 74, 76, 78, 82, 86–88, 96,
    98–102, 110, 112, 114, 116, 118, 120–124,
    130–131, 149–170, 186, 190, 194, 196,

201–203, 210–215, 218, 220–222, 228,
    230–231, 233, 235, 242–246, 248, 254, 261,
    263, 265, 267–268, 273–274, 276–281, 284,
    290–293, 295–302 ; data 110; funnel 15 ;
    hub and spoke 87; integrated marketing
    communication (IMC) 160; lifecycle 23;
    organizational literacy 210; pain points 149;
    strategic thinking 212; targeting 46; sticky
    content 37; *see also* branding
MarketingCharts.com 149, 298
MasterCard 253–254
Martin, R. L. 18, 292
Mathison, R. 91, 298
Matthes, J. 131, 292
McKenna, K. 6, 290
McWilliams, A. 196, 298
measurement xix–xxiii, 4, 8–12, 14, 19–20,
    24, 35–40, 42–44, 46, 53–54, 57–58,
    61, 75–80, 82–90, 95, 98, 102, 105–106,
    117–120, 127, 131, 149, 155, 163, 172, 234,
    242, 255, 261–262, 275, 280–282, 284, 286,
    289, 301; error 11, 42; *see also* data
media cluster xxi, 81, 86, 113, 117, 119, 124,
    139, 188–190, 197, 255–256, 267
Mediakix 159, 298
media literacy 4, 75–76, 179
media storytelling xxii, 20, 22, 88, 115, 164,
    201, 212, 215, 248–249, 262, 268–269, 281;
    rich media 20
Meltwater 76–77, 94, 102, 124, 153, 158
memes 60, 62, 91, 160, 172, 233, 281, 301; *see
    also* Richard Dawkins
Mersey, R. D. 128, 298
Messenger 61, 87, 175, 260, 302; *see also*
    Facebook
messenger bot sequences 260; *see also* chat
    bots
metadata 117, 135
metrics xxii–xxiii, 10, 12, 19, 21, 36, 40, 44,
    54, 57–60, 73, 7679, 101–102, 105–107,
    109–110, 116–117, 121–122, 125,
    149–150, 153, 155, 157–158, 165–166,
    168, 210, 214, 233, 238, 244, 248, 255–256,
    267, 269, 275, 281, 286, 301; buzz 58; vanity
    metrics 60
Metzger, M. J. 62, 291

Meyerson, Charlie 169–170
Miami 245
Microsoft xix, 24, 32, 82, 178, 185, 189, 215, 242, 247, 281, 300; *see also* Excel
Microsoft Sites 82
Millennials 28, 128, 216–217, 244, 246, 294
Miller, P. 78, 118, 197, 298
Mills, J. L. 173–174, 298
mindshare 154
Minnesota v. Tatro 183, 298
Mississippi State University xvi, 95
MIT CFO Forum 234
MIT Computer Science and Artificial Intelligence Lab (CSAIL) 231
MIT Media Lab 234
mobile xx, 6–7, 9, 11–12, 14, 21–22, 38, 43–44, 61,73, 77, 82, 98, 100, 107, 111, 115, 122, 139, 158, 163, 172–173, 177–181, 183, 196, 214–216, 243–244, 247, 249, 254, 276, 279, 281, 284–285, 287, 291, 297–298; apps 21, 61; Apple iPhone 61
monetization 13, 106, 153, 159, 281
motivation 11, 41, 105, 130, 132, 141–144
Moz 76, 124, 154
Mulrennan, D. 134, 298
multimodal discourse analysis 243, 293
Murdoch, A. 18, 298
Murphy, Juan José López 241
Murphy, Todd xvi, 78, 254–256
MySpace 21, 232, 300

Nakashima, R. 177, 298
Narjes, Charlotte xxiii
National Opinion Research Center (NORC) 114
Neely, Jennifer 213
Negroponte, Nicholas 234–237
Netflix 61, 185
network analyses xvii–xxii, 5, 16, 19, 60, 78. 86–87, 112–113, 115–116, 119, 124, 132–133, 136–139, 174, 188–191, 197, 213, 267, 282, 284–285, 290–292, 294–295, 297, 300–301, 303; betweenness 189; centrality 189; social graph 284; structure 197, 213; visualize 267, 282; *see also* influence

Newhouse School of Public Communications xvi, 232, 237
Ni, L. 4
Nichols, A. 18
Nielsen 124, 247, 265, 298
NodeXL xvii, 16, 113, 124, 136–137, 158, 188–191, 294; *see also* social network analysis
Noelle-Neumann, E. 23, 299
Non-disclosure agreements (NDAs) 29
nonprofit 15, 65, 196
Nuvi 78, 124, 266

Oath 82
objectivity 188
O'Brien, M. 129, 302
ObservePoint 3, 35, 73, 299
Oelrich, P. A. 234, 237
operational definition 15, 271, 282
optimization xix, 5, 14, 20, 24, 43, 45, 52, 58, 60, 67–68, 70, 72–73, 76, 79, 81, 83, 101, 119, 124, 156, 158, 163, 180, 243, 282, 284, 294; *see also* Google Analytics
opinion leaders 6, 10, 113–114, 132, 213, 299, 301
organic content xix–xxii, 5–6, 13, 17, 24, 27, 33, 36, 43–44, 46, 78, 87, 96, 98, 111, 120, 123, 131, 157–158, 163–164, 168, 194, 214, 246, 252, 271, 282–283, 286
organizational communication 3–8, 10, 13–15, 17–19, 21–23, 35, 39–40, 43–45, 57–60, 72–73, 106,115, 124, 128–130, 141–170, 193–197, 201, 204, 209–215, 218, 228, 230, 241, 248, 285, 292, 295, 299; cohesion 197; thought leadership 212; *see also* social media policy
Osberg, S. R. 18, 298
Ouyang, A. 133, 303
owned media i, 4–5, 22, 40, 45, 49, 58, 106, 111, 119–120, 124, 149, 152, 154, 156, 162, 173, 195, 211, 242, 255–256, 265, 272, 276, 281–282; *see also* PESO
Oxford, Kelly 134, 136–137

Packingham v. North Carolina 182
Page, J. T. 211, 299

pageviews 13, 44–46, 48, 50, 53, 84, 87, 282; *see also* Google Analytics
Park, S.-Y. 17, 303
Parnell, L. J. 211, 299
participation marketing 4, 196, 218, 291; *see also* marketing
Patashnick, M. J., 219, 230
Patel, D. 252
Patel, Neil 5, 13–14, 76–77, 252, 299
pay-per-click (PPC) 4, 87, 282
PayPal 56–57, 82, 209, 294
paywall 78, 282
PBS 4, 299
perceived relationship investment (PRI) 129
Periscope 232, 271; *also see* Twitter
Persson, A. 130, 291
PESO 22, 119–120, 211, 255
Petto, Sam xvi, 141–144
Pew Internet 124, 139–140, 189, 289, 300–301
photographs 21, 24, 26, 28, 30–32, 36, 59, 77, 87, 90, 96, 123, 125, 142, 157–158, 160, 172, 178, 182–184, 190, 201, 224–226, 244, 268–269, 280–281, 283–285, 290; photography 49; *see also* Instagram; selfies
Phunware 177–180; *see also* Alan Knitowski
Pinterest 20, 74, 82, 96, 142, 155, 276, 282; community 96; pins 96
play 231–233
Pompper, D. 197, 299
Porter, Jay 204, 216–218
Porter, C. 12, 299
Porter, L. 132, 295
PostControlMarketing.com 76, 299; *see also* Keith Quesenberry
posting 9, 20, 23, 25, 28, 109, 129, 143, 159, 201, 228, 239, 244, 282–285, 297, 303
predictive analytics 58, 101–102, 130, 185, 245, 293, 297
Presnell, Donna xvi, 218–230
privacy xx, 4, 12, 38, 44, 59, 85, 95, 130, 171–173, 175–177, 179, 181, 183–184, 186–188, 214, 218, 248, 262, 269, 279, 283, 291–292, 296–298, 301; data 44, 59, 95, 171, 181, 188, 214, 218, 262, 269; future 179; law 172, 175, 279; ownership 38; policy 12;

protection 130, 172; settings 177; *see also* California Act 291; GDPR 248, 279; RTBF
profile clicks 169
propaganda 128–129; *see also* public relations
ProPublica 17
PRSA Strategies & Tactics 242
Pryor, J. B. 138
psychographics 11, 298
public relations (PR) xv–xvii, xix, xxii, 4, 9, 15–16, 24, 30, 38–39, 54, 59, 115, 119–120, 127–129, 134, 139, 144, 149–170, 185–186, 192, 200, 211, 216, 220–221, 230, 242, 246, 255–256, 278, 283–284, 291–296, 298–299, 301; content, 246; ethics 185–185; manipulation 128–129; non-profit 15; reputation management 129, 154; strategic communication 128; tone, 59; *see* also earned media; trust
Public Relations Society of America 24, 185–186, 192; *see also* ethics: PRSA Code of Ethics
Purdue University i, xvi, xxiii, 92, 95, 98, 152

Quesenberry, K. A. 4–5, 8, 44, 59, 165, 263, 265, 299

Raacke, J. 21, 300
Radian6 (SalesForce) 124, 212, 234, 281
Ramirez, A. 8, 300
Rainie, L. 37, 139
Rasmussen, J. 220, 230
reach xix, xx, 4, 13–14, 16–17, 19–24, 26, 36–38, 42, 54, 58–59, 67–74, 82, 87–88, 90, 96–97, 105–106, 110–11, 120, 122, 124–125, 132, 135, 141, 150–152, 157–158, 164–165, 195, 209, 212–214, 218–219, 221, 245–246, 248, 260, 262–263, 265–267, 270, 276, 280–281, 283
real-time 6, 17–18, 28, 58, 71, 77, 81, 101–102, 105, 111, 121–124, 153, 155, 172, 178–179, 190, 232, 234, 248, 260, 265, 267, 275, 278, 279, 283, 286; engagement 278, 283; metrics 105; monitoring 81, 155, 267; social media listening 6, 155, 283
Recode 10, 300

Reddit 13, 20, 97, 132, 294; Redditors 97; subreddit 132; up-vote and down-vote 97

Reeder. G. D. 138

relationships xxii, 4, 7–10, 14, 19, 21, 23, 26, 29, 30, 33, 42, 52, 56–58, 60–62, 72, 77, 87, 91, 102, 106, 112–113, 116, 119, 127–131, 151, 154, 161, 170, 175–176, 186, 246; brand 91; long-term 246; relationship-building 61; trust 23, 29, 113

Reno v. ACLU 181, 300

research questions 11, 15, 56, 144, 217

RetweetRank.com 76

Rey, B. 138–139

return on investment (ROI) 13–14, 35, 87, 93, 120, 131, 155, 165, 212, 245, 283

request for proposals (RFP) 25

Rheingold, H. 23, 75,300

right to be forgotten (RTBF) 130–131, 183, 284, 303; *see also* privacy

Robella, B. 76

Rogers, E. M. 5, 61, 112–113, 197, 210, 232, 237, 300

Roose, K. 4, 61, 300

Roquemore, Rylee xvi, 218–230

Rosen, A. 265

Rosenberg, J. 12, 300

Rosenthal, L 159, 297

Rubel, S. 14, 300

rural i, xxii, 7, 9, 92–94, 98, 112, 196

Rural Futures Institute (RFI) i, xxiii, 93

Russo, T. C. 119, 300

ROSTIR 211

Salesforce 124, 212

Samuels, R. 60, 300

Sanderson, J. 21, 296

Sandes, F. S. 118, 197, 300

Sandoval, G. 243, 300

Saudi Arabia 84

Schulman, Dan 135, 209, 294

Scott, M. 93, 95

search engine optimization (SEO) xx, 4–5, 14, 21, 42, 51–52, 76, 86–87, 101, 121, 261, 282, 284; clicks 86, 101, 130; marketing 86; page rank 165; *see also* keywords, pageviews

search engine marketing (SEM) 4, 87, 284; audit 87

search engine results pages (SERPs) 5, 284

Seattle 201–203

Seiden, Krista 35

self-status seeking 142–143

SEO Analyzer 76; *see also* Neil Patel

Sha, B.-L.197

Shankman, Peter 198–200

share of voice (SoV) xxii, 4, 33, 131, 154, 193, 248, 284, 290

ShareRocket 110, 112, 124, 300

Shearer, E. 140, 300

Shen, H. 132, 301

Shifman, L. 62, 301

Shneiderman, B. 139, 294

Shulman, Stu xvii, 117–118, 121, 139

Siegel, D. 196, 298

Signal 172

Silicon Prairie 248–252

Silicon Valley 22, 30, 230, 244, 248 ; *see also* entrepreneurship

Silverman, Craig xxi,

Simon, S. 129, 301

Singer, N. 173, 184, 265, 301

Slack 124, 215

Slashdot 10, 301

SMART goals 40, 162–164, 170, 270–271, 273–274

Smith, A. 140, 301

Smith, B. G. 127, 160, 301

Smith, Marc A. xvii, 119, 139, 189–191, 294–295, 301; *see also* NodeXL

Snapchat 24, 31, 33, 61, 74, 82, 95–96, 132, 140, 160, 162, 172, 242, 246, 284–285, 290, 292; AR lenses 242; data 95; Snaps 95; unique views 95

Social Assurity 179

Social Bakers 124

social business 16, 33, 72, 233–234, 284, 295

social capital 23, 116, 119, 128, 133, 197, 212, 243, 296–297, 301

social equity index 111, 124; *see also* ShareRocket

socializing 142–143

social media audit 24, 59, 120, 156, 161

social media calendar 36, 60, 155, 158
social media communication (SMC) i,
    xix–xxi, 7–8, 37, 42, 61, 119, 182–183, 193,
    201, 212, 214, 230, 242, 247, 268, 285, 287,
    297
social media emergency management
    (SMEM) 93, 285
social media health 133
social media listening xxi, 6, 17, 122, 124, 270,
    283, 290
social media policy 21–22, 279, 285;
    boundaries 22; governance 21; policies 22;
    rules 22
social media strategy, strategies xvi, 54, 119,
    150, 155–156, 166, 168, 213, 220, 222, 265,
    269, 290, 299
Social Media Today xx, 246, 268, 290–291,
    295–296, 299–300, 302
Social Mention 124
social movements 133, 292
Social network analysis (SNA) xvii, xxi, 16,
    78, 112–113, 116, 119, 124, 133, 136, 188,
    191, 213, 285, 291, 300, 303; theory and
    methods 133; visualization 78; *see also*
    social networks
social networks 38, 81; authentic 81; SoMe 81
social network sites (SNS) 16, 81–102, 243;
    data 87; Facebook 87; *see also* computer–
    mediated communication
Sohn, D. 133, 297
Solis, Brian 24
SoMe 81, 197
Soriano, C. R. R. 21, 297
SourceWatch 39, 301
Southwest Airlines 6
Sutherland, T. 36, 295
spammer 26
Spellings, Margaret 220
Spotify 61, 185
Sprout Social 6, 31, 42, 77, 125, 149, 269, 281,
    290–291, 295, 300
stakeholders i, 22, 40–41, 57, 59, 128,
    130–131, 162, 166, 170, 186, 193, 197, 212,
    229, 242, 248
Starbucks 178–179, 217
Statista 86

Statistical Package of the Social Sciences
    (SPSS) 142
Steinfeld, C. 243, 301
Stelzner, M. 88, 252, 268, 301
Sterne, Jim 57–59, 72–75, 78, 116, 210–211,
    301–302
Stewart, D. R. 171, 302
Stitt, G. 60, 302
St. Louis 175–176, 251
St. Louis Post-Dispatch 175–176
Stucke, M. E. 8, 293
Stutterheim, S. E. 138
subject matter experts (SMEs) 42, 285
Subramanian, Roma xvii, 134–139
Sun, A. 263–264
Sundar, S. S. 133, 289
sustainability 92, 299
Syracuse University xvi, 232, 237
SWOT analysis 161–162, 170, 270–271

tactics xvi, xxii, 6, 11, 16, 19–20, 22–24,
    35, 37, 40, 44, 52, 54, 58–60, 62, 71–72,
    82, 92, 150, 154–155, 159–160, 194, 211,
    223, 242, 245, 248, 268–269, 271, 276,
    283–286, 295, 300; *see also* public relations,
    marketing
tagging 143, 154, 213, 285
Talbot, K. 268, 302
Tanner, L. 129, 296, 302
Target (retailer) 8, 267
TED 93, 95
terms of service (ToS) 173, 192, 285
text analytics 118, 132, 294
The Daily Beast 197, 291
The New York Times 95, 138, 173, 175–176,
    185, 237, 292, 294, 298, 300–302
The Weather Channel xx, 173, 302
Thyng 269; *see also* augmented reality
TikTok 61, 98, 300
T-Mobile 172
Tompkins, Matt xvii, 257–260
tracking calls 12, 286, 299
Tran, D. 6, 260, 302
Trejo, Beth 237–238
Trendkite 125, 153–154, 302; *see also* Union
    Metrics

Trump, Donald J. 58, 132, 134, 136, 138, 231, 294, 298
trust 9, 12, 17, 22–23, 25–26, 29, 42, 58, 61, 79, 81, 93, 112–116, 118, 122, 127, 129–132, 151, 156, 160, 186, 196–197, 199, 212–213, 216–219, 243, 252, 261, 268, 278, 286, 293–296; satisfaction 127; *see also* credibility; public relations; relationships
Tucker, R. 237
TV 13, 246, 257
Twitch 60, 175–176, 203
Twitter i, xix, 4, 9–11, 13–14, 20, 25, 54, 58, 61, 67–71, 74, 76–78, 82, 84, 86, 90–93, 95, 105, 108–110, 112, 116–117, 119, 124–125, 128–129, 132, 134–140, 151–153, 155, 158, 162–163, 166–169, 178–179, 188–191, 195–196, 200–201, 210, 213, 219, 227, 234–235, 237–238, 246–247, 252, 257–258, 263–266, 269–272, 275–276, 279, 284, 286, 289–291, 294–295, 300–301; analytics 68, 90–91, 105, 116, 152, 188; chat 91; impressions 169; networks 134–139; Tweetdeck 77
Twitter Analytics 68, 76, 90–91, 105, 124–125, 167, 263, 272, 286
Twitter Assistant 77, 125, 238, 266; *see also* Union Metrics
Twitter Counter 9
Twitter Tweetdeck 125

Uber 175–176
UberSuggest 5, 77; *see also* Neil Patel
UK Tech Nation Exceptional Talent Visa 202, 204
Uniform Resource Locator (URL) 12, 285
Union Metrics 77, 125, 238, 263, 266–267
Unique Identity Number (UID) 85
Universal Information Services xvi, xxiii, 78, 124, 254–256; *see also* Alpha Clips, 124, 255; Todd Murphy
University of Illinois xxiii
University of Nebraska–Lincoln i, xxiii
University of Nebraska at Omaha i, xv–xxiii, 5, 45, 47, 106–109, 134–139, 141–144, 162, 265

University of North Carolina xv, 195, 220, 230
University of Southern California 242
UNO Social Media Lab i, xv, xxiii, 31, 88–90, 94, 97, 100, 110, 134–139, 141–144, 151, 265
urban 7, 9, 17, 67, 92–93, 196
Urdan, A. T. 118, 197, 300
United States v. American Library Association 181

Valentino-DeVries, J. 173, 302
Valmont 155, 302
Vargas, Anna xvii, 24–30
Vasileva, T. 20, 302
Vaynerchuk, G. xx, 18, 41, 78, 242, 302
VaynerMedia 41, 242
Verheyden, M. 128, 302
Verizon 82, 183
video xx, xxii, 7, 11, 14, 20–25, 32–33, 45–46, 59, 61, 65, 74, 77–78, 87, 90, 97–98, 123, 125, 129, 131, 152, 157, 159–160, 164, 168, 175–176, 183–184, 201, 215, 223–229, 238, 242, 244, 246, 257, 259–262, 265, 267–269, 271, 277, 279–281, 283–285, 287, 299–302; *see also* viral 77
virtual communities 8, 75–76, 93, 178, 181, 190, 287, 296, 300
virtual reality (VR) 202, 231, 241, 262
Vitak, J. 243, 301
voice-activated 241–242, 247

Walker, Russell 35, 38, 303
Ward, S. J. A. 188, 191, 303
Weare, Andrea xvii, 134–139
WeAreSocial 6
Weber Shandwick 17
Website Grader 77
Webster, J. G. 111, 303
Weeks, B. E. 140, 303
Western Carolina University xv–xvi, 218–230
Wellman, B. 119, 294
Welsh, D. 128, 303
WhatsApp 61, 175, 203; *see also* Facebook
Wiklund, J. 236–237
Wilkins, Carey 57

Wille, Alan 99–102
Williams, Ev 10, 300
Wiselytics 139
WLS-AM 211
word-of-mouth (WOM) xxii, 16, 21–22, 28, 30, 118, 197, 213, 278, 287, 292–293, 300
WordPress 19–20, 33, 49, 159

Yahoo 82
Yang, F. 133, 303
Ye, L. 139, 296
Yelp 197, 291
YouTube xxii, 9, 13–14, 20–21, 25, 31–33, 61, 74–75, 78, 82, 97–98, 109, 121, 123–125, 140, 144, 159, 162, 169–170, 183, 191, 204, 237, 244, 246, 252, 257–259, 267, 269, 271, 281, 285, 287
YouTube Studio 97, 124–125, 159
Yu, W. 237
Yun, G. W. 17, 303

Zacharilla, L. 94
Zalman, Randa xvii, 62–71, 75
Zamith, R. 86, 132, 303
Zaveri, M. 176
Zhao, S. 243, 293
Zhong, B. 133, 303
Zuckerberg, Mark 174
Zuboff, 3. Xix, 303